THE DEBATE
OVER
SLAVERY

Stanley Elkins and His Critics

EDITED BY
Ann J. Lane

UNIVERSITY OF ILLINOIS PRESS
Urbana, Chicago, London

ACKNOWLEDGMENTS

The editor wishes to thank the following publishers and journals for permission to reprint the designated selections. Rights in all cases are reserved by the owner of the copyright:

Negro History Bulletin for "Chattel Slavery and Concentration Camps," by Earl E. Thorpe (published in the May 1962 issue, pages 171–76); *Civil War History* for three selections, all published in the December 1967 issue: "Rebelliousness and Docility in the Negro Slave: A Critique of the Elkins Thesis," by Eugene D. Genovese (pages 293–314), "A Note on Elkins and the Abolitionists," by Aileen S. Kraditor (pages 330–39), and "Resistance to Slavery," by George M. Fredrickson and Christopher Lasch (pages 315–29); *American Quarterly* for "Slavery and Personality," by Mary Agnes Lewis (published in the Spring 1967 issue, pages 114–21); Cornell University Press for an excerpt from *The Problem of Slavery in Western Culture*, by David Brion Davis, 1966 (Chapter Eight, pages 223–61); Cambridge University Press for "Anglicanism, Catholicism, and the Negro Slave," by Herbert S. Klein (published in *Comparative Studies in Society and History*, April 1966 issue, pages 295–330); Walker and Company for an excerpt from *Patterns of Race in the Americas*, by Marvin Harris, 1964 (Chapter Six, pages 65–78); Macgibbon & Kee and Associated University Presses for an excerpt from *The Sociology of Slavery*, by Orlando Patterson, 1967 (pages 174–81); *The Massachusetts Review* for "Through the Prism of Folklore: The Black Ethos in Slavery," by Sterling Stuckey (published in the Summer 1968 issue, pages 417–37); and *The New York Review of Books* for "American Slaves and Their History" (originally published as "On Writing the History of Black Slaves," Dec. 3, 1970, pages 34–42), by Eugene D. Genovese.

Special thanks to Stanley Elkins for having written such a provocative essay that it elicited years of lively criticism and to Eugene D. Genovese for having offered inspiration and advice from the beginning.

Contents

THE DEBATE
OVER
SLAVERY

Stanley Elkins
and His Critics

Introduction

ANN J. LANE

Stanley M. Elkins published *Slavery*[1] more than a decade ago; each year witnesses increasing testimony to its importance and influence. Whatever the limitations of the book, and there is no lack of critics to point them out, it has without doubt extended the examination of slavery in the United States in permanent and profound ways. Asking in effect the barest and simplest question one could ask about slavery—what did slavery do to the slave?—Elkins has offered ways of probing that question that are sometimes astonishing in their subtlety and sophistication. He forced the discussion of the slave system in this country to be examined within the larger view of slavery in the Caribbean and Latin America. He extended disciplines, as well as geography, by utilizing tools of sociology, psychology, and anthropology. In the introduction to the first edition of *Slavery* he expressed the hope that his study would alter the traditional ways in which slavery in the United States was viewed. He has accomplished that aim,

[1] Elkins, *Slavery: A Problem in American Institutional and Intellectual Life* (Chicago, 1959). Paperback editions were published in 1963 by Grosset & Dunlap and in 1968 by the University of Chicago Press. All three editions have the same pagination. References to specific pages in this book will appear in the text in parentheses.

a major undertaking considering the one hundred years or so in which the debate had been locked.

In an effort to examine "the old subject in new ways," Elkins used comparative analysis as the center of his argument. He began with the assertion that slavery in the United States was unique in many important ways. To explore those ways he built on Frank Tannenbaum's enormously influential book *Slave and Citizen*[2] to compare the liberal, Protestant, secularized, capitalist culture of the United States with the conservative, paternalistic, Catholic, quasi-medieval culture of Spain and Portugal and their New World colonies. Slavery in the United States was not imported from elsewhere, but was created here, "fashioned on the spot by Englishmen in whose traditions such an institution had no part." There was nothing here to prevent unmitigated capitalism from becoming unmitigated slavery. The emerging institution of slavery was, in effect, unchallenged by other institutions, Elkins contended.

In the Spanish and Portuguese world, slavery had long been familiar, so that for the Iberian New World there was already established a legal and social setting that was heavy with the traditions of centuries. The "tension and balance" among church, crown, and plantation in Latin America prevented slavery from being carried by the planter class to its ultimate logic. These three powerful interests—the crown, the planter, and the church—were all deeply involved with the system and had concerns that were "distinct and not always harmonious." This balance of power left its profound mark on the "sanctions governing the status and treatment of slaves." For example, unlike in the United States, there was high social approval given to freeing slaves, marriage was a rite protected by law, and the "master did not enjoy powers

---

[2] Frank Tannenbaum, *Slave and Citizen: The Negro in the Americas* (New York, 1947).

of life and death over the slave's body." The master owned a man's labor but not the man, "for master and slave were brothers in Christ." The question on which Elkins focused throughout is not the severity or laxness of the slave systems but the completeness with which the decisions concerning the life of the slave were under the master's control.

Thus in Latin America the slave had space to develop; it was, in Elkins' term, an "open" system that permitted the development of the rights of personality. In the United States slavery developed virtually unchecked by institutions. Slavery here operated as a "closed" system. Did not living in such a closed system, Elkins asked, "produce noticeable effects upon the slave's personality?"

The widespread and uniform description of the slave, docile but irresponsible, loyal but lazy, the "perpetual child incapable of maturity"—a "Sambo"—is uniquely North American, Elkins asserted. Sambo has no Latin American counterpart. The question of personality, then, becomes crucial to the problem of slavery in the United States, having something to do with the difference between open and closed systems of slavery. Elkins suggested that there were elements in the very nature of the plantation system in the United States—its closed character—that could "sustain infantilism as a normal feature of behavior." Sambo could thus be viewed as a plantation type, not a universal type. Was the Sambo personality a product of the powerless position in which slaves in the United States were placed, and did the plantation system in this country create childlike and servile personalities?

Descriptions of Africans bought by European slavetraders, said Elkins, indicate an absence of any particular "African" type at all and least of all anything resembling a Sambo. An examination of African culture suggested that Sambo was not an African type. Elkins then recreated what must have been the assault upon the personality suffered by the first generation of Africans brought here: the shock of capture, the long march to the sea, sale, the Middle Passage, the introduction to the New World. Undoubtedly, old guides for action were no longer valid; there was a detachment from prior cultural sanctions, a psychological numbing. The detachment was completed, though, Elkins said, by the kind of closed authority system into which the slave was introduced and to which he would have to adjust if he were to survive.

"The more diverse the symbols of authority" the greater is the possible variety of adjustment to them and, consequently, "the wider the margin of individuality." How wide or narrow was the margin on the antebellum plantation? Elkins used two kinds of material to probe the mechanisms of adjustment to absolute power: theoretical knowledge drawn from psychology and an analogy derived from literature on German concentration camps. It is the analogy with the adjustment to absolute power in the concentration camp that became the most controversial aspect of his study. Despite the many differences between the two systems, which Elkins carefully delineated, he was drawn to the concentration camp experience because the data indicated that "infantile personality features could be induced in a relatively short time among adults from diverse backgrounds." The concentration camp was not only a perverted slave system, but "a perverted patriarchy." He brought the two institutions together—the concentration camp and the antebellum slave plantation—to show the psychological effects of closed systems of control.

In studying the concentration camp, Elkins described the shock of arrest, the transportation to camp, the loss of control over physical needs, the prospect of interminable imprisonment. While most inmates perished, for others the concentration camp became a way of life. In the process of rapid assimilation to a drastically different form of social organization, the psychological consequences of being powerless or dependent, according to many observer-inmates, was the "reduction to infantilism or the rapid creation of childlike qualities." To relate the effect of social structure on the formation of personality, Elkins used three theories of personality: the Freudian, which describes the new values acquired by the superego, the new father-image in the form of the S.S. guard, and the process of identification with the aggressor; the interpersonal theory of Harry Stack Sullivan, which describes the estimations and expectations of "significant others" in the course of which the attitudes of the guards became internalized and the prisoners became as children; and role psychology, which places greater emphasis on the individual's cultural and institutional environment to explain similar observations of identification and infantilization.

Again, cruelty is not the key, but "closedness," in which all lines of authority descend from the S.S. guard or the master. The mechanism which inspires devotion even to a cruel S.S. guard or planter "father" is the abnormal dependency. In the concentration camp, Elkins said, some inmates had alternative roles; these are the people who have described the camps. Similarly, Latin American slaves entered a society where alternatives were more diverse than those awaiting slaves to the north. For the slave on the plantation in the United States, virtually all avenues of communication to the society at large originated and ended with the master. Of all the roles available on the North American plantation, "Sambo was by far the most pervasive."

In the final section of *Slavery* Elkins compared the structures of American and British society in mid-nineteenth century to explain the different role and function of abolitionists here and abroad. American society offered no proper chan-

nels—no national church, university system, national focus
of social and financial power, or national bar—no national
institutions, through which conflicting interests could be
mediated. In England men could hardly avoid thinking and
acting institutionally. In the United States the abolitionists
did not, and could not, analyze slavery as an institution, and
did not, and could not, exploit institutional means for subverting it, for in this country there was no way yet provided
for intellectuals to be "located institutionally and thus be
sensitized to power and the meaning of power."

The critical responses to *Slavery* have been many and varied
through the years and have touched upon the major concerns
of the book.

Although Tannenbaum's essay was published more than
twenty years ago, it has become central to a growing debate
over the comparative view of North American and Latin
American slavery. On one side are Marvin Harris and David
Brion Davis, who emphasize the similarities among modern
slave systems, Iberian or Anglo-Saxon. On the other side are
Tannenbaum, Elkins, and Herbert Klein, who utilize the
comparative method to highlight the contrasts between the
two systems.

Davis and Harris both directly challenge Tannenbaum,
and by extension, Elkins, at various points. Davis maintains
that there is too little evidence available to warrant generalizations on the relative functioning of slave systems. He also
points to the possibility of large gaps between the legal status
of the slave and the actual working of the institution. "Comparative analysis of historical forms of servitude reveals," he
asserts, "precedents for most of the striking traits of American
slavery." Despite great historical diversity, the very ways of
defining and regulating the institution show that "slavery has

always raised certain fundamental problems that originate in the simple fact that the slave is a man." Marvin Harris shares the notion that in examining legal treatment, reality, not law, is paramount. "The Crown could publish all the laws it wanted," he says, "but in the lowlands, sugar was king." In Brazil, as everywhere in the colonial world, he asserts, law and reality bore equally small resemblance to each other. All slaveowners of whatever nationality always seem to have been convinced that "their" slaves were the happiest. Perhaps what explains the notions about Anglo-Saxon slavery, he suggests, is that English planters had a bad press.

One empirical investigation denies the assertion that there was a great distinction between the model of the law and the reality of the practice. Herbert Klein, in a study of the operation of two colonial powers, Cuba and Virginia, concludes that the Cuban church did "modify the harsh rigors of plantation servitude"; as a result the black was allowed to merge fully into Cuban society when slavery was destroyed. His case, which supports Tannenbaum and Elkins, indicates that while the church in Cuba played an important part in mediating treatment of the slave, the Anglican church did not play a comparable part in Virginia life, with the result that "the Virginia slave faced a harsh world dominated by his master and with little protective intervention from outside institutions."

The view of the abolitionists as developed in *Slavery* has proven to be the least controversial aspect of Elkins' analysis. It has, as a result, attracted the least amount of criticism. Aileen S. Kraditor has been the only voice challenging his assertion that the abolitionists suffered from an antiinstitutional bias. She insists that the abolitionists did value institutions as weapons to be used in their struggle to break the political power of the slaveowners, and where existing institutions were deemed by them to be too corrupted, they tried to replace them with new institutions. Abolitionists were anti-institutional, she says, only in the sense that they recognized that the abolition of slavery required a reorganization of the entire social structure of the South.

Elkins' acceptance of the Sambo stereotype as an accurate description of the plantation personality, and particularly his use of the term "Sambo," have elicited the most extensive and most critical responses over the years. What Elkins may have set forth as an abstraction for analytical purposes, some of his critics have taken for the concrete historical reality and challenged within that context. Where Elkins refers to the "broad belt of indeterminacy between 'mere acting' and the 'true self,' " many of his critics maintain that Sambo was a mask the slave wore to protect himself and which he could remove at will. Both Mary Agnes Lewis and Earl E. Thorpe, for example, claim that the antebellum plantation provided more room to maneuver than Elkins allowed and that Sambo was, indeed, simply the face shown to the white man. It was the slaveowners who created the myth of Sambo to justify their institution and not the system that created a Sambo personality, says Thorpe, suggesting at the same time that perhaps the mask did not even exist. Lewis speaks of "compliance as a valid defensive function" which could be carried on without serious personality distortion. The use of force in the antebellum South, she asserts, is an indication that the Sambo personality was not internalized to the extent Elkins claimed. She maintains, along with several others in this book, that there were many more "significant others" in the life of the slave than the master, that a self-perpetuating, viable slave culture did emerge to compete with the slave-owner's authority and significance, a slave culture which the slaveowners were unable to perceive and therefore unable to pass down to historians as reality. Sterling Stuckey tries to delineate that subculture with the use of folk songs and folk tales. Stuckey suggests, on the basis of his evidence, that slaves were able "to fashion a life style and a set of values—an ethos"—which kept them from being imprisoned altogether by the definitions which the larger society sought to impose. This ethos, he says, an amalgam of Africanisms and New World elements, helped the slaves to endure.

Others challenge Elkins not on the basis that the Sambo personality did not exist, but rather because it was more widespread than Elkins recognized. Elkins' descriptions of the Sambo personality, says Orlando Patterson, bear a remarkable resemblance to those which existed in Jamaica. The term used in Jamaica to designate this personality pattern was "Quashee." Having drawn attention to the similarities, Patterson goes on to describe them, but in the process seems inadvertently to demonstrate subtle but not unimportant differences between Quashee and Sambo, particularly in the recurrence in Jamaica of traits of ambiguity and evasiveness in the slave personality. To Eugene D. Genovese, Sambo is a universal slave-type, a slavish personality, not simply a product of North American slavery. At the same time, Genovese contends, this slavish personality is much more complicated than Elkins' deterministic model describes. While Elkins was aware of alternatives and deviants and tried to explain their origin, he was forced to do so outside the model he had constructed.

The imaginative possibilities inherent in the way Elkins examined his subject are demonstrated by the variety of ways others have been inspired to deal with related questions. Several authors, for example, were drawn to Erving Goffman's

notion of a total institution. Goffman defines a total institution, a concept strikingly similar to Elkins' earlier characterization of a closed system, as a "place of residence and work
where a large number of like-situated individuals, cut off
from the wider society for an appreciable period of time,
together lead an enclosed, formally administered round of
life."[3] Roy Simon Bryce-Laporte uses Goffman's concept in a
systematic way to examine slavery over time. Christopher
Lasch and George Fredrickson also use Goffman's analysis
but in a somewhat different way. They offer as useful tools
Goffman's various strategies of accommodation, which are
possible in most total institutions but not in concentration
camps. Such strategies can explain a variety of possible responses from slaves aside from the infantilization process,
which they reject as being an inadequate explanation for
much of what we know about slave behavior. They discuss
another, and perhaps more appropriate, analogy, the prison,
for additional insights into ways total institutions operate
and affect the behavior of their inmates.

The impact of the slave plantation on the personality of the
slave can be better explained by the use of learning theory,
according to another critic whose work is not included here.
Stanley S. Guterman, a sociologist at Rutgers University, in
an unfinished essay entitled "Personality Theory and Sociological Explanation, A Critique of Elkins' *Slavery*," asserts
that Elkins' use of Freudian, Sullivanian, and role theories
explains behavior less satisfactorily than an examination of
the varied responses as products of different content of learning experience in plantation and concentration camp. Still
another provocative suggestion comes from Norman R.
Yetman, a sociologist at the University of Kansas. In an un-

---

[3] Goffman, *Asylums: Essays on the Social Situation of Mental Patients
and Other Inmates* (Chicago, 1961).

published paper based on work drawn from his doctoral dissertation,[4] he maintains that an empirical examination of the Sambo thesis can be undertaken, even with the limited data available. Since Elkins maintained that Sambo should appear with greater frequency among certain categories of the slave population, it is, says Yetman, a statistical concept. Before it is assumed that the data is inadequate, the voluminous slave narratives, autobiographies, and interviews should be examined carefully. Yetman's concerns are pertinent, because although Elkins has placed great reliance upon the comparison with Latin American slavery and the analogy to the concentration camp to support his contentions, neither is really indispensable to his thesis.

Although Elkins emphatically states that he is not relating the Sambo personality of slavery to the current Afro-American population, others, black and white, have made such connections. Daniel Moynihan, Charles Silberman, and Genovese, among others, have used this frame of reference, for which they have frequently received hostile reactions from within the black community.[5] A recent essay by Genovese, included here, indicates a shift from his earlier position, however. Where he in the past concentrated on rebelliousness versus facility, he now stresses black culture. He traces the positive aspects of the slaves' responses: ingenuity, self-expression, and the continuity in black culture as a foundation upon which the increasingly self-conscious black community is able to build.

4 "The Slave Personality: A Test of the 'Sambo' Hypothesis," University of Pennsylvania, 1969.
5 Daniel Moynihan (with Nathan Glazer), *Beyond the Melting Pot; the Negroes, Puerto Ricans, Jews, Italians and Irish of New York City* (Cambridge, Mass., 1963); Charles Silberman, *Crisis in Black and White* (New York, 1964); Eugene D. Genovese, "The Legacy of Slavery and the Roots of Black Nationalism," *Studies on the Left* 6, no. 6 (1966), 3-26.

Although the focus of this collection is on those critiques that extend or challenge Elkins' ideas, there is a growing body of literature that accepts and uses his analysis. Two black psychiatrists, William H. Grier and Price M. Cobbs, in their book, *Black Rage*,[6] apparently accept the Elkins analysis in large part and then apply it to the present. Early in their study they say that "we must conclude that much of the pathology as seen in black people had its genesis in slavery. The culture that was born in that experience of bondage has been passed from generation to generation." In a retrospective examination of slave childrearing, they assert that all slaves initially had been confronted with the option to submit or die, and obviously those who survived reared their children to live and therefore to submit. The attack on the autonomy of the slave child must have been relentless:

> Once the mother opts for her child's life she . . . had to take particular pains to crush any defiant aggressive traits. No maturity could be allowed; no independence could be encouraged. . . . He must learn to fear and exalt the owner and to hate himself.[7]

Referring specifically to reactions of Jews under Nazi persecution, they go on to conclude that

> the institution of slavery will call forth a tendency on the part of the enslaved to identify with the oppressor. . . . the victim . . . takes on the personal characteristics of the oppressor and treats his fellow sufferers with the same cruelty he has himself only recently suffered. . . . This phenomenon, however, must have been a regular occurrence . among slaves who lived permanently in a hopeless state.[8]

[6] New York, 1968.
[7] *Ibid.*, 143–44.
[8] *Ibid.*, 145.

James P. Comer, also a black psychiatrist, has examined individual development and black rebellion and traced the origin of many present problems in the black community to slavery.[9]

> Slavery—whether pleasant and paternalistic or harsh and rejecting—reduced most of the African captives to a state of psychological childhood. The captive was rendered helpless and totally dependent on an all-powerful master by a set of overwhelming circumstances. . . . the masters' total control enabled them to infantilize many slaves.[10]

Grier and Cobbs claim that the key to a functioning family is the ability of the adults to protect the weaker members, and that under slavery "there could be no functioning family." The entire matter of slave families is an unsettled one, but it is by implication an important aspect of Elkins' evaluation of slave personality. Two unpublished examinations of slave families, one by Willie Lee Rose and the other by Herbert Gutman, suggest a considerably more stable family life among slaves than has previously been recognized. Gutman, for example, on the basis of Freedmen's Bureau marriage records, suggests that significant numbers of slaves lived as husband and wife for many years, raised children, and in many ways functioned in two-parent households. Gutman also indicates that there is substance to the assertion that the movement of large numbers of freedmen after the Civil War was for the purpose of reuniting families. Willie Lee Rose suggests that although both parents were frequently present in the slave family, and that indeed the family was consider-

[9] James P. Comer, "Individual Development and Black Rebellion: Some Parallels," *Midway: A Magazine of Discovery in the Arts and Sciences* 9, no. 1 (1968), 33–48.
[10] *Ibid.*, 40–41.

ably more stable than previously imagined, there were aspects
of childrearing ill designed for the development of secure
personalities and well designed for the Sambo personality.
Both parents had something to do with the process of social-
izing the child to survive in slavery.

Amidst the impressive outpourings of criticism directed at
Slavery what is curious are those areas left untouched. There
is, first, the word "Sambo," which has contributed much to
the controversial nature of Elkins' book. It is of some historical interest because although Sambo is now a word imbued with specific and shared preconceived notions, it was
not always so. Harriet Beecher Stowe's Sambo is not at all
Elkins' Sambo. Sambo existed in the antebellum period—that
is, the name was used commonly—but it was applied to all
kinds of slaves with all kinds of personalities. The docile,
impassive, humble, obedient, childlike slave had been described
by slaveowners in the Old South, but he was not precisely
labeled as Sambo until considerably later.

An even more curious lack of attention has been demonstrated in relation to the concentration camp analogy. With
few exceptions (see Bryce-Laporte's essay), critics have focused their energies on the slave plantation rather than on the
Nazi camps. Elkins relied heavily on Bruno Bettelheim's
study, "Individual and Mass Behavior in Extreme Situations,"[11] and the historians who responded to the challenges
Elkins raised were specialists in American history and were
willing to assume the validity of Bettelheim's descriptions and
analyses. The sociologists and social psychologists who have
been intrigued by Elkins' efforts to use the tools of their fields
to analyze his own have usually been drawn to the subject
by an interest in slavery and have therefore shown little interest in the concentration camp description.

[11] *Journal of Abnormal Psychology* 38 (October, 1943), 417–52.

Bettelheim was in a concentration camp for a relatively short time, he operated from a privileged position, and he used his work as therapy to help him retain his sanity—obviously useful for him, but not necessarily conducive to scholarly detachment or even to accurate perceptions. Other survivors tell different stories and have different insights. Even Elkins' other sources, Eugen Kogon in *The Theory and Practice of Hell,* and Elie A. Cohen in *Human Behavior in the Concentration Camp,* provide descriptions of a wider range of responses.[12] Cohen, for example, carefully describes the inmates' identification with the S.S. as "partial" for most prisoners. The greater number of the prisoners identified not with the moral standards of the S.S., he concludes, but with their aggressive manifestations. Thus the prisoners may have adopted aggressive behavior but not the standards or values of the S.S., which is a different kind of identification than the slaves presumably had. Some inmates escaped identification successfully, particularly the political prisoners, who organized their subculture and underlife, to use the language applied to slave society. Said one woman inmate: "I never felt bound by a single one of the rules laid down by the S.S. I observed them only as far as I considered them of benefit to the prisoners and felt free to break them whenever I was unobserved." Those who seemed to have conformed more completely to Bettelheim's description were the Kapos, those inmates who functioned as liaison to the concentration camp apparatus, somewhat comparable to the slave drivers of the antebellum plantations. None of these comments challenge Elkins' thesis, but had he used a wider range of concentration

12 Eugen Kogon, *The Theory and Practice of Hell: The German Concentration Camps and the System behind Them* (New York, 1958); Elie A. Cohen, *Human Behavior in the Concentration Camp* (New York, c. 1953).

camp response he might have had a wider latitude in examining the plantation as well.

Another aspect of Elkins' analysis surprisingly neglected is the notion of infantilization. Different societies rear their young in different ways. What infantilized behavior meant for a slave born and reared on a Southern plantation must have been profoundly different from the regression as expressed by a reasonably well educated, relatively sophisticated concentration camp inmate. And so indeed was their behavior quite different, although Elkins may be quite right in recognizing infantilized, or more accurately, slavish, behavior in both situations. If Cohen's explanation is valid, then concentration camp inmates accepted the manifestation of the aggressive behavior of their S.S. guards but not the moral standards or the image of themselves the S.S. projected. Whatever the force of their regression, concentration camp inmates usually knew they were superior to their oppressors. The process of infantilization of the slaves, to accept Elkins' hypothesis, was different, because they not only accepted and identified with the authority of their masters, but many accepted, in one way or another, the description of themselves as created by the rulers of their society.[13]

Stanley Elkins, in his lengthy rejoinder, "Slavery and Ideology," groups the many criticisms *Slavery* has aroused through the years into three broad categories: the differences between Latin American and North American slavery; the Nazi concentration camp analogy; the significance of anti-institutionalism in American life for abolitionism. After ex-

[13] These remarks are not meant to add to the accumulated criticisms, for that is neither my intent nor my role; indeed, the different quality of the infantilization may even add greater force to the validity of Elkins' analogy.

amining them in some detail he offers predictions about the future course of the argument. Once again, as he did a dozen years ago, he hopes to reinvigorate and redirect the study of slavery by offering new and altered perspectives. How successful he will be the coming years will tell.

PART ONE

APPRAISALS

Chattel Slavery and Concentration Camps

EARL E. THORPE

After criticizing the historical writings of Ulrich Bonnell Phillips as being strongly biased and based on faulty sources, Richard Hofstadter wrote in 1944:

> Let the study of the Old South be undertaken by other (unbiased) scholars who have absorbed the viewpoint of modern cultural anthropology, who have a feeling for social psychology . . . , who will concentrate upon the neglected rural elements that formed the great majority of the Southern population, who will not rule out the testimony of more critical observers, and who will realize that any history of slavery must be written in large part from the standpoint of the slave—and then the possibilities of the Old South as a field of research and historical experience will loom larger than ever.[1]

In 1959 the University of Chicago Press published a book entitled *Slavery: A Problem in American Institutional and Intellectual Life*, which was written by a scholar who states that he accepted certain of the Hofstadter challenges as incentives for his study of the institution. This scholar, Stanley

[1] Richard Hofstadter, "U. B. Phillips and the Plantation Legend," *Journal of Negro History*, XXIX (April, 1944), 109–24.

M. Elkins, in an opening chapter entitled "Slavery as a Problem in Historiography," opines that studies of the Negro in
American history made by Negroes themselves, as well as
those by Phillips, James Ford Rhodes, Kenneth Stampp,
Gunnar Myrdal, Herbert Aptheker, and just about everyone
who has previously written on the subject have the serious
defect of being biased, polemical, and overly dominated by
moral considerations. Thus Professor Elkins clearly indicates
that he is going to beware of the heavy hand of prejudice
which he feels has done damage to previous writings about
the Negro.

Elkins makes it clear that he does not believe the old charge
that Negroes are biologically inferior. Although he shares the
conviction that the slaves were indeed culturally inferior,
this scholar goes to considerable length to disagree with
Phillips and others who contended that plantation slaves in
America were inferior because the African cultures from
which they came were inferior. Unlike Phillips, Melville J.
Herskovits, and others, Elkins agrees with those scholars who
believe that very little of the African heritage survived in
North America.[2] "No true picture . . . of African culture,"
he concludes, "seems to throw any light at all on the origins
of what would emerge, in American plantation society, as the
stereotyped 'Sambo' personality" (97).

On one aspect of his own thesis, Elkins writes:

> An examination of American slavery, checked at certain
> critical points against a very different slave system, that of
> Latin America, reveals that a major key to many of the
> contrasts between them was an institutional key: The

[2] See Melville J. Herskovits, *The Myth of the Negro Past* (New York,
1941), and E. Franklin Frazier, *The Negro in the United States* (New
York, 1949).

presence or absence of other powerful institutions in society made an immense difference in the character of slavery itself. In Latin America, the very tension and balance among three kinds of organizational concerns—church, crown, and plantation agriculture—prevented slavery from being carried by the planting class to its ultimate logic. For the slave in terms of the space thus allowed for the development of men and women as moral beings, the result was an "open system": a system of contact with free society through which ultimate absorption into society could and did occur with great frequency. The rights of personality implicit in the ancient traditions of slavery and in the church's most venerable assumptions on the nature of the human soul were thus in a vital sense conserved, whereas to a staggering extent the very opposite was true in North American slavery [which] operated as a "closed" system (81).

This scholar seeks to further buttress his conclusion with a contention that the impact of enslavement on the personality and character of Nazi concentration camp inmates was substantially identical with that which plantation slavery in North America had on the personality and character of Negroes. Utilizing the excellent and abundant literature which describes and analyzes the behavior of concentration camp inmates, Professor Elkins gives a concise but thorough picture of this behavior (103 ff.). *Without any effort at all* to enumerate the *differences* between plantation slavery and the concentration camp, Elkins admits that there are differences but contends that this does not make comparison impossible (104). He characterizes Negro slaves in North America as a "society of helpless dependents" (98). The dominant slave type, Elkins states, "corresponded in its major outlines to 'Sambo.'" This dominant type existed, he declares, because "there were

elements in the very structure of the plantation system—its
'closed' character—that could sustain infantilism as a normal
feature of behavior."[3] Of what he feels was the dominant
slave type, he writes: "Sambo, the typical plantation slave,
was docile but irresponsible, loyal but lazy, humble but
chronically given to lying and stealing; his behavior was full

[3] When he holds that the Sambo stereotype is a factual representation
of the plantation slave personality, Elkins apparently fails to perceive that
he may at the same time be ascribing that same personality to the masses
of antebellum Southern whites. Bruno Bettelheim (see Chapter Seven of
his *The Informed Heart: Autonomy in a Mass Age* [Glencoe, Illinois,
1960]), and other observers state that the same psychological forces operative within the concentration camps were the dominant ones operative on
the German populace outside the camps, and the effect was the same, with
the difference being largely one of degree. Wilbur Cash and other critics of
Southern culture have pointed out that the masses of Southern whites were
subjected to the same frontier forces, similar patterns of control, paternalism, general illiteracy, and exclusion from the political, social, and cultural mainstream as was the Negro slave, with the difference being one of
degree. These same critics have often ascribed to Southern whites, antebellum and postbellum, virtually the same negative personality traits and
characteristics as those often ascribed to the Negro.
    It is doubtless true, as Professor Elkins writes, that certain situations or
settings put premiums on certain types of behavior (228). In order for the
rigid Sambo stereotype to emerge as the true slave personality, however, a
high degree of constancy or consistency in behavior would have to be
maintained. Such has never been the case where race relations in the South
are concerned. The strange career of Jim Crow did not begin with Ap-
pomattox, as Elkins thinks (133), but was a prominent feature of Old South
culture.
    Also, the rather common belief which Elkins appears to accept com-
pletely (82 ff.) to the effect that the Old South accepted the Negro only
in the posture of a child is an erroneous over-simplification. Here again
consistency was too lacking for the image to be true, for it is largely in
the social relations or amenities that the child-posture was insisted on. At
working time, which existed far more frequently and lasted much longer
than the brief periods of what may be termed points of social contact, the
white South sought to get the bondsman to give a very efficient and adult-
like performance. The same is true where the matter of obeying the laws
was concerned, for here the white South wanted not child-like irresponsibility but adult-like respect for the law. The notion that the Old South
always encouraged and wanted the child-posture from Negroes needs considerable revision.

of infantile silliness and his talk inflated with childish exaggeration. His relationship with his master was one of utter dependence and childish attachment" (82). Of his acceptance of this stereotype, Professor Elkins writes: "The picture has far too many circumstantial details, its hues have been stroked in by too many brushes, for it to be denounced as counterfeit. Too much folk-knowledge, too much plantation literature, too much of the Negro's own lore, have gone into its making to entitle one in good conscience to condemn it as 'conspiracy'" (84). "Why should it be, turning once more to Latin America," he continues, "that there one finds no Sambo, no social tradition, that is, in which slaves were defined by virtually complete consensus as children incapable of being treated with the full privileges of freedom and adulthood?" "There," he answers, "the system surely had its brutalities [but] there . . . the system was not closed" (134).

The position taken in this article is that the Sambo stereotype was not the real Negro personality because, unlike the concentration camp, plantation slavery in North America had enough "elbow room" for the development of a more complex, better-rounded personality; that Sambo was often the side of his personality which the Negro chose to present to the white man; that although the child-posture is the one which whites generally sought to effect in their relationship with Negroes, because of the contradictions and "elbow room" in the system most bondsmen never internalized many of the planters' values. Elkins fails to recognize properly the complexity of slave personality. The bondsman wore many faces, of which Sambo usually was only his public and not his private one.[4]

---

[4] On the more positive side, it may be pointed out that Elkins' discussion of the role of guilt in liberal and reform movements is highly provocative. Too, unfortunately for the scholar who is interested in plantation slavery

With reference to the so-called Latin American contrast, it seems that there are at least three effective answers to the Elkins thesis. First, despite their differences, because of the high degree of similarity, it is erroneous to categorize Latin American slavery as an "open system" and the North American variety as the "closed system." A second point hinges on this scholar's often-repeated assertion that "one searches in vain through the literature of the Latin American slave systems for the 'Sambo' of our tradition—the perpetual child incapable of maturity" (84). This is so not because there were no slaves in Latin America who evidenced clear Sambo characteristics as one side of their personalities. Rather, the

---

in America, there were no professional psychologists and psychiatrists among the Negro bondsmen. Therefore, if the student of this institution will avoid the pitfalls into which Elkins stumbled, from a careful study and comparison of the behavior of concentration camp inmates he may gain great insight into many aspects of this "problem in American institutional and intellectual life."

The growth of anthropology, psychoanalysis, social psychology, and related disciplines, and the significance of the new insights into human behavior which they offer, means that the historian of the second half of the twentieth century will probably not be counted adequately literate who does not have an acquaintance with these disciplines. In calling for this broader approach to the study of the Negro in American history, Professors Hofstadter and Elkins are correct. In his December 1957 address before the American Historical Association, entitled "The Next Assignment," William L. Langer had as his central concern "the directions which historical study might profitably take in the years to come." (In *American Historical Review*, LXII, No. 2 [January, 1958], 284.) Here he urged historians to cease to be "buried in their own conservatism" and to recognize "the urgently needed deepening of our historical understanding through exploitation of the concepts and findings of modern . . . psychoanalysis and its later developments and variations as included in the term 'dynamic' or 'depth psychology.'" The whole of Professor Langer's Presidential Address was an attack on what he called the "almost completely negative attitude toward the teachings of psychoanalysis" which historians have traditionally held, together with some illustrations and suggestions as to specific applications of this knowledge which historians may make. The present writer believes that scholars who are interested in Afro-American studies would do well to take Professor Langer's suggestions seriously.

omission reflects Professor Elkins' own admission that in contrast to the situation in North America, Latin American culture *accepted the institution of slavery as a necessary evil.* Elkins fails to see that there was thus no need to create myths and stereotypes to justify the institution. In other words, the existence of the stereotype in North America is rooted not in a true estimate of slave personality but in the peculiar psychological needs of the slave owners. By their effort to convince themselves, and everyone else, that the institution was a positive good, the planters of North America were compelled to claim that Sambo was indeed the true slave personality.[5] Literature can be very misleading.

In addition to the objection that the personality differences are usually little more than mystical literary inventions created to satisfy the North American slave owners' conscience, one reviewer of the Elkins volume shows that when the capitalist system matured in Latin America, there was practically no difference between treatment of slaves and freedmen there and the treatment meted out in North America. The reviewer concludes:

[5] Any historian who denies that Sambo, often feigned but sometimes genuine, was one side of the bondsman's personality is probably guilty of being unrealistic. What is now known about both human behavior and totalitarian systems calls for a change in some aspects of the slave image which some Negro historians have favored. Since these were their immediate blood and cultural forebears, and in view of the overly narrow image of them which the Slavocracy projected, it is understandable that they sometimes have given great stress to the neater side of the bondsman's personality and character. Thus in reaction against one stereotype, they have been in danger of creating another one, equally false.

Contemporary knowledge ought to have put beyond the bounds of controversy that slavery is generally debasing and degrading to human personality. Rather than fly in the face of this fact and deny the whole of the Slavocracy's propaganda, the truths that should be insisted upon are: (1) These negative behavior characteristics are not innate racial traits; (2) They indict the slave system and not the enslaved; and (3) They do not constitute the whole picture.

The slave plantation . . . was a special, emergent capitalist form of industrial organization, which appeared earlier, and with more intensity, in the colonies of the north European powers than in the colonies of Spain. . . . The differentials in growth of slave plantations in different colonies are to be understood as resulting from different ecologies, differential maturation of metropolitan markets and industries, and different political relationships between creole governing bodies and the metropolitan authorities. The rate of growth of the slave plantation . . . did not hinge on matters of race, civil liberties, protection of the rights of individuals slave and free, or the presence or absence of one or several religious codes.[6]

As dark as the picture of chattel slavery in North America was, because the theory, literature, law, and actual practice were frequently at variance, the results on personality development were not as extreme as Professor Elkins would have us believe.[7]

[6] S. W. Mintz, in *American Anthropologist*, LXIII, No. 3 (June, 1961), 586. Professor Elkins appears to be essentially correct in his contention that in the case of plantation slavery and the concentration camps each became "a kind of grotesque patriarchy" (104, 113). The present observer does not find this the startling discovery which Professor Elkins seems to think it is. There is a sense in which practically every highly authoritarian system is a grotesque patriarchy, and Elkins seems to miss Wilbur Cash's often-repeated assertions in his volume, *The Mind of the South* (New York, 1941), that the total Southern culture, both antebellum and postbellum, has been essentially such a grotesque patriarchy. The present observer has even noticed that in several small colleges and universities the college president represents for a number of students and faculty members a father image and paternalism is the dominant basis of their relationships. This paternalistic factor is the major argument against highly authoritarian systems and, therefore, the major argument in favor of democracy as a way of life which does not treat adults as if they are children.

[7] Apparently the only subject on which Professor Elkins is willing to accept the judgment of the slave owners is their conclusion that Negroes constitute an inferior human type. As indicated, to be sure he does not accept the reasoning on which his conclusion rests, but he devotes one-half of his book to an effort to prove that the slave owners' conclusion was a

It is wrong to study in an institution or culture, as he does, "the infantilizing tendencies of power" without pointing out the counter-tendencies which were operative and which tended to minimize, negate, or eliminate many of the infantilizing tendencies. This omission makes his conclusions about the personalities of plantation slaves in North America erroneous in their simplicity. Some of the significant omissions which would have to be included in a valid analogy are discussed below.

A major difference between the two systems is to be found in the extent of resistance to enslavement. Many observers

---

correct one. Yet, near the end of his volume, when discussing "Slavery, Consensus, and the Southern Intellect," he is well-nigh completely denunciatory of the Southern intellect which he says, mainly because of its rigidity, single-mindedness, and hysterical fears (207), was not able to think objectively about slavery. "At most," he writes, the Southern intellect "thought in the vicinity of slavery." On this point, Elkins further states:

> The existence of thoroughgoing consensus in a democratic community appears to create two sorts of conditions for the functioning of intellect. One is sternly coercive, the other, wildly permissive. On the one hand, consensus narrows the alternatives with which thought may deal; on the other, it removes all manner of limits—limits of discrimination, circumspection, and discipline—on the alternatives that remain. The former function is probably better understood than the latter; both, however, were fully at work in the intellectual life of the ante-bellum South (212-13).

Elkins declares that the Southern intellect made "a general agreement" to stop "[objective] thinking about slavery altogether," and points up the ineffectiveness of pro-slavery propaganda by reminding us that though the slave's way of life was declared to be a better one than that of Northern industrial workers, there was an absolute failure of "any free workers to present themselves for enslavement" (216). "In reality," he concludes, "the contour of this body of thought was governed by the fact that the South was talking no longer to the world, or even to the North, but to itself. It is this fact—the fact of internal consensus and the peculiar lack of true challenge-points at any level of Southern society—that gives the pro-slavery polemic its special distinction" (217). In this chapter Elkins is clearly describing the Southern mind as a diseased one and he rejects its conclusions on practically all points except one, this being the concept of Negro inferiority.

have noted the almost complete lack of resistance among inmates of the concentration camps, pointing out that although
guards were usually few the prisoners walked meekly into
the gas chambers or quietly dug their graves and lined up
beside them to be shot.[8] Bruno Bettelheim is severely critical
of the prisoners for what he feels was their unrealistic lack
of resistance.[9] Elkins agrees with this depiction of the behavior of camp inmates, but gives a similar characterization of
the plantation slaves, whom he calls "a society of helpless
dependents" (98). That he takes this statement literally can
be seen in the disparaging remarks which he makes about
Herbert Aptheker's study of slave revolts[10] and in his own
comparison of slave revolts in North and South America.
Elkins does not perceive that, despite the absence of pro-
tracted large-scale slave revolts in North America, the many
forms of persistent resistance by the bondsmen to their enslavement is dramatic evidence of the very significant difference between the two systems.

Professor Elkins offers as one proof that Negro slaves were
a docile mass the statement that "the revolts that actually did
occur were in no instance planned by plantation laborers but
rather by Negroes whose qualities of leadership were developed well outside the full coercions of the plantation authority-system" (138). So anxious is he to prove his thesis that he
apparently discounts the possibility that this may be so not
because of the lack of leadership qualities among plantation

[8] See Otto Kurst, *Auschwitz* (New York, 1960); Eugen Kogon, *The
Theory and Practice of Hell*, tr. by Heinz Norden (New York, 1960);
Rudolf Hoess, *Commandant of Auschwitz*, tr. by Constantine FitzGibbon
(New York, 1961); Victor Frankl, *From Death Camp to Existentialism*, tr.
by Ilse Lasch (Boston, 1959).

[9] Bettelheim, *The Informed Heart;* see especially the last three chapters.

[10] Aptheker's sources he calls "unsubstantiated rumors gleaned from
rural Southern newspapers."

slaves but because the opportunity to plan revolts was greater in or near towns or cities. Furthermore, although, as Elkins points out, Denmark Vesey was a freed artisan, Nat Turner a literate preacher, and Gabriel a blacksmith who lived near Richmond, their hundreds and thousands of co-conspirators were not of this category, but were mostly the plantation slaves whom Elkins describes as humble, lazy, silly, immoral, docile, and loyal. In other words, to Elkins the leaders of the plots and revolts were the unusual or exceptional individuals. This and similar arguments lead the present writer to the conviction that Professor Elkins is here utilizing a version of the old argument which attributed the intelligence and achievements of some light-skinned Negroes to the amount of so-called white blood in their veins, thereby eliminating them from the race.[11]

Several observers have written of the manner in which the Nazis thought of and sought to operate the concentration camps with the same organization and administrative emphases

[11] For other examples of the evidence of slave resistance which Elkins treats as of little significance, see Harvey Wish, "American Slave Insurrections before 1861," *Journal of Negro History*, XXII (July, 1937), 299–320; R. A. and A. H. Bauer, "Day to Day Resistance of Slavery," *Ibid.*, XXVII (October, 1942), 388–419; Kenneth W. Porter, "Florida Slaves and Free Negroes in the Seminole War, 1825–1842," *Ibid.*, XXVIII (October, 1943), 390–421; John Hope Franklin, *From Slavery to Freedom* (New York, 1947); and Earl E. Thorpe, *The Mind of the Negro* (Baton Rouge, 1961), Chapters III, IV, and V.

Not only is Elkins' picture of what oppression did to the personality and character of plantation slaves overdrawn, but the same is true of the picture which he paints of the results of oppression in the concentration camp. On this Victor Frankl has written:

> The sort of person the prisoner became was the result of an inner decision, and not the result of camp influences alone. Fundamentally, therefore, any man can, even under such circumstances, decide what shall become of him—mentally and spiritually. He may retain his human dignity even in a concentration camp. (In his *From Death Camp to Existentialism*, 66.)

as are found in the most modern factory.[12] Absence of the mid-twentieth-century level of organizational knowledge and efficiency was a major factor which kept plantation slavery from being as dehumanizing as was the case with concentration camps. It is not without justification that modern man uses the word "totalitarianism" to describe this century's mass state. "Every single moment of their lives was strictly regulated and supervised," one critic says of the camp inmates. "They had no privacy whatsoever."[13] Even after the work day was over, the camp inmate lived in barracks-style quarters which did not afford anything like the amount of freedom from the surveillance and oppressions of the ruling elite that slave quarters on the plantation usually offered. It is because he was so constantly under surveillance and oppression, together with the chronic possibility and fear of momentary extermination, that the camp inmate presents the classic picture of the ever-regressed personality and character which Elkins mistakenly attributes to plantation slaves.

Many camp inmates were made the subject of barbarous medical experiments.[14] Plantation slaves were not so used as human guinea pigs. A highly literate former camp inmate states that at the peak of its development, the "slave labor and extermination policy [of the concentration camps] did away with all considerations for the value of a life, even in terms of a slave society. . . . In the Hitler state slaves [did not even have an] investment value. That was the *great difference* between exploitation by private capitalists and exploitation by a state answering only to itself."[15] Are we to

[12] See, for example, works already cited by Bettelheim, Kurst, Kogon, Hoess, and Frankl.

[13] Bettelheim, *The Informed Heart*, 108.

[14] See A. Mitscherlich and F. Mielke, *Doctors of Infamy* (New York, 1949).

[15] Bettelheim, *The Informed Heart*, 243. Italics supplied.

suppose, as Elkins does, that this "great difference" between the two systems made no difference where the personalities which they bred or allowed is concerned? Whereas the concentration camp inmate, in order to keep from becoming an elected candidate for the incinerators or gas chambers, always had to act and work as if he were physically able to be of some service to the Third Reich, the plantation slave was usually free from this daily and hourly threat of a death sentence. Because he represented economic capital, usually the worst that the plantation slave could expect for dissatisfying the ruling class on such matters was a lashing or being sold, but of the camp inmates, we are told, "Everybody was convinced that his chances for survival were very slim; therefore to preserve himself as an individual seemed pointless."[16] "The prisoners' lives were in such extreme danger," continues this observer, "that little energy or interest was left over" for anything except concern with the problem of sheer survival.[17]

In his 1957 Presidential Address before the American Historical Association, Professor William L. Langer discussed the great psychological impact which the Black Death had on the personality and character of Europeans of the late medieval and early modern periods. A study might well be made of the consciousness of death in Negro thought, but, apart from the horrors of the Middle Passage, there is nothing in the history of plantation slavery to match the impact of the Black Death or the omnipresent hand of death in the concentration camps. This fact is doubtless one of several which kept plantation slavery from being as dehumanizing as were the Nazi internment camps.

16 *Ibid.*, 138.
17 *Ibid.*, 203.

Elkins, Victor Frankl, Bettelheim, and others have commented on the weakness and almost disappearance at times
of the emotional life of the camp inmates.[18] This is a marked
contrast to the emotional life of the plantation slaves, an
emotionality often so variegated and strong that it has added
an indelible heritage of dance, song, laughter, and pathos to
the American way of life. In the literature on concentration
camps, many pages are filled with discussions of the *Musel-*
manner, or Moslems, persons who had completely given up
all interest in life. To this the literature on chattel slavery
stands in marked contrast. A number of scholars state that
throughout the slave era, among other attributes Negroes
manifested "childlike qualities of happiness and good nature."[19] Where were these qualities to be found in the concentration camps? In great contrast to the plantation system,
with concentration camp inmates, *the other side of child be-*
havior, a side which Elkins ignores entirely—that of the happy
child—is missing.

Bettelheim tells us that concentration camp inmates were
deliberately kept on a starvation diet in order to make them
easier to handle. "It is difficult," he writes, "to deeply terror-
ize a people that is well fed and well housed."[20] As inadequate
as their diets usually were, plantation slaves were better fed
than concentration camp inmates. Largely because of the
poor quality and inadequate amounts of food given, after a
few months of imprisonment, most of the latter were mere
skin and bones suffering chronically from diarrhea and dysen-
tery.[21]

---

[18] *Ibid.*, passim; Elkins, 115.
[19] Otto Klineberg, ed., *Characteristics of the American Negro* (New
York, 1944).
[20] Bettelheim, *The Informed Heart*, 297.
[21] Elkins states that in the concentration camps, because of chronic
hunger due to the scanty meals, "even the sexual instincts no longer func-

The fact that most antebellum Negroes were *born into slavery*, while the concentration camp inmates were born and reared as free men and women, must have considerable significance where the development of personality is concerned. Also, there were no state laws in Nazi Germany comparable to the "Black Codes" of the Old South. Although they were often honored more in the breach than in the observance, are we to suppose that the existence of laws setting limits to the cruelty which plantation slaves could be made the objects of, and actual court cases which resulted from the existence of these laws, had no effect on the personality and character development of the slave?

We are informed that "No prisoner was told why he was imprisoned, and never for how long."[22] In contrast to this, are we to suppose that the elaborate biblical, historical, and other justifications for his race's enslavement which were constantly presented to the plantation bondsman had no effect on the development of his personality and character? As ridiculous as these justifications now appear, may it not be that such rationalizations given to an enslaved race may affect their personality development in a more positive way than is the case with enslavement of selected members of a free populace, with no justification at all given?

Professor Elkins calls both the concentration camps and antebellum plantations highly similar "closed systems." Yet where in the concentration camps was there anything comparable to the ebony-hued slave women suckling white infants at their breasts, or free white children and slave children

---

tioned" (107). Bettelheim denies this and states that both homosexuality and masturbation were practiced in the camps, though often more because of anxiety as to whether one had lost his sexuality than for any other reason.

22 Bettelheim, *The Informed Heart*, 108.

playing together, or planters paying high cash prices for
colored mistresses and concubines? Where in Nazi Germany
was there an Underground Railroad, or a geographically
contiguous region rife with abolitionism, or anything even
comparable to the colonization society? How many S.S.
officers or Kapos encouraged the camp inmates to sing while
they worked as was the case with the Negro slaves? While the
plantations produced the enchanting slave songs and tales,
and eternally beautiful spirituals, what of comparable beauty
has come out of the concentration camps?[23] And can we
imagine inmates being in such physical and psychical condition so as to be considered for last-ditch military service in
the manner of the Confederate Congress voting to enlist and
arm Negro slaves? Because their fruits were so different, we
must conclude that the personalities of slaves and camp inmates were different.

So absolute and unmitigated was the cruelty of the concentration camps that they were indeed the closed systems to
which Elkins refers. In them it is true that prisoners had to
make a total adjustment to enslavement, and for most dehumanization was well nigh complete. But in the United
States even the slaves knew that the basic national creed as
couched in such documents as the Declaration of Independence and the Federal Constitution ran counter to the

[23] There were, of course, similarities in the reactions of inmates of the
concentration camps and the plantation slaves. Among those similarities,
both groups tended to be highly interested in food and other bodily needs,
to day-dream a lot as an escape from the harsh realities of their lives, and
to internalize the values of the ruling class. Because of fear of the ruling
elite, both tended to direct many of their aggressions against one another,
and, as was the case with the camp prisoner-leaders known as Kapos, sometimes Negroes put in positions of leadership outdid the Slavocracy in manifestations of anti-Negroism. Among both, stealing from or cheating the
ruling elite was often considered as honorable as stealing from fellow
slaves was thought despicable.

prospect of their remaining eternally in bondage. Where in Nazi Germany did a similar conflict exist between ideal and reality?

Professor Elkins' failure adequately to consider these differences means that his conclusion that the effect which the concentration camp had on its inmates is the same effect that plantation slavery in North America had on Negroes is in need of drastic revision. While he seems to understand fairly well the mind and personality of the camp inmate, his understanding of the mind of the Negro slave leaves much to be desired.

Despite their similarities, the differences between the two systems are so significant that, for the development of a more healthy or adult personality, when compared to the concentration camps the plantation system in North America had considerably more "elbow room." It was not on the plantations of North America, as Elkins claims, but in such products of Occidental efficiency and technology as Belsen, Sachsenhausen, Dachau, and Buchenwald that our Christian civilization first saw the institution of slavery "carried to its ultimate logic."[24]

24 A number of psychologists and psychiatrists have pointed out that the radical alterations in personality and character which occurred in concentration camps prove that some long-accepted Freudian concepts, valid under normal life-circumstances, are invalid where the behavior of man under extreme stress is concerned. Here is a situation roughly analogous to that of Newtonian physics, which twentieth-century scientists have shown to break down at both of the extreme ends of the matter and space continuities. It has been pointed out that much in Freudian psychology was peculiarly applicable to the nineteenth-century society in which Freud lived, "the stability of whose institutional and status relationships could always to a large extent be taken for granted," but less appropriate for a dynamic culture such as that long characteristic of the United States (119). That Freud failed to perceive these particular limitations of his psychology Elkins attributes in part to the fact that in modern Occidental civilization, before the Nazi concentration camps, chattel slavery in America was the only large-scale social laboratory which might have given Freud the evi-

It is not without significance that plantation slavery existed in a culture which was peace-oriented, while the concentration camps were vital parts of a war-oriented culture. Just as the twentieth century has produced total war, in these camps it also has produced total enslavement. However, although the Nazis may be said to have perfected the institution of slavery, from the long record of North America's treatment of Africans and their descendants the Nazis could have and probably did learn much.

Because his own biases blurred his vision,[25] and because

---

dence that he needed for a more inclusive psychology. Thus it seems that Freud might have benefited greatly from a close study of slavery in America. For other comments on the changes in Freudian psychology wrought by the concentration camp experiences, see Elie Cohen, *Human Behavior in the Concentration Camp* (New York, 1953); Bettelheim, *The Informed Heart*, 14 and passim; Leo Alexander, "War Crimes: Their Social-Psychological Aspects," *American Journal of Psychiatry*, CV (September, 1948), 173; and Frankl, *From Death Camp to Existentialism*, passim.

On the subject of this paper, see also Kenneth Stampp, "The Historian and Southern Negro Slavery," *American Historical Review*, LXII (April, 1952).

[25] Although Professor Elkins usually has rejected the mood and methodology of the Slavocracy, he makes the mistake of accepting its conclusions about the nature of the bondsman's personality and character. Throughout the volume Professor Elkins reveals himself as a staunch elitist and conservative, in whose philosophy, like that of most conservatives, the word "gradualism" is sacrosanct. Further evidence of his biases in favor of the Slavocracy are evident in the strongly denunciatory tone which he takes where the American abolitionists are concerned. Calling them "Intellectuals without Responsibility," he writes as if they were all hate- and guilt-ridden neurotics who should have been incarcerated for their own sake and for that of society (see 140-92). Elkins erroneously states that the "loftiest manifestation" of slave religion was "at about the level of Green Pastures" (195), and he feels that had not irresponsible extremists, such as the abolitionists, had their way slavery would have been eliminated by a gradual, hence to him more adult, approach. This adult approach would have had as one step the insistence that each slave "be offered a spiritual life marked by dignity and be given instruction in Christian morality" (195). That this would have involved a denial of the "positive good" argument of the South, or how a slave society can effectively teach Christian morality, are points on which Elkins is silent.

of the too-loose fashion in which Elkins handles his analogy, we must conclude that the challenge laid down for historical scholars in 1944 by Professor Hofstadter has not yet been met. Professor Elkins should have been more impressed with the words of Herbert J. Aptheker, written in 1943, which state: "The dominant historiography in the United States either omits the Negro people or presents them as a people

---

Professor Elkins has great admiration for the English abolitionists and thinks that they were realistic, objective, and dispassionate about their cause because they were men of wealth who operated through parliament and other well-established institutions, in contrast with the American abolitionists who were a displaced elite, anti-institutional, and each speaking for no one but himself. He ignores the fact that declining profits from slave-produced products were a key factor in the success which English abolitionists had, while abolitionism in the United States was fighting a system which could boast of almost steadily rising prices from about 1810 to 1860. Too, he omits the fact that when England abolished slavery she had a diversity of economic interests while the Old South's economy rested almost exclusively on cotton culture. Finally, Elkins fails to consider another significant difference between the two abolitionist movements. "The United States alone, of all the great powers," comments one observer, "had to fight for the abolition of slavery within its own national territory. . . . The irreducible conflict, in the case of other nations, was fought by under-mining mercantilism, pushing free trade, and shifting power to the industrial capitalists. . . . this was accomplished within the metropolis, far from the colonies themselves. The American South, however, was integrated with United States institutions in a way that the British West Indies never were, and never could be, with the institutions of Great Britain" (Mintz, *American Anthropologist*, 587).

Professor Elkins repeatedly makes it clear that he detests uncompromising idealists, and has great admiration for "men with specific stakes in society, men attached to institutions and with a vested interest in one another's presence, men aware of being engaged with concrete problems of power" (146–47). By his standards, not only do Margaret Fuller, Ralph Waldo Emerson, William Ellery Channing, Orestes Browning, Theodore Parker, James Freeman Clark, Bronson Alcott, Henry David Thoreau, and other persons mentioned flunk the course, but Socrates, Jesus Christ, and similar non-propertied idealists and reformers who worked largely outside of institutional frameworks also fail to appreciate the fact that a dynamic society probably needs critics operating without as well as within the institutional framework, for if the man outside of institutions is liable to exaggerate the role of the individual, those who operate within institutions are liable to become organization- and institution-bound and lose sight of human beings.

without a past, as a people who have been docile, passive, parasitic, imitative."[26] "This picture," Aptheker declares, "is a lie." Elkins should have been more impressed with the words of a planter who wrote in 1837: "The most general defect in the character of the Negro is hypocrisy: and this hypocrisy frequently makes him pretend to more ignorance than he possesses; and if his master treats him as a fool, he will be sure to act the fool's part."[27] Finally, Professor Elkins should have been more impressed with the work of the Association for the Study of Negro Life and History, which has devoted almost a half century of labor directed toward disproving the Sambo and similar stereotypes.

[26] Herbert J. Aptheker, *American Negro Slave Revolts* (New York, 1943).
[27] In Kenneth Stampp, *The Peculiar Institution* (New York, 1956), quoting *The Farmer's Register*, V (1837), 32.

Rebelliousness and Docility in the Negro Slave: A Critique of the Elkins Thesis

EUGENE D. GENOVESE

Despite the hostile reception given by historians to Elkins' *Slavery*,[1] it has established itself as one of the most influential historical essays of our generation. Although Elkins ranges widely, we may restrict ourselves to his most important contribution, the theory of slave personality, and bypass other questions, such as his dubious theory of uncontrolled capitalism in the South. His psychological model would fit comfortably into other social theories and may, up to a point, be analytically isolated.

Elkins asserts that the Sambo stereotype arose only in the United States. He attempts to explain this allegedly unique personality type by constructing a social analysis that con-

[1] For a brief critique of the book as a whole see Genovese, "Problems in Nineteenth-Century American History," *Science & Society*, XXV (1961). This present paper shall, so far as possible, be limited to questions of method and assumption. A much shorter version was read to the Association for the Study of Negro Life and History, Baltimore, Maryland, Oct., 1966, where it was incisively criticized by Professor Willie Lee Rose. Mrs. Rose was also kind enough to read and criticize the first draft of this longer version. I do not know whether or not my revisions will satisfy her, but I am certain that the paper is much better as a result of her efforts.

trasts a totalitarian plantation South with a feudal Latin America in which church, state, and plantation balanced one another. To relate this ostensible difference in social structure to the formation of slave personality he invokes an analogy to Nazi concentration camps to demonstrate the possibility of mass infantilization and proceeds to apply three theories of personality: (1) the Freudian, which relates the growth of a personality to the existence of a father figure and which accounts for the identification of a tyrannized child with a tyrannical father; (2) Sullivan's theory of "significant others," which relates the growth of a personality to its interaction with individuals who hold or seem to hold power over its fortunes; and (3) role theory, which relates the growth of a personality to the number and kinds of roles it can play.[2] Elkins assumes that Sambo existed only in the United States and that our task is to explain his unique appearance in the Old South. I propose to show, on the contrary, that Sambo existed wherever slavery existed, that he nonetheless could turn into a rebel, and that our main task is to discover the conditions under which the personality pattern could become inverted and a seemingly docile slave could suddenly turn fierce.

Elkins asserts that the United States alone produced the Sambo stereotype—"the perpetual child incapable of maturity." He does not, as so many of his critics insist, equate childishness with docility, although he carelessly gives such an impression. Rather, he equates it with dependence and, with a subtlety that seems to elude his detractors, skillfully accounts for most forms of day-to-day resistance. His thesis, as will be shown later, is objectionable not because it fails to account for hostile behavior, but because it proves too much

---

[2] Elkins, *Slavery*, 115-33 and the literature cited therein.

and encompasses more forms of behavior than can usefully be managed under a single rubric.

Elkins' assumption that the existence of a stereotype proves the reality behind it will not stand critical examination either as psychological theory or as historical fact. As psychological theory, it is at least open to question. John Harding and his collaborators have argued that stereotypes, under certain conditions, may in fact be without foundation;[3] this side of the problem may be left to specialists and need not alter the main lines of the argument. Historically, Sambo was emerging in the United States at the same time he was emerging in the French colonies. Negroes, if we would believe the French planters, were childlike, docile, helpless creatures up until the very moment they rose and slaughtered the whites. Accordingly, I have a sporting proposition for Elkins. Let us substitute French Saint-Domingue for the United States and apply his logic. We find a Sambo stereotype and a weak tradition of rebellion. True, there was a century of maroon activity, but only the efforts of Mackandal constituted a genuine revolt. Those efforts were, in the words of C. L. R. James, "the only hint of an organized attempt at revolt during the hundred years preceding the French Revolution."[4] Boukman's revolt ought properly to be regarded as the first phase of the great revolution of 1791 rather than a separate action. In short, when the island suddenly exploded in the greatest slave revolution in history, nothing lay behind it but Sambo and a few hints. Now, let us rewrite history by having the French Jacobins take power and abolish slavery in 1790,

[3] John Harding *et al.*, "Prejudice and Ethnic Relations," *Handbook of Social Psychology*, ed. Gardner Lindzey (Cambridge, 1954), II, 1021–62, esp. 1024.
[4] C. L. R. James, *The Black Jacobins: Toussaint L'Ouverture and the San Domingo Revolution* (Vintage ed.; New York, 1963), 21.

instead of 1794. With the aid of that accident the slaves would have been freed as the result of the vicissitudes of Jacobin-Girondist factionalism and not by their own efforts. We would then today be reading a Haitian Elkins whose task would be to explain the extraordinary docility of the country's blacks. As the rewriting of history goes, this excursion requires little effort and ought to make us aware of how suddenly a seemingly docile, or at least adjusted, people can rise in violence. It would be much safer to assume that dangerous and strong currents run beneath that docility and adjustment.

Reaching further back into history, we find an identification of Negroes, including Africans, with a Sambo-like figure. As early as the fourteenth century—and there is no reason to believe that it began that late—so learned and sophisticated a scholar as Ibn Khaldun could write:

> Negroes are in general characterized by levity, excitability, and great emotionalism. They are found eager to dance whenever they hear a melody. They are everywhere described as stupid. . . . The Negro nations are, as a rule, submissive to slavery, because (Negroes) have little (that is essentially) human and have attributes that are quite similar to those of dumb animals.[5]

In 1764, in Portugal, a pamphlet on the slavery question in the form of a dialogue has a Brazilian slaveowning mine operator say: "I have always observed that in Brazil the Negroes are

[5] Ibn Khaldun, The Muqaddimah (tr. Franz Rosenthal; New York, 1958), I, 174, 301; the parentheses were inserted by the translator for technical reasons. David Brion Davis maintains that as Muslims extended their hegemony over Africa, they came to regard black Africans as fit only for slavery: The Problem of Slavery in Western Culture (Ithaca, 1966), 50. Cf. Basil Davidson, Black Mother (Boston, 1961), xvii, 7, 45, 92–93, for Sambo's appearance in Africa.

treated worse than animals. . . . Yet, withal the blacks endure this." The conclusion drawn was that this submissiveness proved inferiority.[6]

Sambo appears throughout Brazilian history, especially during the nineteenth century. In the 1830s the ideologues of Brazilian slavery, significantly under strong French influence, assured planters that the black was a "man-child" with a maximum mental development equivalent to that of a white adolescent. This and similar views were widespread among planters, particularly in the highly commercialized southern coffee region.[7] Brazilian sociologists and historians accepted this stereotype well into the twentieth century. Euclides da Cunha, in his masterpiece *Rebellion in the Backlands*, described the Negro as "a powerful organism, given to an extreme humility, without the Indian's rebelliousness."[8] Oliveira Lima, in his pioneering comparative history of Brazil and Spanish and Anglo-Saxon America, described the Negro as an especially subservient element.[9] Joao Pandía Calógeras, in his long-standard *History of Brazil*, wrote:

> The Negro element in general revealed a perpetual good humor, a childish and expansive joy, a delight in the slightest incidentals of life. . . . Filled with the joy of youth, a ray of sunshine illumined his childlike soul. Sensitive, worthy of confidence, devoted to those who treated him well, capable of being led in any direction by affection and kind

[6] C. R. Boxer (ed.), "Negro Slavery in Brazil" [trans. of *Nova e Curiosa Relacao* (*1764*)], *Race*, V (1964), 43.

[7] Stanley J. Stein, *Vassouras: A Brazilian Coffee County, 1850–1900* (Cambridge, Mass., 1957), 133.

[8] Euclides da Cunha, *Rebellion in the Backlands* (*Os Sertoes*) (tr. Samuel Putnam; Chicago, 1944), 71; for a critical review of some of this literature see Arthur Ramos, *The Negro in Brazil* (Washington, 1939), 22–24.

[9] Manoel de Oliveira Lima, *The Evolution of Brazil Compared with That of Spanish and Anglo-Saxon America* (Stanford, 1914), p. 122.

words, the Negro helped to temper the primitive harshness of the Portuguese colonists.[10]

One of the leading interpretations in Brazil today regards the blacks as having been subjected to a regime designed to produce alienation and the destruction of the personality by means of the exercise of the arbitrary power of the master. The account given in Kenneth M. Stampp's *The Peculiar Institution* of the efforts to produce a perfect slave has a close parallel in Octavio Ianni's *As Metamorfoses do Escravo*, which analyzes southern Brazil during the nineteenth century.[11]

Nor did Sambo absent himself from Spanish America. The traditional advocacy of Indian freedom often went together with a defense of Negro slavery based on an alleged inferior-

[10] Joao Pandía Calógeras, *A History of Brazil* (Chapel Hill, 1939), 29. Even today, when Negroes face discrimination in Brazil, whites insist that it is a result of their own incapacities and sense of inferiority. See Fernando Henrique Cardoso and Octavio Ianni, *Côr e Mobilidade em Florianópolis* (Sao Paulo, 1964), 231.

[11] Kenneth M. Stampp, *The Peculiar Institution* (New York, 1956), 148: "Here, then, was the way to produce the perfect slave: accustom him to rigid discipline, demand from him unconditional submission, impress upon him his innate inferiority, develop in him a paralyzing fear of white men, train him to adopt the master's code of good behavior, and instill in him a sense of complete dependence. This at least was the goal."

Octavio Ianni, *As Metamorfoses do Escravo* (Sao Paulo, 1962), 134–35: "Essential to the full functioning of the regime [was] a rigorous, drastic system of control over the social behavior of the enslaved laborer; . . . mechanisms of socialization appropriate to the dominant social strata . . . ; the impossibility of vertical social mobility; . . . rules of conduct ordered according to a standard of rigid obedience of the Negroes in front of white men, whether masters or not."

See also Fernando Henrique Cardoso, *Capitalismo e Escravidao no Brasil Meridional* (Sao Paulo, 1962), 312–13. Davis follows Ianni and others and speaks of Brazilian slaves as having been reduced "to a state of psychic shock, of flat apathy and depression, which was common enough in Brazil to acquire the special name of *banzo*." *Problem of Slavery*, 238; cf. Ramos, *Negro in Brazil*, 22, 135–36.

ity that suggests a Sambo stereotype.[12] In 1816, Simón Bolívar wrote to General Jean Marión of Haiti:

> I have proclaimed the absolute emancipation of the slaves. The tyranny of the Spaniards has reduced them to such a state of stupidity and instilled in their souls such a great sense of terror that they have lost even the desire to be free!! Many of them would have followed the Spaniards or have embarked on British vessels [whose owners] have sold them in neighboring colonies.[13]

Elkins cites evidence that the Spanish regarded the Indians as docile and the Negroes as difficult to control, but evidence also exists that shows the reverse. The view of the Indian or Negro as docile or rebellious varied greatly with time, place, and circumstance.[14] Sidney Mintz, with one eye on Cuba and Puerto Rico and the other eye on Brazil, has suggested that, regardless of institutional safeguards, the more commercialized the slave system the more it tended to produce dehumanization. This thesis needs considerable refinement but is at least as suggestive as Elkins' attempt to construct a purely institutional interpretation.[15]

On close inspection the Sambo personality turns out to be neither more nor less than the slavish personality; wherever slavery has existed, Sambo has also.[16] "Throughout history,"

[12] Davis, *Problem of Slavery*, 171.
[13] *Selected Writings of Bolivar* (New York, 1951), I, 131.
[14] For an interpretation of the Spanish slave law as holding Negroes to be an especially revolutionary people see Augustín Alcalá y Henke, *Esclavitud de los negros en la América espanola* (Madrid, 1919), 51. For a view of Brazilian Indians that sounds much like Sambo see the comments of the famous Dutch sea captain, Dierck de Ruiter, as reported in C. R. Boxer, *Salvador de Sá and the Struggle for Brazil and Angola* (London, 1952), 20.
[15] Sidney Mintz, review of Elkins' *Slavery*, *American Anthropologist*, LXIII (1961), 585.
[16] "Slavery is determined 'pas par l'obeissance, ni par rudesse des labeurs,

David Brion Davis has written, "it has been said that slaves,
though occasionally as loyal and faithful as good dogs, were
for the most part lazy, irresponsible, cunning, rebellious, un-
trustworthy, and sexually promiscuous."[17] Only the element
of rebelliousness does not seem to fit Sambo, but on reflection, even that does. Sambo, being a child, could be easily
controlled but, if not handled properly, would revert to
barbarous ways. Davis demonstrates that by the fifth century
B.C. many Greeks had come to regard the submission of
barbarians to despotic and absolute rulers as proof of inferiority.[18] By the end of the eighteenth century, America
and Europe widely accepted the image of the dehumanized
black slave, and even Reynal believed that crime and indolence would inevitably follow emancipation.[19]

Sambo has a much longer pedigree and a much wider range
than Elkins appreciates. Audrey I. Richards, in 1939, noted
the widespread existence of "fatal resignation" among primitive peoples in Africa and suggested that their psychological
and physical sluggishness might be attributable in a large
part to poor diet and severe malnutrition.[20] Josué de Castro,
former head of the United Nations Food and Agriculture
Organization, has made the same point about Brazilian slaves
and about people in underdeveloped countries in general.[21]
As Jean-Paul Sartre has suggested, "Beaten, under-nourished,
ill, terrified—but only up to a certain point—he has, whether

mais par le statu d'instrument et la réduction de l'homme a l'etat de chose.'"
François Perroux, *La Coexistence pacifique*, as quoted by Herbert Marcuse,
*One-Dimensional Man: Studies in the Ideology of Advanced Industrial So-
ciety* (Boston, 1964), 32–33.
[17] Davis, *Problem of Slavery*, 59–60.
[18] *Ibid.*, 66–67.
[19] *Ibid.*, 420.
[20] Audrey I. Richards, *Land, Labour and Diet in Northern Rhodesia: An
Economic Study of the Bemba Tribe* (London, 1939), 400.
[21] Josué de Castro, *The Geography of Hunger* (Boston, 1952), *passim*.

he's black, yellow, or white, always the same traits of character: he's a sly-boots, a lazy-bones, and a thief, who lives on nothing and who understands only violence."[22] By constructing a single-factor analysis and erroneously isolating the personality structure of the Southern slave, Elkins has obscured many other possible lines of inquiry. We do not as yet have a comparative analysis of slave diets in the United States, Brazil, and the West Indies, although it might tell us a great deal about personality patterns.

It is generally believed that Elkins merely repeated Tannenbaum when he declared Sambo to be a native of the Old South; in fact, the assertion is, for better or worse, entirely his own. I would not dwell on this point were it not that I cannot imagine Tannenbaum's taking so one-sided a view. I intend no disrespect to Elkins by this observation, for, as a matter of fact, his single-mindedness, even when misguided, has helped him to expose problems others have missed entirely. Elkins' greatest weakness, nonetheless, is his inability to accept the principle of contradiction, to realize that all historical phenomena must be regarded as constituting a process of becoming, and that, therefore, the other-sidedness of the most totalitarian conditions may in fact represent the unfolding of their negation. If Sambo were merely Sambo, then Elkins must explain how an overseer could publicly defend his class, without challenge, for having "to punish and keep in order the negroes, at the risk of his life."[23]

Elkins recognizes a wide range of institutional factors as having contributed to the contrast between the Latin and

[22] Jean-Paul Sartre, preface to Frantz Fanon, *The Wretched of the Earth* (New York, 1965), 14.
[23] Quoted from the *Southern Cultivator*, VII (Sept., 1849), 140, by William K. Scarborough, "The Southern Plantation Overseer: A Re-evaluation," *Agricultural History*, XXXVIII (1964), 16.

52 EUGENE D. GENOVESE

Anglo-Saxon slave systems, but he places special emphasis on the system of law in relation to the structure and policies of Church and Crown.[24] Although in this way Elkins follows Tannenbaum, he necessarily must go well beyond him, and therein lies his greatest difficulty. Tannenbaum's well-known thesis need not be reviewed here, but we might profitably recall his suggestive comment on *Las Siete Partidas:*

> *Las Siete Partidas* was formed within the Christian doctrine, and the slave had a body of law, protective of him as a human being, which was already there when the Negro arrived and had been elaborated long before he came upon the scene.[25]

The essential point of Tannenbaum's contrast between this legal tradition and that of the Anglo-Saxon lies in its bearing on the problem of emancipation. Whereas the Hispanic tradition favored and encouraged it, the Anglo-Saxon blocked it.[26] So long as a general contrast can be demonstrated, Tannenbaum's thesis obtains, for he is primarily concerned with the social setting into which the Negro plunged upon emancipation. His thesis, therefore, can absorb criticism such as that of Arnold A. Sio, who argues that the Romans assimilated the rights of their slaves to property despite a legal code which respected the moral personality of the slave. Sio finds evidence of a similar tendency in Latin as well as Anglo-Saxon America.[27] Tannenbaum's thesis would fall only if the tendency

[24] See his explicit summary statement, "Culture Contacts and Negro Slavery," *Proceedings of the American Philosophical Society,* CVII (1963), 107–10, esp. 107.
[25] Frank Tannenbaum, *Slave and Citizen: The Negro in the Americas* (New York, 1946), 48.
[26] *Ibid.*, 65, 69, and *passim.*
[27] Arnold A. Sio, "Interpretations of Slavery: The Slave Status in the Americas," *Comparative Studies in Society and History,* VII (1965), 303,

were equally strong everywhere; but obviously it was not.[28] Elkins, however, cannot absorb such qualifications, for he necessarily must demonstrate the uniqueness of the Southern pattern as well as the absoluteness of the contrast with Latin America. If the contrast could be reduced to a matter of degree, then we should be left with more American than Latin American Sambos, but Elkins' notion of a special American personality pattern and problem would fall.

Elkins, like Tannenbaum, ignores the French slave colonies, but nowhere was the gap between law and practice so startling. The *Code Noir* of 1685 set a high standard of humanity and attempted to guarantee the slaves certain minimal rights and protection. It was treated with contempt in the French West Indies, especially when the islands began to ride the sugar boom. It is enough to quote a governor of Martinique, one of the men charged with the enforcement of these laws: "I have reached the stage of believing firmly that one must treat the Negroes as one treats beasts."[29] On the eve of the Haitian Revolution probably not one of the protective articles of the *Code Noir* was being enforced.[30]

---

308. For a fresh consideration of the problem of slave law in the islands see Elsa V. Goveia, "The West Indian Slave Laws in the Eighteenth Century," *Revista de Ciencias Sociales* (1960), 75–105.

[28] Marvin Harris has counterposed an economic viewpoint to Tannenbaum's. Despite considerable exaggeration and one-sidedness, he does demonstrate the partial applicability of an institutional approach. For a critical analysis of Harris' polemic and the literature it touches see Genovese, "Materialism and Idealism in the History of Negro Slavery in the Americas," *Journal of Social History*, forthcoming.

The experience of the Dutch demonstrates how much religious and national attitudes gave way before the necessities of colonial life. The Dutch experience in Surinam, New Netherland, Brazil, etc. varied enormously. See e.g., C. R. Boxer, *The Dutch in Brazil* (Oxford, 1957), esp. 75; Edgar J. McManus, *A History of Negro Slavery in New York* (New York, 1966), Ch. I.

[29] Quoted by James, *Black Jacobins*, 17.

[30] *Ibid.*, 56; Davis, *Problem of Slavery*, 254 and the literature cited therein.

Elkins offers Brazil as a counterpoint to the Old South and invokes the Iberian legal tradition, together with the power of Church and Crown. Yet, even Gilberto Freyre, on whom Elkins relies so heavily, writes of the widespread murders of slaves by enraged masters.[31] As late as the nineteenth century, slaves were being whipped to death in the presence of all hands. The law might say what it would, but the *fazendeiros* controlled the police apparatus and supported the doctors who falsified the death certificates.[32] The measures designed to prevent wanton killing of slaves do not seem to have been better in Latin America than in Anglo-Saxon America.[33] If Brazilian slaves went to the police to complain about unjust or illegally excessive punishment, the police would, in Freyre's words, give them a double dose.[34] If the law mattered much, we need to know the reason for the repeated reenactment of legislation to protect slaves. The famous Rio Branco Law of 1871, for example, granted slaves rights they were supposed to have enjoyed for centuries, and these too remained largely unrespected.

The Portuguese Crown could legislate in any manner it wished, and so later could the Emperor of Brazil; local power resided with the *fazendeiros*, as the emissaries of the Crown learned soon enough. We may imagine conditions in the first three centuries of colonization from Freyre's succinct comment on conditions in the middle of the nineteenth century: "The power of the great planters was indeed feudalistic,

[31] Gilberto Freyre, *The Masters and the Slaves: A Study in the Development of Brazilian Civilization* (2nd English Language ed., rev.; New York, 1956), xxxix.

[32] Stein, *Vassouras*, 136.

[33] See, e.g., the discussion of the law of 1797 in Antigua in Elsa V. Goveia, *Slave Society in the British Leeward Islands at the End of the Eighteenth Century* (New Haven, 1966), 191.

[34] Gilberto Freyre, *The Mansions and the Shanties: The Making of Modern Brazil* (New York, 1963), 226.

their patriarchalism being hardly restricted by civil laws."[35]
Not until that time did a strong central government arise to
challenge effectively the great planters.[36] That the contrast
with the Old South might have been the reverse of what
Elkins thinks is suggested by the diary of an ex-Confederate
who fled to Brazil after the war. George S. Barnsley, formerly
a Georgia planter and Confederate army surgeon, complained
as late as 1904 of the lack of government and the prevalence
of virtually feudal conditions.[37]

Las Siete Partidas constituted a theoretical work and standard of values, the importance of which ought not to be
minimized, but it had little to do with the actual practice on
which Elkins' thesis depends.[38] The kind of protection that
transcended the theoretical and might have conditioned decisively the personality development of the slave population as
a whole probably did not appear until the *Real Cédula* of
1789. As Davis suggests, "There are many indications, moreover, that Spanish planters paid little attention to the law."[39]

Elkins assumes that the strongly centralized Spanish state
could and did prevail over the planters. No doubt it did in
matters of prime importance to its survival and income. In
most matters, notwithstanding its best efforts at institutional
control, the planters continued to have their way on their own
estates. The Spanish court promulgated humane legislation to

[35] Gilberto Freyre, "Social Life in Brazil in the Middle of the Nineteenth Century," *Hispanic American Historical Review*, V (1922), 597–
628; see also Freyre, *Masters*, xxxiii, 24, 42; *New World in the Tropics: The
Culture of Modern Brazil* (Vintage ed.; New York, 1963), 69.

[36] Alan A. Manchester describes 1848 as the turning point. See *British
Pre-Eminence in Brazil* (Chapel Hill, 1933), 261–62.

[37] George S. Barnsley MS Notebook in the Southern Historical Collection, University of North Carolina, Chapel Hill.

[38] For a penetrating discussion of these two sides of *Las Siete Partidas*
see Davis, *Problem of Slavery*, 102–5.

[39] *Ibid.*, 240.

protect the natives of the Canary Islands, but attempts at
enforcement so far from home proved futile. The problem
swelled enormously when transferred to the West Indies, not
to mention to the mainland.[40] The fate of the protective features of the Laws of Burgos (1512) and of similar legislation
is well known.[41] The British and other foreigners who did
business in Spanish America ridiculed the mass of laws and the
clumsy administrative apparatus designed to enforce them. As
the agent of the South Sea Company at Jamaica noted in
1736, he who wants to deal illegally with the Spanish officials
needs only the cash necessary to bribe them.[42] The lot of the
slaves could, under such conditions, hardly reflect other than
the disposition of the masters. A case study by Jaime Jaramillo
Uribe of the judicial system of New Grenada shows that
even the reform laws of the eighteenth century could not
reach down into the plantations to protect the slaves.[43]

Much of Elkins' treatment of Spanish law deals with Cuba
and flows from the work of Herbert Klein.[44] Without attempting a close examination of the intricacies of the Cuban
case, we ought to note that it presents a striking picture of a
bitter struggle between planters and state officials. The
planters, there too, usually won the day. The liberal Governor

[40] Arthur Percival Newton, *The European Nations in the West Indies,
1493–1688* (London, 1933), 3.
[41] For a useful recent summary discussion of the literature see Harris,
Patterns of Race, 18–20.
[42] Cf. Arthur S. Aiton, "The Asiento Treaty as Reflected in the Papers
of Lord Shelburne," *Hispanic American Historical Review*, VIII (1928),
167–77, esp. 167.
[43] Jaime Jaramillo Uribe, "Esclavos y senores en la sociedad colombiana
del siglo XVIII," *Anuario colombiano de historia social y de cultura*, I
(1963), 1–22.
[44] Herbert Klein, "Anglicanism, Catholicism, and the Negro," *Comparative Studies in Society and History*, VIII (1966), 295–327, included in this
volume; *Slavery in the Americas: A Comparative Study of Cuba and Virginia* (Chicago, 1967).

Concha finally admitted that the resistance of the slaveowners
to government intervention was justified by the necessity for
controlling the blacks and avoiding any ambiguity in authority. In 1845 the government did seriously challenge the
masters' power, but the uproar proved so great that the
militant officials had to be removed.[45]

The fate of the law during the sugar boom requires more
attention than Elkins and Klein have given it. In its earlier
phases Cuban slavery was exceptionally mild and fit much of
Elkins' schema. When the Haitian Revolution removed the
Caribbean's leading sugar producer from the world market,
Cuba entered into a period of wild expansion and prosperity.
The status of the slave declined accordingly. The old institutional arrangements did not disappear, but their bearing on
the life of the great mass of slaves became minimal or nonexistent.[46]

The legal and political structure of Spanish America in
general and of Cuba in particular helped ease the way to freedom by providing a setting in which the slave might be
abused brutally but retained a significant degree of manhood
in the eyes of society. For Tannenbaum's purpose, this distinction establishes the argument: the slave was abused as a
slave but only incidentally as a Negro. The master might rule
with absolute authority, but only because he could get away
with it, not because it was, by the standards of his own class,
church, and society, just and proper. Tannenbaum and Freyre
do make too much of this argument. The persistence and

[45] See H. H. S. Aimes, *A History of Slavery in Cuba, 1511 to 1868* (New
York, 1907), 150–51, 175–77.
[46] On this point see Sidney Mintz, foreword to Ramiro Guerra y
Sánchez, *Sugar and Society in the Caribbean* (New Haven, 1964), and his
review of Elkins' book in the *American Anthropologist*, LXIII (1961), 579–
87. Klein, Tannenbaum, and Elkins make much of the practice of *coartación*.
For a critical assessment see Davis, *Problem of Slavery*, 266–67.

depth of racial discrimination and prejudice in twentieth-century Brazil and Cuba ought to remind us that the enslavement of one race by another must generate racist doctrines among all social classes as well as the intelligentsia. Qualitative and quantitative distinctions nonetheless obtain, and Tannenbaum's argument requires correction and greater specificity, not rejection. For Elkins, Tannenbaum's distinction, however qualified, is not enough. If, as seems likely, the great majority of the slaves labored under such absolutism, theoretical or not, their personalities would have been shaped in response to conditions equivalent to those he describes for the United States.

In the United States, as in the British West Indies and everywhere else, custom and conventional moral standards had greater force than the law, as Ulrich B. Phillips long ago argued. Just as the vast range of rights granted the slaves in Latin America usually proved unenforceable in a society in which power was largely concentrated in local planter oligarchies, so in Anglo-Saxon America the quasi-absolute power of the master was tempered by the prevailing ethos. Tannenbaum, and especially Elkins, go much too far in denying that English and American law recognized the moral personality of the slave. As Davis has demonstrated, the double nature of the slave as thing and man had to be, and in one way or another was, recognized in law and custom by every slave society since ancient times. As a result, every Southern planter knew intuitively the limits of his power, as imposed by the prevailing standards of decency. If he exceeded those limits, he might not suffer punishment at law and might even be strong enough to prevent his being ostracized by disapproving neighbors. For these reasons historians have dismissed community pressure as a factor. In doing so, they err badly, for the point is not at all what happened to a violator of conven-

pursuing slave-trade profits and to the generally venal character of priests, secular officials, and laymen.[48] The governor
of Angola, the troops, the bishop, and the entire staff of civil
and ecclesiastical officials drew their salaries from the direct
and indirect proceeds of the slave trade. The Holy House of
Mercy (*Misericordia*) at Luanda, as well as the Municipal
Council (*Camara*), lived off the trade. Since the *Junta das
missoẽs*, the chief missionary agency, was supported by these
proceeds we need not be surprised that it accomplished little.[49]

In Brazil itself the decisive questions concern the number,
character, and relative independence of the priests.[50] We have
little data on numbers, but in the mid-twentieth century,
Brazil, with a population of fifty million, of whom 95 per cent
were nominal Catholics, had, according to Vianna Moog, only
six thousand priests.[51] We may, nonetheless, assume for a
moment that a high ratio of priests to slaves existed. There is
good reason to believe that a significant percentage of the
priests who ventured to the colonies had questionable characters and that many of good character succumbed to the indolence, violence, and corruption that marked their isolated,
quasi-frontier environment. It is no insult to the Church to

[48] C. R. Boxer, *Race Relations in the Portuguese Colonial Empire,
1415–1825* (Oxford, 1963), 7–8, 11–12, 21.

[49] C. R. Boxer, *Portuguese Society in the Tropics: The Municipal Councils of Goa, Macao, Bahia, and Luanda, 1510–1800* (1965), 131–32; Davidson,
Black Mother, 158.

[50] Elkins certainly errs in ascribing a protective role to the Jesuits, whose
efforts on behalf of the Indians were not repeated with the Negroes. Jesuit
treatment of those Negroes within their reach does not constitute one of the
more glorious chapters in the history of the order. The literature is extensive; for a good, brief discussion see Joao Dornas Filho, *A Escravidao
no Brasil* (Rio de Janeiro, 1939), 105.

[51] Vianna Moog, *Bandeirantes and Pioneers* (New York, 1964), 209. Cf.
Percy Alvin Martin, "Slavery and Abolition in Brazil," *Hispanic American
Historical Review*, XIII (1933), 168: "On most plantations the spiritual life
of the slaves received scant attention. Priests were found only on the larger
estates."

tion but the extent to which the overwhelming majority of slaveholders internalized conventional values. In this respect the legal structures of Brazil and the United States were important in conditioning those conventional values. Once again, the difference between the two cases suffices for Tannen-baum's thesis but not for Elkins'—which depends entirely on the experience of absolute power by the slave.

Elkins follows Tannenbaum in ascribing a special role to the Catholic Church in the development of Ibero-American slave societies. The Church defended the moral personality of the slave from a position of independent institutional strength, whereas in the Anglo-Saxon world the separation of church and state, the bourgeois notion of property rights, and divisions within the religious community largely excluded churches from the field of master-slave relations. The religion as well as the legal structure helped generate a particular climate of moral opinion into which the Negro could fit as a man. The difference in structure and result satisfies Tannen-baum's argument; it does not satisfy Elkins' argument, which turns on the specific role played by the priesthood in the life of the slave.

Since Brazil, as the largest Catholic slaveholding country, ought properly to serve as a test case, we might profitably begin with a consideration of developments in Angola, which supplied a large part of its slaves. The clergy, including Jesuits and Dominicans, participated in every horror associated with the slave trade; there is little evidence of their having played a mediating role.[47] By the middle of the seventeenth century Catholic proselytism in the Congo and Angola had spent its force. Contemporary Catholic sources admit that much of the failure was due to the greed of the

[47] Boxer, *Salvador de Sá*, 279.

affirm this state of affairs, for the Church has had to struggle for centuries to raise the quality of its priests and to maintain high standards of performance. Like other institutions of this world it has consisted of men with all the weaknesses of men, and in the difficult circumstances of colonial life the adherence of its men to the high standards of the Church Militant proved erratic and uncertain.

Even if we grant the Brazilian clergy a higher quality than it probably deserved, we confront the question of its relationship to the master class. The local chaplain depended on and deferred to the planter he served more than he depended on his bishop. The Brazilian Church never achieved the strength and cohesion of the Church in Spanish America. The typical sugar planter, in Freyre's words, "though a devout Catholic, was a sort of Philip II in regard to the Church: he considered himself more powerful than the bishops or abbots." Under these conditions the interposition of priest between master and slave was probably little more significant than the interposition of the mistress on a plantation in Mississippi. The analogy assumes particular force when we consider that, increasingly, the Brazilian priesthood was recruited from the local aristocracy.[52] In coffee-growing southern Brazil, in which slavery centered during the nineteenth century, few priests resided on plantations at all and visits were possibly less common than in the United States. The large number of Africans imported during 1830–1850 received little attention from the Church.[53]

The situation in Spanish America worked out more favorably for Elkins' argument because the Church there came much closer to that independence and crusading spirit which has been attributed to it. Even so, the ruthless exploitation of Indians and Negroes by large sections of the clergy is well

[52] Freyre, *New World in the Tropics*, 70–71, 87–88; *Mansions*, 244.
[53] Stein, *Vassouras*, 196–99.

documented. The position of the Church as a whole, taken over centuries, demonstrates its growing subservience to state and secular power in respects that were decisive for Elkins' purposes. The bulls of Popes and the decrees of kings proved inadequate to temper the rule of the great planters of the New World, although they did play a role in shaping their moral consciousness.[54] In Cuba the clergy acted more boldly and, according to Klein, had a numerical strength adequate to its tasks. However, the effective interposition of even the Cuban clergy during the sugar boom of the nineteenth century has yet to be demonstrated, and if it were to be, Cuba would stand as an exception to the rule.

That more Brazilian and Cuban slaves attended religious services than did Southern is by no means certain, the law to the contrary notwithstanding. That the Catholic clergy of Latin America interposed itself more often and more effectively than the Protestant clergy of the South cannot be denied. On balance, Tannenbaum's case is proven by the ability of the Catholic Church to help shape the ethos of slave society and the relative inability of the Protestant to do the same. But Elkins' case falls, for the difference in the potentialities for and especially the realities of personal interposition remained a matter of degree.

Despite the efforts of law and Church in Latin America it is quite possible that as high or higher a percentage of Southern slaves lived in stable family units than did Latin American. The force of custom and sentiment generally prevailed over the force of law or institutional interference. In Brazil, as in the Caribbean, male slaves greatly outnumbered female; in the

[54] Cf. Rene Maunier, *The Sociology of Colonies* (London, n.d), I, 293–94.

United States the sexes were numerically equal. This factor alone, which derived primarily from economic and techno-logical conditions, encouraged greater family stability in the United States and therefore casts great doubt on Elkins' thesis. To the extent that participation in a stable family life encouraged the development of a mature personality, the slaves of the South probably fared no worse than others. Elkins argues that the Latin American families could not be broken up because of Church and state restrictions. In fact, they often were broken up in open defiance of both. The greatest guarantee against sale existed not where the law for-bade it, but where economic conditions reduced the necessity.

The attendant argument that Latin American slaves could function in the roles of fathers and mothers, whereas Southern slaves could not, is altogether arbitrary. The feeling of secur-ity within the family depended on custom and circumstance, not law, and a great number of Southern slaves worked for masters whose economic position and paternalistic attitudes provided a reasonable guarantee against separate sales. In any case, all slaves in all societies faced similar problems. When a slaveowner beat or raped a slave woman in Brazil or Cuba, her husband was quite as helpless as any black man in Missis-sippi. The duties, responsibilities, and privileges of father-hood were, in practice, little different from one place to another.

The point of Elkins' controversial concentration camp analogy is not altogether clear. Sometimes he seems to wish to demonstrate only the possibility of mass infantilization, but if this were all he intended, he could have done so briefly and without risking the hostile reaction he brought down on himself. At other times he seems to intend the analogy as a direct device. Although he denies saying that slavery was a concentration camp or even "like" a concentration camp, he does refer to concentration camps as perverted patriarchies and extreme forms of slavery; he finds in them the same total power he believes to have existed on the Southern plantations. In the first, restricted, sense the analogy, used suggestively, has its point, for it suggests the ultimate limits of the slave experience. In the second, and broader, sense it offers little and is generally misleading. Unfortunately, Elkins sometimes exaggerates and confuses his device, which only demonstrates the limiting case, with the historical reality of slavery. His elaborate discussion of detachment offers clues but is dangerously misleading. The process did not differ for slaves bound for different parts of the New World; only the post-shock experience of the slave regimes differed, so that we are led right back to those regimes. No doubt Elkins makes a good point when he cites concentration camp and slave-trade evidence to show that many participants were spiritually broken by the process, but he overlooks the contribution of newly imported Africans to slave disorders. Everywhere in the Americas a correlation existed between concentrations of African-born slaves and the outbreak of revolts. The evidence indicates that creole slaves were generally more adjusted to enslavement than those who had undergone the shock and detachment processes from Africa to America.[55]

The fundamental differences between the concentration camp and plantation experience may be gleaned from a brief

---

[55] Elkins seems troubled by this—see p. 102 but he does not pursue it. K. Onwuka Dike points out that Guineans brought to the trading depots of the Niger Delta had already been prepared psychologically for slavery by the religious indoctrination accompanying the cult of the Aro oracle. See "The Question of Sambo: A Report of the Ninth Newberry Library Conference on American Studies," *Newberry Library Bulletin*, V (1958), 27, and Dike's *Trade and Politics in the Niger Delta, 1830–1885* (Oxford, 1956), Ch. II.

consideration of some of the points made in Bruno Bettelheim's study, on which Elkins relies heavily.[56] Prisoners received inadequate clothing and food in order to test their reaction to extremities of inclement weather and their ability to work while acutely hungry. Slaves received clothing and food designed to provide at least minimum comfort. Slaves suffered from dietary deficiencies and hidden hungers, but rarely from outright malnutrition. In direct contrast to prisoners, slaves normally did not work outdoors in the rain or extreme cold; usually, they were deliberately ordered to stay indoors. Pneumonia and other diseases killed too many slaves every winter for planters not to take every precaution to guard their health. Therein lay the crucial differences: prisoners might be kept alive for experimental purposes, but slaves received treatment designed to grant them long life. Prisoners often did useless work as part of a deliberate program to destroy their personality; slaves did, and knew they did, the productive work necessary for their own sustenance. Prisoners were forbidden to talk to each other much of the day and had virtually no privacy and no social life. Slaves maintained a many-sided social life, which received considerable encouragement from their masters. The Gestapo deliberately set out to deny the individuality of prisoners or to distinguish among them. Planters and overseers made every effort to take full account of slave individuality and even to encourage it up to a point. Prisoners were deliberately sub-

---

[56] Bruno Bettelheim, "Individual and Mass Behavior in Extreme Situations," *Journal of Abnormal and Social Psychology*, XXXVIII (1943), 417–52. On the general problem of the concentration camp analogy see the remarks of Daniel Boorstin as reported in the *Newberry Library Bulletin*, V (1958), 14–40, and Earl E. Thorpe, "Chattel Slavery and Concentration Camps," *Negro History Bulletin*, XXV (1962), 171–76, included in this volume. Unfortunately, Mr. Thorpe's thoughtful piece is marred by a clumsy discussion of the problem of wearing a mask before white men.

jected to torture and arbitrary punishment; those who followed orders endured the same indignities and blows as those
who did not. Slaves, despite considerable arbitrariness in the
system, generally had the option of currying favor and avoiding punishment. As Hannah Arendt has so perceptively observed: "Under conditions of total terror not even fear can
any longer serve as an advisor of how to behave, because
terror chooses its victims without reference to individual
actions or thoughts, exclusively in accordance with the objective necessity of the natural or historical process."[57] Concentration camp prisoners changed work groups and barracks
regularly and could not develop attachments. Slaves had families and friends, often for a lifetime. The Gestapo had no
interest in indoctrinating prisoners. They demanded obedience,
not loyalty. Masters wanted and took great pains to secure the
loyalty and ideological adherence of their slaves. In general,
the slave plantation was a social system, full of joys and sorrows and a fair degree of security, notwithstanding great
harshness and even brutality, whereas the concentration
camp was a particularly vicious death-cell. They shared a
strong degree of authoritarianism, but so does the army or a
revolutionary party, or even a family unit.

    With these criticisms of data we may turn to Elkins' discus-
sion of personality theory. His use of Sullivan's theory of
"significant others" breaks down because of his erroneous notion of the absolute power of the master. In theory the
master's power over the slave in the United States was close
to absolute; so in theory was the power of Louis XIV over

---

[57] Hannah Arendt, "Ideology and Terror: A Novel Form of Government," *Review of Politics*, XV (1953), 314. I am indebted to Professor
Daniel Walden of the Pennsylvania State University for calling this illuminating article to my attention and for suggesting its relevance to the
subject at hand.

the French. In practice, the plantation represented a series of compromises between whites and blacks. Elkins' inability to see the slaves as active forces capable of tempering the authority of the master leads him into a one-sided appraisal.[58]

According to Elkins, the Latin American slave could relate meaningfully to the friar on the slave ship; the confessor who made the plantation rounds; the zealous Jesuit who especially defended the sanctity of the family; the local magistrate who had to contend with the Crown's official protector of the slaves; and any informer who could expect to collect one-third of the fines. In general, it would not be unfair to say that, notwithstanding all these institutional niceties, the Latin American slaveowners, especially the Brazilian, ruled their plantations as despotically as any Southerner. Priest, magistrate, and anyone careless enough to risk his life to play the informer came under the iron grip of the plantation owners' enormous local power.

Various other persons did affect meaningfully the lives of slaves in all systems. The plantation mistress often acted to soften her husband's rule. The overseer did not always precisely reflect the master's temperament and wishes, and slaves demonstrated great skill in playing the one against the other. The Negro driver often affected their lives more directly than anyone else and had considerable authority to make their lives easy or miserable. Slaves who found it difficult to adjust to a master's whims or who feared punishment often ran to some other planter in the neighborhood to ask for his intercession, which they received more often than not. Elkins ignores these and other people because they had no lawful right to intervene; but they did have the power of

[58] For a perceptive and well-balanced discussion of this side of plantation life see Clement Eaton, *The Growth of Southern Civilization* (New York, 1961), 74 and *passim*.

persuasion in a world of human beings with human reactions. To the vast majority of slaves in all systems, the power of the master approached the absolute and yet was tempered by many human relationships and sensibilities. To the extent that slavery, in all societies, restricted the number of "significant others," it may well have contributed toward the formation of a slavish personality, but Latin America differed from the South only in permitting a somewhat larger minority to transcend that effect.

Similar objections may be made with reference to the application of role theory. The Latin American slave could ordinarily no more act the part of a husband or father than could the Southern. The typical field hand had roughly the same degree of prestige and authority in his own cabin in all societies. Legal right to property did not make most Latin American slaves property owners in any meaningful sense, and many Southern slaves were de facto property owners of the same kind. The theoretical right of the one and the mere privilege of the other did not present a great practical difference, for the attitude of the master was decisive in both cases. For Tannenbaum's social analysis the significance of the difference stands; for Elkins' psychological analysis it does not.

The theory of personality that Elkins seems to slight, but uses to greatest advantage, is the Freudian, perhaps because it offers a simple direct insight quite apart from its more technical formulations. We do not need an elaborate psychological theory to help us understand the emergence of the slaveowner as a father figure. As the source of all privileges, gifts, and necessaries, he loomed as a great benefactor, even when he simultaneously functioned as a great oppressor. Slaves, forced into dependence on their master, viewed him with awe and identified their interests and even their wills with his. Elkins' analogy with concentration camp prisoners who began to imitate their SS guards indicates the extreme case of this tendency. All exploited classes manifest something of this tendency—the more servile the class the stronger the tendency. It is what many contemporary observers, including runaway slaves and abolitionists, meant when they spoke of the reduction of the slave to a groveling creature without initiative and a sense of self-reliance. Elkins, using Freudian insight, has transformed this observation into the politically relevant suggestion that the slave actually learned to see himself through his master's eyes.

Elkins has often been criticized for failing to realize that slaves usually acted as expected while they retained inner reservations, but he did recognize this possibility in his discussion of a "broad belt of indeterminacy" between playing a role and becoming the role you always play. The criticism seems to me to miss the point. The existence of such reservations might weaken the notion of total infantilization but would not touch the less extreme notion of a dependent, emasculated personality. The clever slave outwitted his master at least partly because he was supposed to. Masters enjoyed the game: it strengthened their sense of superiority, confirmed the slaves' dependence, and provided a sense of pride in having so clever a man-child. On the slave's side it made him a devilishly delightful fellow but hardly a man. The main point against Elkins here is the same as elsewhere—when he is sound he describes not a Southern slave but a slave; not a distinctly Southern Sambo personality but a slavish personality.[59]

Elkins' general argument contains a fundamental flaw, which, when uncovered, exposes all the empirical difficulties

[59] Brazilian slaves saw their masters as patriarchs and, in Freyre's words, "almighty figures." Freyre, *Mansions*, 234. See also Celso Furtado, *The Economic Growth of Brazil* (Berkeley, 1963), 153–54.

under review. In his model a regime of total power produces a Sambo personality. Confronted by the undeniable existence of exceptions, he pleads first things first and waives them aside as statistically insignificant. Even if we were to agree that they were statistically insignificant, we are left with a serious problem. Elkins did not construct a model to determine probabilities; he constructed a deterministic model, which he cannot drop suddenly to suit his convenience. The notion of "total power" loses force and usefulness and indeed approaches absurdity in a world of probabilities and alternatives. If Elkins were to retreat from this notion and consequently from his determinism, he could not simply make an adjustment in his model; he would have to begin, as we must, from different premises, although without necessarily sacrificing his remarkable insights and suggestions. If the basic personality pattern arose from the nature of the regime, so did the deviant patterns. It would be absurd to argue that a regime could be sufficiently complex to generate two or more such patterns and yet sufficiently simple to generate them in mutual isolation. The regime threw up all the patterns at once, whatever the proportions, and the root of every deviation lay in the same social structure that gave us Sambo.

This range of patterns arose from the disparity between the plantations and farms, between resident owners and absentees, and above all between the foibles and sensibilities of one master and another. They arose, too, within every slaveholding unit from the impossibility of absolute power—from the qualities, perhaps inherited, of the particular personalities of slaves as individuals; from the inconsistencies in the human behavior of the severest masters; from the room that even a slave plantation provides for breathing, laughing, crying, and combining acquiescence and protest in a single thought, expression, and action. Even modern totalitarian regimes, self-consciously armed with unprecedented weapons of terror, must face that opposition inherent in the human spirit to which Miss Arendt draws attention. The freedom of man cannot be denied even by totalitarian rulers, "for this freedom —irrelevant and arbitrary as they may deem it—is identical with the fact than men are being born and that therefore each of them *is* a new beginning, begins, in a sense, the world anew."[60] We need not pretend to understand adequately that remarkable process of spiritual regeneration which repeatedly unfolds before our eyes. The evidence extends throughout history, including the history of our own day; its special forms and content, not its existence, constitute our problem. Miss Arendt therefore concludes her analysis of terror wisely: "Every end in history necessarily contains a new beginning. . . . Beginning, before it becomes a historical event, is the supreme capacity of man; politically, it is identical with man's freedom. . . . This beginning is guaranteed by each new birth; it is indeed every man."[61]

Sambo himself had to be a product of a contradictory environment, all sides of which he necessarily internalized. Sambo, in short, was Sambo only up to the moment that the psychological balance was jarred from within or without; he might then well have become Nat Turner, for every element antithetical to his being a Sambo resided in his nature. "Total power" and "Sambo" may serve a useful purpose in a theoretical model as a rough approximation to a complex reality, provided that we do not confuse the model with the reality itself. Neither slavery nor slaves can be treated as pure categories, free of the contradictions, tensions, and potentialities that characterize all human experience.

Elkins, in committing himself to these absolutist notions,

[60] Arendt, *Review of Politics*, XV (1953), 312.
[61] *Ibid.*, 327.

overlooks the evidence from his own concentration camp analogy. Bettelheim notes that even the most accommodating, servile, and broken-spirited prisoners sometimes suddenly defied the Gestapo with great courage. Eugen Kogon devotes considerable space in his *Theory and Practice of Hell* to the development and maintenance of resistance within the camps.[62] In a similar way the most docile field slaves or the most trusted house slaves might, and often did, suddenly rise up in some act of unprecedented violence. This transformation will surprise us only if we confuse our theoretical model with the reality it ought to help us to understand.

Elkins has not described to us the personality of the Southern slave, nor, by contrast, of the Latin American slave; he has instead demonstrated the limiting case of the slavish personality. Every slave system contained a powerful tendency to generate Sambos, but every system generated countervailing forces. Elkins, following Tannenbaum, might properly argue that differences in tradition, religion, and law guaranteed differences in the strength of those countervailing forces; he cannot prove and dare not assume that any system lacked them.

Elkins accounts for such forms of deviant behavior as lying, stealing, and shirking by absorbing them within the general framework of childish response. He is by no means completely wrong in doing so, for very often the form of a particular act of hostility degraded the slave as much as it irritated the master. Elkins' approach is not so much wrong as it is of limited usefulness. Once we pass beyond the insight that the form of rebelliousness might itself reveal accommoda-

---

[62] Bettelheim, *Journal of Abnormal and Social Psychology*, XXXVIII (1943), 451; Eugen Kogon, *The Theory and Practice of Hell* (New York, 1950), esp. Chs. XX, XXXI.

tion, we cannot go much further. If all behavior short of armed revolt can be subsumed within the framework of childishness and dependence, then that formulation clearly embraces too much. Our historical problem is to explain how and under what conditions accommodation yields to resistance, and we therefore need a framework sufficiently flexible to permit distinctions between accommodating behavior that, however slightly, suggests a process of transformation into opposite qualities; such a framework must, moreover, be able to account for both tendencies within a single human being and even within a single act.

It has become something of a fashion in the adolescent recesses of our profession to bury troublesome authors and their work under a heap of carping general and specific complaints; it is no part of my purpose to join in the fun. Elkins' book has raised the study of Southern slavery to a far higher level than ever before, and it has done so at a moment when the subject seemed about to be drowned in a sea of moral indignation. It has demonstrated forcefully the remarkable uses to which psychology can be put in historical inquiry. It has brought to the surface the relationship between the slave past and a wide range of current problems flowing from that past. These are extraordinary achievements. To advance in the direction Elkins has pointed out, however, we shall first have to abandon most of his ground. We cannot simply replace his psychological model with a better one; we must recognize that all psychological models may only be used suggestively for flashes of insight or as aids in forming hypotheses and that they cannot substitute for empirical investigation. As the distinguished anthropologist, Max Gluckman, has observed, respect for psychology as a discipline requiring a high degree of training in the acquisition and interpretation of data forces us to bypass psychological analyses whenever possible.[63] Or, to put it another way, if we are to profit fully from Elkins' boldness, we shall have to retreat from it and try to solve the problems he raises by the more orthodox procedures of historical research.

[63] Max Gluckman, *Order and Rebellion in Tribal Africa* (New York, 1963), 2–3.

Slavery and Personality

MARY AGNES LEWIS

This paper will explore Stanley Elkins' treatment of the
American plantation system as a factor in the formation and
perpetuation of distinct slave personality traits.[1] In his book
Slavery, Elkins combines role psychology and the interpersonal approach to personality formation.[2] The interpersonal
theory asserts that in any group certain people are influential
in the formation of the personalities of individual members of
that group. Sullivan[3] has designated this influential or refer-

[1] This paper was originally published under the title "Slavery and Personality: A Further Comment," in *American Quarterly* 19 (Spring, 1967),
114–21. It was prepared as an independent study project in consultation with
Dr. Robin Brooks, History Department, California State College at Hay-
ward.

[2] Elkins' much-debated thesis on individual and group adjustment has
received considerable attention in recent years. The most important uses of
the "Sambo" stereotype are to be found in the literature dealing with concepts of identity. The emergence of the slaveowner as the sole significant
other within the American slave system is discussed in W. Haywood Burns,
The Voices of Negro Protest (New York and London, 1963). The psychological consequences of the slave's and freedman's dependence on white
authority-figures is summarized in Charles Silberman's *Crisis in Black and
White* (New York, 1964) and Thomas F. Pettigrew's *A Profile of the
Negro American* (Princeton, 1964). In *The New World of Negro Americans* (New York, 1963), Harold R. Isaacs finds the major element in Afro-
American group identity to be "identification with the aggressor"—the desire
to be white.

[3] Harry Stack Sullivan, *Conceptions of Modern Psychiatry* (Washing-

ence group *significant others*. The individual internalizes the
reactions of others toward his performance of certain roles.
Personality is acquired through social interaction as the individual continually adjusts his behavior to conform to the
expectations and evaluations of significant others.

The role system, on the other hand, de-emphasizes the factor of individual choice since roles are defined and assigned by
society and not by the individual. Role theory focuses on the
ways in which a society determines how social intercourse is
to be conducted.[4]

Elkins writes, "In the slave system of the United States—
so finely circumscribed and so cleanly self-contained—virtually
all avenues of communication to the society at large, originated
and ended with the master. The system was unique, *sui ge-
neris*" (63). The essence of this unique system was its "closedness," that is, the near-total domination of slaves by owners.
The psychological consequence of this closed system was the
creation and fostering of a distinct slave personality of which
the principal element was the slave's "total" dependence on a
single authority-figure, the owner.

Elkins characterizes this personality type: "Sambo, the
typical plantation slave, was docile but irresponsible, loyal but
lazy, humble but chronically given to lying and stealing; his
behavior was full of infantile silliness and his talk inflated with
childish exaggeration. His relationship with his master was
one of utter dependence and childlike attachment: it was
indeed this childlike quality that was the very key to his
being" (82).

---

ton, D.C., 1947), 95–96; see also Sullivan's *The Interpersonal Theory of
Psychiatry* (New York, 1953).
    [4] Theodore M. Newcomb, *Social Psychology* (New York, 1950), 280–83.

The assumption we are asked to accept is that a group of atomized, childlike individuals had no means by which to relate themselves and others save the integrative framework provided by the owner's authority. The Self (slave) they related to was a direct function of the Other (owner).

The owner, then, was the sole significant other in that he provided the ways in which the slave viewed himself and the rest of society. Moreover, the owner set the social goal to which the slave aspired—to become an obedient and "loved" servant. The slave manifested his gratitude for this love and approval by his loyalty and service to the owner.

For a paradigm of the effective "closed system" Elkins turns to the German concentration camps of the Second World War. Here, compliance and the appropriate patterns of behavior were exacted in a relatively short period of time. The effectiveness of the camp experience in structuring personality is measured by the lack of organized resistance among prisoners, the infrequency of suicides, and the absence of hatred toward the guards (114–15). Elkins acknowledges exceptions to submissive, childlike behavior among camp inmates. These were notably people who performed roles *other than* that of prisoner. They were orderlies, clerks, and the like. Thus, even in such a "perverted patriarchy" many of the inmates escaped identification with the SS guards (134–35).[5]

Elkins also acknowledges that exceptions to Sambo obtained under plantation slavery. However, he insists that the most important factor in conditioning the personalities of the majority of slaves was identification with a benevolent patri-

---

[5] Here Elkins writes that "to a prisoner so engaged, there were others who mattered, who gave real point to his existence—the SS was no longer the only one. Conversely, the role of the child was not the only role he played. He could take initiative; he could give as well as receive protection; he did things which had meaning in adult terms."

78   MARY AGNES LEWIS

arch. Elkins informs us that it was because the system was closed that "the individual, consequently, for his very psychic security, had to picture his master in some way as the 'good father,' even when, as in the concentration camp, it made no sense at all" (128–29).

As the plantation system became more elaborate, race relations came to be governed by patterns of behavior which differentiated black and white into distinct and irrevocable categories.[6] The crystallization of a truly "closed" structure was prevented by permitting two racially autonomous groups of people to exist. The link between the races was economic rather than one based on social reciprocity.[7]

Once the system sanctioned the existence of an independent slave community the possibility that the owner would remain the only significant other vanished. For, while the slave remained an object in his relations with whites, within his own community the slave performed roles other than those required by the "institution" of slavery. The structure and values of the slave community were sufficiently separate from those of whites. Kenneth Stampp has noted that "the resulting unique patterns of slave behavior amused, or dismayed, or appalled the whites and convinced most of them that Negroes were innately different."[8] It was possible for a woman to

[6] These behaviors served to separate rather than to join people together. See E. Franklin Frazier, *The Negro in the United States* (New York, 1949), chap. 3, "The Plantation as a Social Institution"; and Bertram W. Doyle, *The Etiquette of Race Relations in the South* (Chicago, 1937), chaps. 2 and 3.

[7] Slave and owner were bound together in an economic venture and its failure could have grave consequences for both parties. "The most grotesque aspect of plantation paternalism lay in the fact that if a planter took *too* complaisant an attitude toward the performance of field work, he courted financial failure, and with failure would come the sale of his slaves to pay his indebtedness." Willie Lee Rose, *Rehearsal for Reconstruction: The Port Royal Experiment* (Indianapolis, 1964), 127.

[8] Kenneth Stampp, *The Peculiar Institution* (New York, 1964), 334.

work all day in the fields and return to her cabin in the evening and poison her baby rather than have it live in bondage.[9] In the field she worked as did other slaves; in the cabin her considerations were those of a mother. Some of the roles validated only within the slave community were those of conjurer, teacher, and parent.

Reports of ex-slaves indicate that considerations having no relation to the approval of a benevolent patriarch were instrumental in shaping the aspirations of slaves. Of these aspirations, the most notable was, of course, the desire for freedom. Any slave who conceived of freedom was, at that moment, outside the system.[10] James L. Smith reported that on his escape several friends accompanied the escape party part of the way—thus, vicariously participating in the escape each may have wished for himself.[11] There are also numerous reports of slaves rendering assistance to fugitives.[12] The danger of these ventures should indicate that participation on any

[9] Such an incident is recorded in *Lay My Burden Down: A Folk History of Slavery*, ed. B. A. Botkin (Chicago, 1945), 154.

[10] Compare with concentration camp inmates, who, according to Bruno Bettelheim, "frequently admitted that they could no longer visualize themselves living outside the camps, making free decisions, taking care of themselves and their families." "Individual and Mass Behavior in Extreme Situations," *Journal of Abnormal and Social Psychology*, XXXVIII (Oct. 1943), 439.

It appears that the major difference between camp inmates and slaves was a vitality that the former entirely lacked. Harvey Wish has noted that while "ex-slaves took issue with the impression of plantation visitors that the slaves must have been contented, . . . the constant outbreak of hearty Negro laughter, the improvised singing, and the vigorous dancing. . . . All this did show an impressive zest for life and a level of existence undoubtedly higher than that of the inmates of a twentieth-century concentration camp." *Slavery in the South: First-Hand Accounts of the Ante-Bellum American Southland*, ed. Harvey Wish (New York, 1964), xix.

[11] James L. Smith, *Autobiography* (Norwich, 1881), 41.

[12] For activities of the underground railroad see Austin Bearse, *Remembrances of Fugitive Slave Days* (Boston, 1880); William Wells Brown, *Narrative* (London, 1849); and William Still, *The Underground Railroad* (Philadelphia, 1872).

level was more meaningful to the slave than the presumed "total" identification with the values of the owner and his household.

Frederick Douglass, like many slaves, had a variety of black significant others. These ranged from "Doctor" Isaac Cooper, the slave who taught him "religion," to the artisans on the plantation.[13] Along this continuum were also to be found those who persisted in defying the authority of the owner and his underlings.[14]

Nichols has rightly observed that "the Negro lived in two worlds in both of which he strove to gain status. Among other Negroes he was often expected to act against his owner's interest or to show a manliness which the master would not permit. To his owner the slave was forced to act with the deference expected of the subordinate caste."[15] The conflict emerging between self and role assignment intensified as the slave community defined "freedom" in terms that opposed the interests of the owner. Suicide, escape, and rebellion were some of the consequences of this conflict.

There were those who, after escaping, regrouped in stable communities in the United States and Canada. Any slave having knowledge of successful escapes, uprisings, and especially communities in which black men lived together in freedom had ties beyond slavery. He had significant others who had not only outwitted the owner but with whom he could intimately identify.

[13] Frederick Douglass, *Life and Times of Frederick Douglass* (New York, 1962), 62.

[14] Successful or not, these rebels became the slave's heroes: "When Nat Turner's insurrection broke out, the colored people were forbidden to hold meetings among themselves. Nat Turner was one of the slaves who had a quite large army; he was the captain to free his race." Smith, *Autobiography*, 30.

[15] Charles H. Nichols, *Many Thousand Gone* (Leiden, 1963), 74.

Elkins refuses to accept compliance (accommodation) as a valid defensive function of slave personality (132–33, n. 106). To view compliance as a convenient mechanism employed by several generations would necessarily destroy his assumption of the slave's internalization of the Sambo role. Consequently, the possibility that conformity and compliance might be extorted without significant personality distortion is not considered. If the Sambo role were internalized, then the use of force would not have been as prevalent as the literature reveals. The use and significance of force is well documented in both judicial records and the reports of ex-slaves.[16] Many fugitives commented on the seemingly paradoxical phenomenon that those individuals who most humbly submitted to punishment and the wrath of the owner or overseer were thereafter most frequently and harshly punished:

> They prefer to whip those who are most easily whipped. The doctrine that submission to violence is the best cure for violence did not hold good as between slaves and overseers. He was whipped oftener who was whipped easiest. That slave who had the courage to stand up for himself against the overseer, although he might have many hard stripes at first, became virtually a freeman. "You can shoot me," said a slave to Rigby Hopkins, "but you can't whip me," and the result was he was neither whipped nor shot.[17]

Evidently the slave with whom the owner and overseer could most readily relate was one who performed the role of sub-

[16] See James Roberts, *Narrative* (Chicago, 1858), 11–12; Austin Stewart, *Twenty-two Years a Slave and Forty Years a Freeman* (New York, 1867), 17–18; *Judicial Cases Concerning American Slavery and the Negro*, ed. Helen T. Catterall (5 vols.; Washington, D.C., 1926–37), I, 216–21, 247.

[17] Douglass, *Life and Times*, 52.

missive slave. Confrontations with recalcitrant slaves were avoided; they could be ignored, hired out, sold, or killed, but not confronted.[18]

A concept dealing with the reinforcement of stereotypes is the "self-fulfilling prophecy."[19] This concept treats social perception as an integral part of transactions people define as being real. By predicting the outcome of any situation the perceiver is aware of and responds to only those things relevant to his initial judgment. He is never conscious of the contribution of his behavior and attitudes to the final outcome. He has, in effect, psychological investments in the maintenance of the initial perception. In this and similar ways slaveholders could remain *selectively inattentive* to anything that might lead to their interacting with slaves in terms other than those provided by the stereotype.

An interesting example of selective inattention is provided in the following letter to an escaped slave from his former owner:

> I write you these lines to let you know the situation we are in,—partly in consequence of your running away and stealing Old Rock, our fine mare. Though we got the mare back, she never was worth much after you took her,—and, as I now stand in need of some funds, I have determined to sell you, and I have had an offer for you, but did not see fit to take it. If you will send me one thousand dollars, and pay for the old mare, I will give up all claim I have to you. . . . If you do not comply with my request, I will sell you to some one else, and you may rest assured that the time is not far distant when things will be changed with you. . . .

[18] The concentration camp system did not tolerate these alternative methods of dealing with difficult prisoners. Bettelheim, *Jour. of Abnormal & Soc. Psychology*, XXXVIII, 436.

[19] Robert K. Merton, "The Self-Fulfilling Prophecy," *Antioch Review*, VIII (Summer 1948), 193-210.

You know that we reared you as we reared our own children; . . . that shortly before you ran away, when your
master asked you if you would like to be sold, you said you
would not leave him to go with any body.

Sarah Logue[20]

The man to whom this letter was addressed was certainly no
Sambo! He replied:

you never could have insulted a brother by telling him you
sold his only remaining brother and sister, because he put
himself beyond your power to convert him into money. . . .
Now you have the unutterable meanness to ask me to return
and be your miserable chattel, or, in lieu thereof, send you
$1000 to enable you to redeem the *land*, but not to redeem
my poor brother and sister! . . . You say, 'You know we
raised you as we did our own children.' Woman, did you
raise your *own children* for the market? . . . Did you raise
them to be driven off, bound to a coffle in chains? Where
are my poor bleeding brothers and sisters? Can you tell?
Who was it that sent them off into sugar and cotton fields,
to be kicked and cuffed, and whipped, and to groan and
die; and where no kin can hear their groans, or attend and
sympathize at their dying bed, or follow in their funeral?
. . . But, by the way, where is your husband? You don't
speak of him. I infer, therefore, that he is dead; that he has
gone to his great account, with all his sins against my poor
family upon his head. . . . If you or any other speculator
on my body and rights, wish to know how I regard my
rights, they need but come here, and lay their hands on me
to enslave me. . . .

Yours, etc.,
J. W. Loguen[21]

[20] *The Mind of the Negro as Reflected in Letters Written during the Crisis, 1800–1860*, ed. Carter G. Woodson (Washington, D.C., 1926), 217–18.
[21] *Ibid.*, 218–19.

Another example of the pervasiveness of selective inattention within the plantation system is given by James "Lindsey" Smith who reported:

> My master came as far as Philadelphia to look for me; and my brother says, when he came back without me, he became a very demon on the plantation, cutting and slashing, cursing and swearing at the slaves till there was no living with him. He seemed to be out of his head; and for hours would set looking straight into the fire; when spoken to, he would say: "I can't understand what made Lindsey leave me."[22]

This last example is perhaps the best instance of the self-fulfilling prophecy of the benevolent patriarch. Smith was not a favorite slave. He was lame, had a record of shunning work, feigning illness, and all the other mechanisms employed to "trick" the owner. Why the owner would have gone to so much bother to retrieve Lindsey becomes clear when one considers the psychological investment in the performance of the role of patriarch. For his owner, Lindsey remained the dependent ward whose behavior in running away was unintelligible. In interaction with the slaveholder only that part of Lindsey associated with Sambo was recognized. The slave's true self could be affirmed only by his fellows.

Finally, Elkins' analysis, far from offering new insights into the American slave system, falls comfortably within traditional approaches to the subject. We have been asked to accept the same syndrome of cultural assumptions and have been guided to the same conclusion: though slavery, per se, was "wrong" it did provide the deculturalized African and his progeny with those valuable cues which enabled them to

[22] Smith, *Autobiography*, 23.

make appropriate adjustments to their situation (89–90). Elkins asks that we accept, on the basis of the evidence, the validity of the Sambo stereotype so that the debate can finally be closed.[23]

However, the closed construct employed by Elkins is inapplicable to slavery as it existed in the United States. So long as there was the possibility of the emergence of alternative significant others the owner's control over the psychological security of slaves was not absolute, or even near-absolute. A viable, self-perpetuating slave culture did emerge to compete with the slaveowner's authority and significance. It was from this society that the slave sought approval and affirmation of himself as a man.

In applying his theory of a closed society to slavery, Elkins is forced to treat escapees, rebels, and the like as deviants. From his established framework, he could not recognize that those he would call deviants fulfilled the ideals and aspirations of many slaves, that day to day resistance could be manifested in any number of ways. "Occasional sabotage, self-maiming, and inadequate workmanship were common enough to bring complaints from owners and employers. More frequent still was the slow-down. Masters could never be certain how much of this was a vote against the system itself and how much simply reflected the low incentives that characterized slavery."[24] The Sambo stereotype does not provide any clues to the readiness of slaves to leave the plantation during and after the Civil War. Nor does it explain the behavior of those who remained but who were engaged in subversive activities.

[23] Rose, *Rehearsal for Reconstruction*, 129–30: "although 'Sambo' finds many illustrations . . . he remains a statistical concept, and the record contains as many stories of protest, disloyalty to the late masters, and manly independence as of servile acquiescence. . . ."
[24] Richard C. Wade, *Slavery in the Cities: The South 1820–1860* (New York, 1964), 225–26.

Elkins assumed that the condition of slavery was similarly experienced and responded to by most American slaves. However, the evidence suggests that there were numerous ways in which black people reacted to slavery and exclusion from the larger society. It also suggests that the concept of the self-fulfilling prophecy offers a preferable explanation of the creation and pervasiveness of the Sambo stereotype by revealing the psychological investment of slaveowners (and, indeed, most whites) in its perpetuation.[25]

[25] "There was the hope on the part of most of the non-slaveholders that they would some day become owners of slaves. Consequently, they took on the habits and patterns of thought of the slaveholders before they actually joined that class." John Hope Franklin, *From Slavery to Freedom* (2nd ed.; New York, 1956), 185.

A Note on Elkins
and the Abolitionists

AILEEN S. KRADITOR

Of the varied interpretations of the American abolitionists during the past decade, one of the most interesting appeared in a book dealing primarily with another subject. The volume, *Slavery*, by Stanley Elkins, attracted attention in the historical profession for its bold suggestion that the Sambo personality was not simply an invention by racists to justify the enslavement of Negroes, but that the position in which the Negro slaves in the United States were placed did in fact create childlike and servile personalities in many of them. The suggestion was so provocative that reviewers paid relatively little attention to the other principal thesis of the book, a novel interpretation of the abolitionists. Although this thesis is supported by scanty evidence it has been adopted and expanded in a volume recently published,[1] and the sections that deal with the abolitionists have recently been republished in two

---

[1] George M. Fredrickson, *The Inner Civil War* (New York, 1965), a study of the impact of the Civil War on a small number of Northern intellectuals, including some abolitionists. Those sections that discuss abolitionists are essentially a gloss on the Elkins text, and the author makes what I believe are the same methodological errors. See James M. McPherson's review of *The Inner Civil War* in *Civil War History*, XII (1966), 67-69, for a cogent critique of those errors.

books of readings widely used in college history courses.[2]
Elkins contrasts the structure of American society with the
structure of British society in the middle of the nineteenth
century, and he finds that by then the power of many American
institutions had melted away. The church had broken
into denominational fragments. The legal profession was not
the strong institution it was in England. Political parties were
dissolving and changing their forms. Old classes were declining
and new ones rising. The result, according to Elkins, was
that traditional institutions were so weak, fragmented, and
shifting that Americans of that day easily imagined that institutions
as such were not necessary to a society's stability.
"In the America of the 1830's and 1840's there was no other
symbol of vitality to be found than the individual, and it was
to the individual, with all his promise, that the thinker, like
everyone else, would inexorably orient himself" (34). Individualism,
self-reliance, abstractionism, disregard of the responsibilities
and uses of power—"Such was the state of mind
in which Americans faced the gravest social problem that had
yet confronted them as an established nation," slavery (34).
Elkins seems unable to decide whether to blame the abolitionists
for approaching slavery in this state of mind. On the
one hand he argues that there were insufficient institutional
arrangements within which they could have worked to rid
the country of this problem in a gradual and peaceful manner.
On the other hand he obviously disapproves of their
alleged anti-institutional bias, of their seeing the question as
"*all* moral," and he declares that there was

in principle if not in fact, an alternative philosophical mode.
Slavery might have been approached not as a problem in

[2] Hugh Hawkins (ed.), *The Abolitionists* (Boston, 1964); and Richard
O. Curry (ed.), *The Abolitionists: Reformers or Fanatics?* (New York,
1965).

pure morality but as a question of institutional arrangements—a question of those institutions which make the crucial
difference in men's relationships with one another . . . (28).

The question is whether the abolitionists as a group did
have an anti-institutional bias. Elkins prejudges the issue in his
query: "Why should the American of, say, 1830 have been
so insensitive to institutions and their function?" (28). "The
American" turns out, according to the evidence Elkins provides, to be a tiny group of Concord Transcendentalists and
a handful of abolitionists, whose ideas and attitudes were un-
characteristic not only of the overwhelming majority of
Americans but even of the majority of abolitionists. He discusses such Transcendentalists as Emerson and Theodore
Parker and their refusal to use institutional means to effect
reforms and to think in institutional terms,[3] and he admits
that "their relationship with abolition societies was never
anything but equivocal" (168). But if the Transcendentalists
did not generally join abolition societies their intellectual
affinities with the abolitionists, according to Elkins, were very
significant. It would seem, then, that he discusses the Transcendentalists in order to provide a foundation for his contention that the abolitionists themselves were anti-institutionalists. This inference is strengthened by his reference (166)
to "Transcendentalism and other reform movements," despite
the notorious fact that the Transcendentalists lacked the commitment to action that characterizes movements for change.
Stating that any other movement concerned with social
policy "would have" found no better source of wisdom than
the Transcendentalists, that a formidable abolitionist movement "might thus have" gathered both strength and weakness

---

[3] Pp. 164–75. I might add that they refused to use *any* means to effect reforms; few of them were activists.

from them, and that the abolitionists "could not have dupli-
cated the intellectual pattern of the Transcendentalists more
precisely if they tried," Elkins then transforms all those
conditionals into declaratives (164–65). Moreover, he believes it significant that "the very time at which they [the
Transcendentalists] flourished coincides with the launching
of the great reform impulses." We are half persuaded already;
the Transcendentalists, it appears, were both logical models
for and contemporaries of the abolitionists. Evidence from
the abolitionists' own writings is almost superfluous.

But "evidence" is furnished, from the speeches and writings
of William Lloyd Garrison, Wendell Phillips, and Stephen S.
Foster, and from the doctrines of Nathaniel P. Rogers, the
last two of whom were undoubtedly anti-institutionalists; and
from the writings of Theodore D. Weld, William Jay, and
James G. Birney, who were not. A thorough study of the
latter three and even a cursory glance at the scores of political
abolitionists who worked through such institutions as the
Democratic and Whig parties, or who formed new institutions such as the Liberty party and the Liberty League, would
have destroyed Elkins' thesis.

To test whether most abolitionists were anti-institutionalists
we ought to begin with a definition of institutions. Elkins
does not provide one, but he describes them as follows:

> institutions define a society's culture . . . they provide the
> stable channels, for better or worse, within which the in-
> tellectual must have his business—if, that is, his work is to
> have real consequences for society and if he himself is to
> have a positive function there. Institutions with power pro-
> duce the "things" not only upon which one leans but also
> against which one pushes; they provide the standards
> whereby, for men of sensibility, one part of society may be
> judged and tested against another. The lack of them, more-

over, removes the thinker not only from the places where
power resides but also from the very *idea* of power and
how it is used (143).

Elkins' application of this analysis to the Transcendentalists,
and by later implication and logical leap to the abolitionists, is
suggested in the title of the next section of the chapter in
which that quotation appears: "Intellectuals without Responsibility." The picture is completed in "The Abolitionist as
Transcendentalist," a section containing many highly anti-
institutionalistic statements by some abolitionists, as well as
quotations that could be interpreted otherwise.

All this might justify Elkins' generalization concerning
abolitionist anti-institutionalism if the bulk of the movement
shared Garrison's repudiation of human government (as construed by Elkins), withdrew from all organized churches as
he and Foster did, and relied solely on moral suasion to induce
slaveholders to repent their sin. Unfortunately for the theory,
this was not the case. The Rogerses and Fosters were a tiny
minority of the movement even in New England, their strong-
hold. The Garrisonian perfectionists (who, incidentally, insisted they were not anti-institutionalists) were but a small
coterie even in Massachusetts. The overwhelming majority of
members of antislavery societies evidently believed that slavery
would not be abolished unless the political power of the slaveowners was destroyed by political means, for they continued
to work within the major parties and later in the Free Soil
and Republican parties. Most of them believed that the re-
spectability and influence of the slaveowners could be destroyed not by withdrawing from the compromising churches
but by working within them, to persuade them to exert pressure on their Southern wings and refuse fellowship with
slaveowning clergymen and members. In other words, the

vast majority of abolitionists did not repudiate institutions or
institutional means to effect the desired change; they valued
institutions as potential weapons, and where existing institutions seemed too corrupted they tried to replace them with
new institutions through which collective efforts could be
exerted. Most of them harbored no illusions about the possibility of convincing the slaveowners, by mere exhortation, of
the error of their ways. When they advocated moral pressure
on the owners they usually explained that this meant world-
wide ostracism, disruption of economic and social contacts,
and an unremitting propaganda offensive—something quite
different from the naive sermons on brotherhood that, according to some historians, abolitionists were content to rely
on.[4] And most abolitionists who advocated this tactic urged
that it be accompanied by efforts to win elections, pass laws,
dominate political parties, reform the churches, and in other
ways use institutions to destroy slavery.

How much extreme individualism and "disregard of the
responsibilities and uses of power" can be read into the following sentiments expressed by James G. Birney, abolitionist
candidate for President?

> We have nothing in our political structure that is stable.
> Stability is an *essential* in governments. With us every thing

[4] See, for example, "To the Abolitionists of Massachusetts," an open
letter from the Board of Managers of the Massachusetts Anti-Slavery Society, in *The Liberator*, Aug. 10, 1838: "We would make the public sentiment of the North a tonic, instead of an opiate to southern conscience, we
would unite and concentrate it, until it shall tell, in a manner perfectly
irresistible, upon the sense of right, the pride of social standing, and character, even upon the interest of the slaveholder, until it shall help to make
real to his mind, and he shall feel, in the air around him, the guilt, the
danger, the deep disgrace, the ruinous impolicy of the relation he sustains.
. . ." Frederick Douglass' writings are full of such statements. Another
theme frequently found in abolitionist writings is that abolitionists should
endeavor to ostracize slaveholders at Northern resorts like Newport.

is unstable because subject to popular excitements, and popular excitements can be generated and used by demagogues at their pleasure. No people, I am sure, can advance in moral refinement and true civilization under the univ'l Suffrage.

On another occasion he wrote that changes such as an increase or decrease in the tariff ought to be gradual because, he said, reforms should not be sudden where lawful interests were at stake.[5]

Far from repudiating institutions, most abolitionists wished to purify them. Consider, for example, a passage from William Goodell's *Slavery and Anti-Slavery* (1852), an extremely influential book by a prominent abolitionist:

> This great question is to be decided, mainly, by the concurrent action of the two great social institutions of the country, the Church, and the State, the ecclesiastical and the civil power.
>
> It is for THE PEOPLE of the non-slaveholding States to say whether those two social institutions shall be redeemed from the foul embraces of slavery, and wielded for their heaven-appointed ends, or whether they shall remain, as at present, in the hands of their enemies.[6]

Such statements abound in antislavery literature. Even the Garrisonian, James S. Gibbons, could write: "Organization, Concert, is at the base of the divine economy."[7]

Another sort of statement frequently encountered is the

[5] Birney to Gamaliel Bailey, Apr. 16, 1843, and to Russell Errett, Aug. 5, 1844, in Dwight L. Dumond (ed.), *Letters of James Gillespie Birney* (New York, 1938), II, 733, 832. Emphasis in original.

[6] Goodell, 584. Emphasis in original.

[7] Gibbons to William Lloyd Garrison, Mar. 30, 1841, in Anti-Slavery Letters to Garrison and Others, Boston Public Library.

accusation by some abolitionists that others were anti-institutionalists. At the height of the controversy over the woman
question and perfectionism, the Rev. James T. Woodbury,
an abolitionist, asserted that in the opinion of Garrison and
his friends: "Slavery is not merely to be abolished, but
nearly everything else. . . . *We* are not willing, for the sake
of killing the rats, to burn the house down with all it contains."[8] The "Appeal" of some abolitionists at Andover Theological Seminary, published in *The Liberator* of August 25,
1837, included the statement that the appellants had read, in
antislavery publications, "speculations which lead inevitably
to disorganization and anarchy, unsettling the domestic economy, removing the landmarks of society, and unhinging the
machinery of government."[9] The targets of these accusations
pleaded innocent[10] (sometimes, in my opinion, convincingly),
but Elkins himself could not have penned a severer indictment of anti-institutionalism than this group of abolitionists
directed against their fellows. While many non-Garrisonians
thought the Andover Appeal in bad taste, they agreed with
its substance. What inferences, then, can be drawn concerning
the thinking of the movement as a whole?

   Only a minority of abolitionists reacted to the hostility
they encountered by rejecting not the *compromising* churches
and the *proslavery* government but churches and governments—institutions per se. The vast majority never did so.
And when the Northern wings of some churches and parties,
and later the Federal government, moved closer to their
position, that majority and even some of the minority ceased

<hr />

   [8] *The Liberator*, Sept. 1, 1837. Emphasis added.
   [9] See also letter from "Alethea," *ibid.*, May 26, 1837; and Elizur Wright,
Jr., "Judge Lawless and the Law," *Quarterly Anti-Slavery Magazine*, I
(1836), 400–409, esp. 400–402. Many other examples could be cited.
   [10] See Garrison's reply to Dr. Osgood, *The Liberator*, Aug. 2, 1839; and
"To the Abolitionists of Massachusetts," cited in fn. 4.

their attacks. When abolitionists supported the Union in the Civil War, it was usually because the institutions, not the abolitionists, had changed.

Radicals have always been accused of wanting to undermine institutions. What is true about most radicals, including most Garrisonians and many other abolitionists, is that they did not share the conservatives' reverence for institutions as such. Specific traditions, customs, and institutions they were willing to judge by transcendent ethical criteria and condemn if found wanting. Garrisonians, for example, repeatedly disclaimed hostility to the clergy and the church and reiterated that they deplored only the perversions of these institutions.[11] It may be argued that the Garrisonians were anti-institutionalists despite their disclaimers. In the case of Henry C. Wright, I think that is true. In other cases it is a matter of definition. This question is peripheral, because if the Garrisonians did not represent the entire movement, Elkins' discussion of their attitude toward institutions proves nothing about American abolitionism as a whole. The bulk of the movement, those who followed the more conservative leaders such as Birney and the Tappan brothers, found no need even to make public disclaimers. Unless a desire to abolish completely an inherently evil institution like slavery and an in-

---

[11] See, for example, Garrison's editorial, "Clerical Protest, No. 2," *ibid.*, Sept. 8, 1837; and "To the Abolitionists of Massachusetts," cited in fn. 4: ". . . the abolitionists form the only great party, in our age, who, aiming at a wide social reform, and operating on and through social institutions, yet rest their efforts and their hopes professedly on religious grounds. . . ." The abolitionist Unitarian, Rev. Samuel May, Jr., wrote: "Mr. Garrison has never denied that there has been, is, and should be *a church;* yet has he been represented as aiming to overthrow the Church, Ministry, Gospel, and all. He *has* plainly & vehemently . . . denied that there was a Church of *Christ* which excused Slaveholding & Slave-trading, . . . which apologised for these, nay which claimed for them the sanction of the Old Testament, and the permission at least of the New!" May to J. B. Estlin, Dec. 29, 1845, May Papers, Boston Public Library.

sistence that all other institutions be purged of its influence are defined as anti-institutionalism, the majority of abolitionists do not merit that label. If such desire and insistence do add up to anti-institutionalism, the label must be applied to every movement for change that does not visualize the proposed change as piecemeal, gradual, and reformist. But to do that is to contradict the word's denotation and to attach to it an invidious connotation in the guise of objective historiography.

Elkins regrets that slavery was not ended gradually, by piecemeal adjustments of the institutional arrangements that supported it. He offers "a catalogue of preliminaries—a series of separate short-term reforms rather than root-and-branch abolition" that might have solved the problem. For example, the churches could have insisted that slaves be instructed in Christian morality and given a dignified spiritual life. They could have required regular marriage and guaranteed the sanctity of the family. Laws could have been passed to mitigate cruelty and recognize the slaves' humanity. Slaves might have been given the right to earn enough money to buy their freedom (194–96). He points out that such schemes were in fact proposed in the United States and were put into practice in other countries. As a result slavery died peacefully in the British West Indies and in Latin America. But, he adds, this process was not possible here. There was no national church, no national focus of social and financial power, no national bar—in short, no other national institutions such as existed in other slaveholding countries—that could have mediated the conflicting interests or wielded the necessary power. The absence of such institutions forced the opponents of slavery to see it in abstract terms, in terms of "sin" on the part of slaveholders and of "guilt" on the part of Northerners. Since this view of the abolitionists' conception of sin, guilt, and morality is a principal corollary of Elkins' anti-institutionalism thesis, it is appropriate at this point to consider its validity. The contrast between the United States and other nations in which slavery existed is valid up to a point; certainly institutions here were much more fluid and in the period under discussion were changing drastically. But no society, no matter how structured, provides institutional means or moral justifications for its own subversion.[12] The significant point is not that American society was relatively "devoid of structure," as Elkins correctly states, but that slavery in this country was part of what structure it had, such an integral part that a movement to destroy it was not a reform movement but a radical one. It judged the institution of slavery not by the moral criteria of the society within which slavery had a legitimate place, but by a higher law that rejected those very criteria. Slavery not only was involved inextricably in the economic and political structure of the entire nation, but was also the social and economic base of a class that wielded almost total power in its own section and tremendous influence in the North and the Federal government. The abolitionists' situation was, therefore, different from that of all the other movements for change in that day—women's rights, temperance, trade-unionism, prison reform, and so on. They were reform movements; abolitionism was radical (more radical than many abolitionists realized). The reformers' goals were attainable without touching the basic structure of Amer-

---

[12] The contrast between the fluidity of American society and the institutional stability of British society should not be overstated. The period was one of unaccustomed change and shift of institutions in Britain, too. As to the reasons why slavery ended peacefully in the West Indies and Brazil, Eugene D. Genovese comments on this in his review of Elkins' book in *Science & Society*, XXV (1961), 47: "The peaceful solution in the British Caribbean . . . followed from the political weakness of the ruling planters. In Brazil, the slaveowners lacked a contiguous territory and were isolated and subjected to a crushing defeatism by the failure of the Confederate cause."

ican society; abolition could be attained only by overturning that structure in part of the country and shifting power drastically in the remainder.

Elkins thus misconstrues what he regards as the abolitionists' penchant for moral abstractions, their moral absolutism, and their guilt feelings. He blames these attitudes on a society so unstructured that it exaggerated each individual's sense of his own responsibility.

> Reforming energy, or a sense of social responsibility, could be designated in terms other than "guilt." But the conditions of American society have made such energy peculiarly a personal, an individual, phenomenon. It is the absence of clear channels for the harnessing of these drives that has made it so. . . . Guilt must be borne as an individual burden to a degree not to be observed elsewhere (161).

The guilt feelings of the abolitionists may be explained in terms other than psychological. If slavery was an integral part of the institutional structure of the nation as a whole, the average Northerner had as realistic a basis for guilt feelings as the average German of the 1930s. By the same token, the minority of Northerners who were aware of their section's complicity in the crime of slavery and who worked in a variety of ways to publicize that complicity and end it were no more pathological than German antifascists thirty years ago. The unrealism was not the abolitionists' for feeling guilty but their neighbors' for *not* feeling guilty.

Frank Tannenbaum, in his brilliant study, *Slave and Citizen: The Negro in the Americas*, argues that the piecemeal and peaceful ending of slavery was impossible in the United States

> because the gap between the Negro and the white man had been made so impassable and so absolute that it could not be

bridged by any means of transition, by any natural growth
and adaptation. Revolution was the result because change as
a principle had been denied.[13]

Elkins cites the Tannenbaum volume, and his own emphasis
on the fluidity of American society might have provided him
with insights suggested by this passage, for it was in the
United States, more than in any other slaveholding nation,
that the contrast between the status of the slave and that of
every other inhabitant was sharpest. The anomaly of the most
rigid, institutionalized form of slavery existing within the most
fluid, least institutionalized social structure had to make slavery seem morally wrong to those whites who took the
Declaration of Independence seriously. This anomaly suggests that the abolitionists' reaction was realistic, not a
pathological attitude forced on them by the absence of institutionalized ways to oppose a social anachronism, and that
whatever one may say of the tactics they employed, they
were correct in insisting that individuals who shut their eyes
to the crime of slavery were to that extent guilty of its perpetuation. It may be argued further that slavery was objectively a moral problem precisely because it was anomalous
and anachronistic and involved basic questions of men's relations to one another.[14] And if that is so, a movement to
abolish it could not, without distorting the nature of the

[13] First published in New York in 1946. The quotation is on pp. 109-10.
[14] Acceptance of the objective reality of the moral aspect of slavery is
gaining currency among historians. The most recent statements of it are in
David Brion Davis, *The Problem of Slavery in Western Culture* (Ithaca,
1966). For example: "Despite great historical diversity in such matters as
employment, manumission, and the differentiation of bondsmen from other
classes, the very ways of defining and regulating the institution show that
slavery has always raised certain fundamental problems that originate in the
simple fact that the slave is a man" (31).

problem, have dealt with it other than as largely a moral problem. That is, the charge of "abstractionism" could be leveled at a movement that did *not* make the moral aspect central.

The moral aspect of slavery thus was not something the abolitionists superimposed on a problem that was difficult enough to solve without it; nor was it imposed by the lack of institutional structure in the abolitionists' society. It was inherent in the nature of slavery itself. And it appealed with irresistible force to those who accepted literally the teachings of their religion that God created all men in his own image and that Christ died for all. The central place that the abolitionists gave to the religious and moral aspect of their crusade also explains why they always accompanied their demand for abolition with the demand for equal rights for the Negro and the ending of racial prejudice. Chattel slavery was simply the worst form of the sin they wanted to eradicate, the sin of denying the humanity of the Negro and the equality of all men as children of God. But Elkins' advice was followed a century before it was offered. The nation failed to respond to the moral appeal and preferred to approach the problem of slavery "as a question of institutional arrangements." This meant separating what the abolitionists insisted on combining—the legal status of the Negro, and the moral condition of American society as reflected in its treatment of the Negro. When the nation altered the former and left the latter unchanged, it distorted the nature of the problem and insured fulfillment of an ominous prophecy (somewhat exaggerated) uttered by Lydia Maria Child twenty-three years before the Thirteenth Amendment was ratified.

Great political changes may be forced by the pressure of external circumstances, without a corresponding change in the moral sentiment of a nation; but in all such cases, the change is worse than useless; the evil reappears, and usually in a more aggravated form.[15]

[15] "Dissolution of the Union," reprinted from *The National Anti-Slavery Standard* in *The Liberator*, May 20, 1842.

Questions of Content and Process
in the Perception of Slavery

CHARLES A. PINDERHUGHES

Competition for leadership provides a strong stimulus to scholars, and research designed to develop new understanding offers one traditional avenue of progress toward leadership. Some scholars achieve prominence by improving the organization of existing data and concepts, some by improved applications of theory, some by adding new wrinkles, some by discrediting predecessors, some by combinations of these and other means. It is clear that competitive and affiliative family-like interactions between scholars play a prominent role in the dynamics whereby we add to our knowledge. Relatively primitive issues such as "who is right and who is wrong," "who has the most," "who took what from whom," "whose material should be swallowed and whose discarded," and "whose is most like mine" pervade our ambivalent struggles to sift through and evaluate the ideas of our fellow men.

Each reader of a book may have a combination of professional and personal motivations, some in full awareness, some quite unconscious. Whether it is in search of some dependable truth, of someone to join, of someone to oppose, of a flag around which to rally one's favorite thesis, or a flag against which to fight with one's favorite thesis, one can generally find it by selective reading.

As a black psychoanalyst on the Group for Advancement of Psychiatry's Committee on Social Issues, I developed both personal and professional interest in questions related to slavery and segregation. During 1963, black people in many American cities complained that schools which were de facto segregated were inferior schools. Some school administrators rebutted with the argument that de facto segregated Chinese, Catholics, Jews, Irish, Italians, and other minorities had no complaints, and they concluded that ethnic group concentration per se had no effect upon educational process. It appeared to me that the critical questions were: Within a given broad cultural context, does ethnic group concentration have more adaptive effects for some minority groups than others? Does ethnic group concentration have destructive or maladaptive effects for some minority groups? For historical data relating to these questions, I sought advice from Professor J. Walter Fisher of Morgan State College, who referred me to several sources including Stanley Elkins' book, *Slavery*.

Professor Elkins invited me to think in a new direction which might explain some of the facts of the past, and suggested some psychodynamics and socio-dynamics which might be in operation. The existence of a volume concerning Elkins and his critics indicates that many persons have been induced by him to think, and to become more involved in understanding the psycho-social dynamics of American racism. His volume contributed significantly to my earliest understandings of American racism and it was very useful in my preparation of papers on "Effects of Ethnic Group Concentration on Educational Process, Personality Development and Mental Health," and "Pathogenic Social Structure: A Prime Target for Preventive Psychiatric Intervention."

Professor Elkins re-focused more personalized attention upon the usually dehumanized treatment of slaves by historians. By borrowing Bettelheim's observations and hypotheses on adaptation in concentration camps, he suggested that each enslaved black responded with thoroughly human responses and reinforced the behavior best adapted to survival. Whether the majority of slaves responded with the particular psychodynamic changes described by Elkins seems to me unimportant alongside of the remarkable involvement of the reader in a personalized consideration of the slave experience. This effect was reinforced by the comparison with the concentration camp experience with which our generation has been identified and deeply involved. The vivid imagery associated with the incarceration and murder of millions of Jews superimposed upon the slave experience offered an illusion of a history brought to life for consideration as it might have been. I feel more indebted to Professor Elkins for his meaningful involvement of the reader in an intellectual and emotional process which has obviously carried many readers far beyond the content he makes explicit. In a liberating process, the reader was freed from earlier limited thinking and misconceptions to proceed on toward additional conceptualization.

In my own case the process extended in the direction of a series of related conclusions which I can outline as follows:

a) The cultural press of our slave society, with black mothers functioning as important programming "instruments," altered the reality of black and white personalities, role relationships, group and family structure, and institutions so that they express and promote the pro-white anti-black paranoia that constitutes white racism. While extremely pathogenic in terms of the deaths, illness, and suffering it causes, this paranoia is a group-related, nonpathological process insofar as individual health is concerned.

b) Both the pro-white, anti-black, group-related paranoia and the contrived reality wrought by it become frozen into culture and transmitted from generation to generation as long as a stable segregated pro-white, anti-black social order can be maintained. As long as new cultural development and cultural diffusion are prevented by a restrictive segregated society, each cultural group reproduces similar characteristics in its members generation after generation. Under these circumstances Irish reproduce Irish, Jews reproduce Jews, Indians reproduce Indians, and descendants of slaves reproduce the psychology, role relationships, family and group structure of slaves.

c) When integration movements have been weakened and neutralized, as by the so-called "white backlash" of 1965–66, blacks have recognized that they have shared a pro-white, anti-black paranoia which had been imposed upon them and given the appearance of reality by all the changes wrought in institutions, relationships, group structure, and personalities. Black American descendants of slaves have differed from all other ethnic groups in important ways:

1. Their culture was not developed by the group members but was imposed by outsiders.

2. Bonds of affection and trust were not promoted between members of their own group but were promoted toward outsiders.

3. Destructive aggression could not be directed outside the group but had to be directed against themselves or against their fellow group members.

4. Their culture did not support self-esteem, sense of

entitlement, and sense of worth as does the culture of other ethnic groups but, instead, systematically undermined these.

5. Their culture programmed their group members toward service, surrender, self-sacrifice, and defeat instead of active mastery, while the culture of all other ethnic groups programmed its members toward active mastery in the setting in which the group developed.

Careful analysis reveals that consideration of black American descendants of slaves as an ethnic group is another delusion in the paranoia. It is a non-group, persisting as an oppressed, segregated, exploited, disrupted, and partially destroyed people. As individuals, they have the same anatomical, physiological, and psychological potentials of any other people, but the programming cultural influences which shape their psychology, role relationships, family structure, social structure, educational life, economic life, and political life impair, hinder, disrupt, and defeat many of them in a competitive society oriented to ethnic group strength. Attempts to develop bonds between themselves, to improve self-esteem and sense of entitlement, to direct disruptive aggression away from group members toward outsiders, and to program their members toward mastery, have reflected attempts to develop a group which is similar to other ethnic groups in purposes, functions, and service to the group members. In a paper entitled "Understanding Black Power: Processes and Proposals," I have described this as an attempt to develop for themselves a group-related, nonpathological, pro-black paranoia similar to that enjoyed by every other ethnic group.

Under slavery and subsequent segregation, black individuals were generally prevented from showing signs of worth, or importance in socially valued terms. In American and

Western European cultures, active mastery, masculinity, and competitive ability were idealized while passive mastery, service, and traditionally feminine roles were devalued. Controlling, demanding, self-centered, self-entitling, narcissistic, infantile roles were idealized and assumed by white masters while parental roles of feeding, cleaning, and serving were demeaned and pressed upon black slaves and servants. In this sense, whites were infantilized toward the omnipotent controlling role of infants and blacks were parentalized toward the feeding, cleaning, service-on-demand role of mothers.

Professor Elkins' perception of infantilization of blacks and his neglect of the infantilization of whites, along with his perception of the parentalization of whites and neglect of the parentalization of blacks, is a reflection of the unconscious white racist patterns which influence the thinking of every American in ways of which they are unaware.

In my opinion, the value of Professor Elkins' book does not lie in its accuracy, or completeness, or rationality, since some errors, omissions, and biases are expected and may be observed in the products of any man. More important was the non-segregating, integrating process he employed when he borrowed data and concepts from another discipline in a search for correlations. In doing this he was guilty of a cardinal sin, for he had been taken in by an obvious outsider and now sought to get the outsider accepted in his own group. All exclusive groups function with group-related paranoias which aggrandize their own toward whom there are affectionate bonds while denigrating outsiders toward whom there are aggressive bonds. While other historians have introduced data and concepts from psychology and psychiatry, few have given the outsider as obvious and central a position as Stanley Elkins did. The integrative interdisciplinary process which he employed is, by nature, loaded with misunderstandings and conflict, and many persons have become involved in both the substantive issues and the process issues. My own participation in social and professional processes with historians was initiated by Professor Fisher whom I trusted as a relative and as a friend. The content of *Slavery* surprised me and gave me a feeling that I, with my psychoanalytic language and ideology, was more welcome than I thought psychoanalysts would be in the foreign world of history. My experiences as a participant in programs of the Association for the Study of Negro Life and History and the American Historical Society have strengthened my conviction that historians are also in conflict over whether or not they should integrate with outsiders. For me, Stanley Elkins' book made a simple statement: let's integrate. Predictably, it set in motion all the dynamics involved in the integration process, including a "backlash." In this miniature model, we may observe many of the dynamic events which occur whenever a compartmentalized and closed society becomes more open. The process cannot proceed unless institutions, disciplines, and minds become more open also.

PART TWO

THE HEMISPHERIC
PERSPECTIVE

The Continuing Contradiction of Slavery: A Comparison of British America and Latin America

DAVID BRION DAVIS

Was antislavery, then, a direct outgrowth of slavery itself? We have maintained that the concept of man as a material possession has always led to contradictions in law and custom. In the ancient world these contradictions did not give rise to abolitionism; but in the historical development of American slavery there were deep strains that made the institution a source of dissonance and discontent. Even men whose interests were closely tied to the system expressed occasional misgivings over mounting debts and economic decay, the rising proportion of Negroes to whites, the haunting threat of insurrection, the failure to infuse masters and slaves with a spirit of Christian love, and the growing discrepancy between American servitude and European ideals of liberty. It remains to be asked whether the evolution of colonial laws and customs provided a basis for believing that the worst evils of slavery could be gradually eliminated through wise legislation, or for concluding that slavery by its very nature was beyond reform.

Such a question poses many problems. As a result of differences in economy, social and political institutions, and the ratio of Negroes to whites, the actual status and condition of colonial slaves varied considerably from one region to another. Yet no slave colony had a monopoly on either kindness or cruelty. Slave codes were often enacted with a view to quieting local fears or appeasing a church or government. Travelers were sometimes biased or quick to generalize from a few fleeting impressions. Since we still seriously lack a thorough comparative study of Negro slavery in the various colonies, we must be content with fragmentary evidence and with extremely tentative conclusions. There would seem to be some basis, however, for questioning two assumptions which have been widely accepted by modern historians.

The first is that Negro slavery in the British colonies and Southern United States was of a nearly uniform severity, the slave being legally deprived of all rights of person, property, and family, and subjected to the will of his owner and the police power of the state, which barred his way to education, free movement, or emancipation. The second assumption is that the French, and especially the Spanish and Portuguese, were far more liberal in their treatment of slaves, whom they considered as human beings who had merely lost a portion of their external freedom. Untainted by racial prejudice and free from the pressures of a fluid, capitalistic economy, these easygoing colonists are supposed to have protected the human rights of the slave and to have facilitated his manumission. Some historians have simply held that slavery in North America was much harsher than that in Latin America, but Elkins has argued more persuasively that the great contrast was not in the bondsman's physical well-being but in the recognition of his basic humanity.[1] As a methodological

---

[1] Pp. 27–80. It is not my purpose to question all of Elkins's highly imaginative insights, or to attempt to prove that differences in religion, econ-

device, this distinction has obvious merit, since a master might look upon his slaves as sub-human animals and still provide them with comfortable maintenance. On the other hand, it would be unrealistic to draw too sharp a line between moral status and physical treatment. It is difficult to see how a so-

---

omy, and social structure had no bearing on the institution of Negro slavery. My aim is simply to show that the importance of such national and cultural differences has been exaggerated, and that all American slaveholding colonies shared certain central assumptions and problems. I do not believe that the modern historian can escape what Elkins terms the moral "coercions" of the great nineteenth-century controversies by portraying both American slavery and antislavery as the pathological results of "the dynamics of unopposed capitalism." It should be noted that Elkins borrowed much of his conceptual framework from Frank Tannenbaum's enormously influential *Slave and Citizen: The Negro in the Americas* (New York, 1947). Though Tannenbaum was one of the first historians to emphasize the importance of Negro slavery in the overall development of the Americas, it seems to me that his comparison of Latin and Anglo-American slavery suffers from three basic weaknesses. First, he assumes that North American law, unlike that of Latin America, refused to recognize the slave as a moral personality. But this is an error, as we shall see. Second, he ignores the fact that the "classical" view of slavery, as embodied in Latin culture, drew as much from Plato and Aristotle as from Cicero and Seneca. Nineteenth-century Brazilian reformers, such as José Bonifácio, found it necessary to counter their opponents' use of classical authorities by arguing that Greeks and Romans had been ignorant of divine religion, and that, in any event, slavery in antiquity had not been so severe as that in Brazil, where racial and cultural differences deprived the bondsman of opportunities for equality (José Bonifácio de Andrada e Silva, *Memoir Addressed to the General, Constituent and Legislative Assembly of the Empire of Brazil . . .* [tr. by William Walton, London, 1826], 20–22). As in Roman and North American law, the slave in Latin America was conceived at once as a chattel or instrument, and as a man with a soul. Third, Tannenbaum seems to think of Negro slavery in Latin America as a relatively unchanging institution, and assumes that certain humane laws of the late eighteenth and nineteenth centuries were typical of bondage in all Latin America throughout its long history. Even more questionable is his assumption that the admirable laws of European governments were obeyed by colonial slaveholders. For a thoughtful discussion of the Tannenbaum-Elkins thesis, see Sidney Mintz's long review of Elkins's book in *American Anthropologist*, LXIII (June, 1961), 579–87. An article which appeared after this chapter was written, and which presents a similar thesis, is Arnold A. Sio, "Interpretations of Slavery: The Slave Status in the Americas," *Comparative Studies in Society and History*, VII (April, 1965), 289–308.

ciety could have much respect for the value of slaves as human personalities if it sanctioned their torture and mutilation,
the selling of their small children, the unmitigated exploitation of their labor, and the drastic shortening of their lives
through overwork and inadequate nourishment. While a few
isolated instances of sadistic cruelty would reveal little about
the legal or moral status of slaves, we should not exclude
physical treatment when it is part of a pattern of systematic
oppression which is fully sanctioned by the laws and customs
of a society. We shall find, however, that there is other evidence than physical treatment for challenging the assumption
that Latin Americans were more sensitive than Anglo-Ameri-
cans to the essential humanity of their slaves.

This assumption has important implications for a history of
antislavery thought. If servitude under the Spanish and Portuguese was generally mild and humane, and if the institution
itself tended to promote a gradual achievement of freedom,
then we should not be surprised by the fact that antislavery
agitation began in Britain and British America. The peculiar
severities of British colonial slavery would appear to have
arisen from local economic or social conditions, and we should
have reason to suspect that antislavery movements were a
direct response to an unprecedented evil. And while the extremes of both slavery and antislavery could be explained by
the absence of a stable social structure, we could conclude
that the Anglo-American reformer might well have looked to
Latin America for a rational model. By gradually imposing
the institutional protections of Latin American slavery on
the formless and unregulated slavery of the north, he might
have removed the evils from a necessary system of labor. But
if the contrast between slavery in the various American
colonies was not so clear-cut as has generally been supposed,
we are left with a different set of implications. It would be

likely that the appearance of antislavery agitation was less a direct response to a unique evil than a result of particular cultural and religious developments in the English-speaking world. And if both the evils of slavery and the attempts to ameliorate them were fairly pervasive throughout the Americas, we should look more skeptically at programs for slow and gradual reform. We should expect to find general emancipation often associated with revolutions and civil wars, as was the case in Saint Domingue, the United States, and several of the Spanish colonies, or with political upheaval and the fall of a government, as in Brazil.[2]

A word of explanation is in order regarding the chronological range of selected examples and illustrations. If we are to judge the influence of traditional Catholic culture, the crucial period in Latin American slavery is the early colonial era, before the full impact of the Enlightenment, the American and French Revolutions, and the wars of independence. But when we test the assumption that slavery in the British colonies and Southern United States was of a monolithic character, unmitigated by any recognition of the Negro's rights of personality, it is appropriate to select examples from the nineteenth century, when laws and customs had hardened

[2] The violence of the American Civil War has led some historians to assume that other nations abolished Negro slavery without bitter conflict. Yet even in Brazil, where Dom Pedro II strove consciously to avoid the bloody course taken by the United States, there was a radical abolitionist movement, an underground railroad, and sectional cleavage; the stormy conflict played an important part in bringing the downfall of the monarchy (see especially Percy A. Martin, "Slavery and Abolition in Brazil," *Hispanic American Historical Review*, XIII [May, 1933], 151–96). British planters in the Caribbean frequently threatened secession, and finally submitted to the superior force of the British government only because they were too weak, economically and politically, to resist. They might have acted differently, as did the planters of Saint Domingue during the French Revolution, if Britain had moved to abolish slavery at the time of their greatest power.

to form a self-contained system of values and precedents. If some of the ameliorative elements we usually associate with Latin American slavery were common in North America, even at a time when bondage had grown more formalized and severe, then we should have less reason to suppose that the basic evils of the institution could have been eliminated by mere palliative reforms.

II

By the late eighteenth century most travelers agreed that in Brazil and the Spanish colonies the condition of slaves was considerably better than in British America.[3] Any comparison must consider Negro slavery as a system of forced labor, of social organization, and of class and racial discipline. Numerous accounts from the late eighteenth and nineteenth centuries tell us that the Latin American slave enjoyed frequent hours of leisure and was seldom subjected to the factory-like regimentation that characterized the capitalistic plantations of the North; that he faced no legal bars to marriage, education, or

[3] Sir Harry Johnston, *The Negro in the New World* (New York, 1910), 42–47, 87–94; Henry Koster, *Travels in Brazil* (London, 1816), 385–86, 390, 444; Mary M. Williams, "The Treatment of Negro Slaves in the Brazilian Empire; a Comparison with the United States," *Journal of Negro History*, XV (1930), 313–36; Donald Pierson, *Negroes in Brazil* (Chicago, 1942), 45–46; H. B. Alexander, "Brazilian and United States Slavery Compared," *Journal of Negro History*, VII (1922), 349–64; Gilberto Freyre, *The Masters and the Slaves: A Study in the Development of Brazilian Civilization* (tr. by Samuel Putnam, New York, 1946), 7–11, 40–41, 369 ff. and *passim;* Tannenbaum, *Slave and Citizen*, 56, 100–105. An occasional traveler, such as Alexander Marjoribanks, observed that if Brazilian slaves were as well treated as those in the United States, there would have been no need to rely so heavily on the African trade as an answer to slave mortality (*Travels in South and North America* [London, 1853], 60). Freyre, Johnston, and Pierson have balanced a generally favorable picture of Latin American slavery with references to extreme cruelty and suffering.

eventual freedom; that he was legally protected from cruelty and oppression, and was not stigmatized on account of his race. This relative felicity has quite plausibly been attributed to a culture that de-emphasized the pursuit of private profit, to the Catholic Church's insistence on the slave's right to marry and worship, and to what Gilberto Freyre has termed the "miscibility" of the Portuguese, which submerged sensitivity to racial difference in a frank acceptance of sexual desire.[4]

No doubt there is much truth in even the idyllic picture of the Brazilian "Big House," where slaves and freemen pray and loaf together, and where masters shrug their shoulders at account books and prefer to frolic with slave girls in shaded hammocks. But we should not forget that West Indian and North American planters were fond of idealizing their own "Big Houses" as patriarchal manors, of portraying their Negroes as carefree and indolent, and of proudly displaying humane slave laws which they knew to be unenforceable. Their propaganda, which was supported by travelers' accounts and which long seemed persuasive to many Northerners and Englishmen, has largely been discredited by numerous critical studies based on a wealth of surviving evidence. Many of the records of Brazilian slavery were destroyed in the 1890s, in a fit of abolitionist enthusiasm, and the subject has never received the careful scrutiny it deserves.[5] Only in recent years have such historians as Octávio Ianni, Fernando Henrique Cardoso, Jaime Jaramillo Uribe, and C. R. Boxer begun to challenge the stereotyped images of mild servitude and racial harmony.

[4] Freyre, *Masters and Slaves*, 7-11 and *passim*. But Freyre also maintains that the sexual relations of masters and slaves were authoritarian in character, and often led to sadistic cruelty.

[5] Arthur Ramos, *The Negro in Brazil* (tr. by Richard Pattee, Washington, 1951), 19-20.

There is little reason to doubt that slavery in Latin America, compared with that in North America, was less subject to the pressures of competitive capitalism and was closer to a system of patriarchal rights and semifeudalistic services. But after granting this, we must recognize the inadequacy of thinking in terms of idealized models of patriarchal and capitalistic societies. Presumably, an exploitive, capitalistic form of servitude could not exist within a patriarchal society. The lord of a manor, unlike the entrepreneur who might play the role of lord of a manor, would be incapable of treating men as mere units of labor in a speculative enterprise. But neither would he think of exploring new lands, discovering gold mines, or developing new plantations for the production of sugar and coffee. It is perhaps significant that accounts of Latin American slavery often picture the relaxed life on sugar plantations after their decline in economic importance, and ignore conditions that prevailed during the Brazilian sugar boom of the seventeenth century, the mining boom of the early eighteenth century, and the coffee boom of the nineteenth century. Similarly, Southern apologists tended to overlook the human effects of high-pressure agriculture in the Southwest, and focus their attention on the easygoing and semipatriarchal societies of tidewater Maryland and Virginia. Eugene D. Genovese has recently suggested that while the North American slave system was stimulated and exploited by the capitalist world market, it retained many precapitalistic features, such as a lack of innovation, restricted markets, and low productivity of labor, and actually gravitated toward an uneconomical paternalism that was basically antithetical to capitalistic values.

Although a particular instance of oppression or well-being can always be dismissed as an exception, it is important to know what range of variation a system permitted. If an exploitive, capitalistic form of servitude was at times common in Brazil and Spanish America, and if North Americans conformed at times to a paternalistic model and openly acknowledged the humanity of their slaves, it may be that differences between slavery in Latin America and the United States were no greater than regional or temporal differences within the countries themselves. And such a conclusion would lead us to suspect that Negro bondage was a single phenomenon, or *Gestalt*, whose variations were less significant than underlying patterns of unity.

Simon Gray, a Natchez river boatman, provides us with an example of the flexibility of the North American slave system. During the 1850s, most Southern states tightened their laws and to all appearances erected an impassable barrier between the worlds of slave and freeman. But the intent of legislators was often offset by powerful forces of economic interest and personality. Simon Gray was an intelligent slave whose superior abilities were recognized by both his master and the lumber company which hired his services. In the 1850s this lowly slave became the captain of a flatboat on the Mississippi, supervising and paying wages to a crew that included white men. In defiance of law, Gray was permitted to carry firearms, to travel freely on his own, to build and run sawmills, and to conduct commercial transactions as his company's agent. Entrusted with large sums of money for business purposes, Gray also drew a regular salary, rented a house where his family lived in privacy, and took a vacation to Hot Springs, Arkansas, when his health declined. Although there is evidence that in Southern industry and commerce such privileges were not as uncommon as has been assumed, we may be sure that Simon Gray was a very exceptional slave.[6]

[6] John H. Moore, "Simon Gray, Riverman: A Slave Who Was Almost Free," *Mississippi Valley Historical Review*, XLIX (Dec., 1962), 472–84.

He might well have been less exceptional in Cuba or Brazil. The essential point, however, is that regardless of restrictive laws, the Southern slave system had room for a few Simon Grays. The flatboat captain could not have acted as he did if the society had demanded a rigorous enforcement of the law.

By the time Simon Gray was beginning to enjoy relative freedom, Portugal and Brazil were the only civilized nations that openly resisted attempts to suppress the African slave trade. It has been estimated that by 1853 Britain had paid Portugal some £2,850,965 in bribes intended to stop a commerce whose horrors had multiplied as a result of efforts to escape detection and capture. But despite British bribes and seizures, the trade continued, and was countenanced by the society which has been most praised for its humane treatment of slaves. One of the boats captured by the British, in 1842, was a tiny vessel of eighteen tons, whose crew consisted of six Portuguese. Between decks, in a space only eighteen inches high, they had intended to stow two hundred and fifty African children of about seven years of age.[7] Suspicion of Britain's motives probably prevented more outspoken attacks on a trade that outraged most of the civilized world. But the fact remains that Brazilian society not only permitted the slave trade to continue for nearly half a century after it had

[7] Christopher Lloyd, *The Navy and the Slave Trade; the Suppression of the African Slave Trade in the Nineteenth Century* (London, 1949), 34, 45. The United States showed laxness in suppressing the African trade, and American ships and capital helped to supply slaves to the chief nineteenth-century markets, Cuba and Brazil. But this laxness was quite a different thing from the open approval of the slave trade by Brazilians. And a recent study which takes a more favorable view of American attempts to suppress the slave trade points out that between 1837 and 1862 American ships captured at least 107 slavers (Peter Duignan and Clarence Clendenen, *The United States and the African Slave Trade, 1619-1862* [n.p. (Stanford University), 1963], 54).

been outlawed by Britain and the United States, but provided a flourishing market for Negroes fresh from Africa. During the 1830s Brazil imported more than 400,000 slaves; in the single year of 1848 the nation absorbed some sixty thousand more. That the reception of these newcomers was not so humane as might be imagined is suggested by a law of 1869, six years after Lincoln's Emancipation Proclamation, which forbade the separate sale of husband and wife, or of children under fifteen. Not long before, even children under ten had been separated from their parents and sent to the coffee plantations of the south.[8]

These examples are intended only to illustrate the range of variation that could occur in any slave society, and hence the difficulties in comparing the relative severity of slave systems. Barbados and Jamaica were notorious for their harsh laws and regimentation, but occasional proprietors like Josiah Steele or Matthew Lewis succeeded in creating model plantations where Negroes were accorded most of the privileges of white servants. John Stedman, who provided Europe with ghastly pictures of the cruelty of Dutch masters in Surinam, also maintained that humanity and gentleness coexisted with the worst barbarity. The well-being of any group of slaves was subject to many variables. It seems certain that the few Negroes in eighteenth-century Québec lived a freer and richer life than hundreds of thousands of slaves in nineteenth-century Brazil and Cuba, despite the fact that the latter were technically guarded by certain legal protections, and the

---

[8] Octávio Tarquinio de Sousa, *História dos fundadores do Império do Brasil* (Rio de Janeiro, 1957–58), IX, 74; Stanley J. Stein, *Vassouras: A Brazilian Coffee County, 1850–1900* (Cambridge, Mass., 1957), 20; Williams, "Treatment of Negro Slaves in the Brazilian Empire," 325. Not only did laws protecting the unity of slave families come surprisingly late, but they were for the most part unenforceable. See Stein, *Vassouras,* 155–59; Martin, "Slavery and Abolition in Brazil," *passim.*

former were defined as chattels completely subject to their owners' authority. Islands like Dominica and Saint Lucia, which were disorganized by war and a transfer from one nation to another, had few social resources for restraining the unscrupulous master or curbing slave resistance. In the newly developed lands of captured or ceded colonies, such as Berbice, Demerara, Trinidad, and Louisiana, there were few effective checks on the speculative planter bent on reaping maximum profit in the shortest possible time. And whereas the North American slave frequently lived in a land of peace and plentiful food, his West Indian brother was the first to feel the pinch of famine when war cut off essential supplies, or when his master was burdened by debt and declining profits. On the small tobacco farms of colonial Virginia and Maryland the physical condition of slaves was surely better than in the mines of Minas Gerais or on the great plantations of Bahia, where a Capuchin missionary was told in 1682 that a Negro who endured for seven years was considered to have lived very long.[9]

North American planters were fond of comparing the fertility of their own slaves with the high mortality and low birth rate of those in the West Indies and Latin America, and

[9] Lowell Joseph Ragatz, *The Fall of the Planter Class in the British Caribbean, 1763–1833* (New York, 1928), 66–67, 70–71; John Gabriel Stedman, *Narrative of a Five Years' Expedition, against the Revolted Negroes of Surinam* . . . (London, 1796), I, 201–7; Marcel Trudel, *L'Esclavage au Canada française; histoire et conditions de l'esclavage* (Québec, 1960), 160–92, 232–56; C. R. Boxer, *The Golden Age of Brazil, 1695–1750: Growing Pains of a Colonial Society* (Berkeley, 1962), 174; *Acts of the Assembly, Passed in the Charibbee Leeward Islands from 1690, to 1730* (London, 1732), *passim*; W. L. Burn, *Emancipation and Apprenticeship in the British West Indies* (London, 1937), 64–70. Jean F. Dauxion-Lavaysse, who had traveled widely in the Spanish, French, and British colonies, said that the slaves on Sir William Young's model plantation at Saint Vincent were treated better than any he had seen (*A Statistical, Commercial, and Political Description of Venezuela, Trinidad, Margarita, and Tobago* [tr. by E. Blaquière, London, 1820], 390).

of concluding that theirs was the milder and more humane system. Such reasoning failed to take account of the low proportion of female slaves in the West Indies, the communicable diseases transmitted by the African trade, and the high incidence of tetanus and other maladies that were particularly lethal to infants in the Caribbean. No doubt differences in sanitation and nutrition, rather than in physical treatment, explain the fact that while Brazil and the United States each entered the nineteenth century with about a million slaves, and subsequent importations into Brazil were three times greater than those into the United States, by the Civil War there were nearly four million slaves in the United States and only one and one-half million in Brazil.[10] But after all such allowances are made, it still seems probable that planters in Brazil and the West Indies, who were totally dependent on fresh supplies of labor from Africa, were less sensitive than North Americans to the value of human life. When a slave's life expectancy was a few years at most, and when each slave could easily be replaced, there was little incentive to improve conditions or limit hours of work. According to both C. R. Boxer and Celso Furtado, Brazilian sugar planters took a short-term view of their labor needs, and accepted the axiom, which spread to the British Caribbean,

[10] Gaston Martin, *Histoire de l'esclavage dans les colonies françaises* (Paris, 1948), 124–35; Ragatz, *Fall of Planter Class*, 34–35; Frank W. Pitman, "Slavery on British West India Plantations in the Eighteenth Century," *Journal of Negro History*, XI (Oct., 1962), 610–17; Celso Furtado, *The Economic Growth of Brazil; a Survey from Colonial to Modern Times* (Berkeley, 1963), 127–28. There is a certain irony in the fact that pro-slavery Southerners like Thomas R. R. Cobb accepted the conventional anti-slavery view of the West Indies. In contrast with the cruelty, impersonality, and despotism of the islands, North American masters and slaves worked side by side in clearing forests, building new homes, and hunting game; consequently, there developed a sense of cooperation and mutual sympathy which was unknown in the Caribbean, or so Cobb claimed in his *Inquiry into the Law of Negro Slavery* (Savannah, 1858), clvii–clix.

that it was good economy to work one's slaves to death and then purchase more. In colonial Brazil, Jesuit priests felt it necessary to admonish overseers not to kick pregnant women in the stomach or beat them with clubs, since this brought a considerable loss in slave property.[11]

But what of the benevolent laws of Latin America which allowed a slave to marry, to seek relief from a cruel master, and even to purchase his own freedom? It must be confessed that on this crucial subject historians have been overly quick to believe what travelers passed on from conversations with slaveholders, and to make glowing generalizations on the basis of one-sided evidence.

Much has been made of the fact that the Spanish model law, *las Siete Partidas*, recognized freedom as man's natural state, and granted the slave certain legal protections. But the argument loses some of its point when we learn that the same principles were accepted in North American law, and that *las Siete Partidas* not only made the person and possessions of the bondsman totally subject to his master's will, but even gave owners the right to kill their slaves in certain circumstances.[12] Some of the early Spanish and Portuguese legisla-

[11] Furtado, *Economic Growth of Brazil*, 51, n. 129; C. R. Boxer, *Race Relations in the Portuguese Colonial Empire, 1415–1825* (Oxford, 1963), 101; Boxer, *Golden Age of Brazil*, 7–9; Maurilio de Gouveia, *História da escravidão* (Rio de Janeiro, 1955), 68. In 1823 José Bonifácio noted that while Brazil had been importing some 40,000 slaves a year, the increase in the total slave population was hardly perceptible. Like British and North American reformers of a generation earlier, he was confident that the abolition of the trade would force masters to take better care of their human property (*Memoir Addressed to the General, Constituent and Legislative Assembly*, 26–28).

[12] *Las Siete Partidas de Rey don Alfonso el Sabio* . . . (Madrid, 1807), III, 117–28. Even Elsa V. Goveia exaggerates the liberality of Spanish law, although she rightly emphasizes the importance of an authoritarian government in checking the worst inclinations of slaveholding colonists. In the

tion protecting Indians has erroneously been thought to have extended to Negroes as well. In actuality, the first laws pertaining to Negroes in such colonies as Chile, Panama, and New Granada were designed to prohibit them from carrying arms, from moving about at night, and above all, from fraternizing with Indians.[13] It is true that in the late seventeenth and early eighteenth centuries the Portuguese crown issued edicts intended to prevent the gross mistreatment of Negro slaves. But as C. R. Boxer has pointed out, Brazilian law was a chaotic tangle of Manueline and Filipine codes, encrusted by numerous decrees which often contradicted one another, and which were interpreted by lawyers and magistrates notorious for their dishonesty. Even if this had not been true, slaves were dispersed over immense areas where there were few towns and where justice was administered by local magnates whose power lay in land and slaves. It is not surprising that in one of the few recorded cases of the Portuguese crown intervening to investigate the torture of a slave, nothing was done to the accused owner. This revisionist view receives support from Jaime Jaramillo Uribe's conclusion that the

---

British West Indies, where the colonists long had a relatively free hand in framing their own laws, slaves were for a time deprived of virtually any legal protection. But given the loopholes and ambiguities in the Spanish law, one suspects that any difference in actual protection was more a result of differences in administrative machinery than in legal traditions (see Goveia, "The West Indian Slave Laws of the Eighteenth Century," *Revista de ciencias sociales*, IV [Mar., 1960], 75–105).

13 Rollando Mellafe, *La introducción de la esclavitud negra en Chile: tráfico y rutas* (Santiago de Chile, 1959), 76–82; Richard Konetzke (ed.), *Colección de documentos para la historia de la formación social de Hispanoamérica, 1493–1810* (Madrid, 1962), II, 280, 427–28; Magnus Mörner, "Los esfuerzos realizados por la corona para separar negrese indies en Hispanoamérica durante el siglo XVI" (unpublished paper); Jaime Jaramillo Uribe, "Esclavos y señores en la sociedad colombiana del siglo XVIII," *Anuario colombiano de historia social y de la cultura*, I (Bogotá, 1963), 5, 21.

judicial system of New Granada was so ineffective that even
the reform legislation of the late eighteenth century did little
to change the oppressive life of Negro slaves.[14]
     In theory, of course, the Portuguese or Spanish slave pos-
sessed an immortal soul that entitled him to respect as a
human personality. But though perfunctorily baptized in
Angola or on the Guinea coast, he was appraised and sold like
any merchandise upon his arrival in America. Often slaves
were herded in mass, stark naked, into large warehouses
where they were examined and marketed like animals. As
late as the mid-nineteenth century the spread of disease
among newly arrived Negroes who were crowded into the
warehouses of Rio de Janeiro brought widespread fears of
epidemic. The Spanish, who ordinarily sold horses and cows
individually, purchased Negroes in lots, or *piezas de Indias*,
which were sorted according to age and size. There is
abundant evidence that Brazilians were little troubled by the
separation of Negro families; in the 1850s coffee planters in
the rich Parahyba Valley thought nothing of selling their
own illegitimate children to passing traders. Despite protests
from priests and governors, it was also common practice for
Brazilians to purchase attractive girls who could profitably
be let out as prostitutes.[15]
     In Brazil, as in other slave societies, there were apparently

[14] Boxer, *Race Relations in Portugese Colonial Empire*, 103; Gouveia,
História da escravidão, 69; Boxer, *Golden Age of Brazil*, 7, 138–39, 306–7;
Uribe, "Esclavos y señores en la sociedad colombiana," 22–25. In 1710 the
king of Spain, hearing of the extremely cruel treatment of slaves in Peru
and New Spain, issued orders allowing the governors to intervene and sell
slaves who had been abused to kinder masters (Konetzke [ed.], *Colección
de documentos*, III, pt. 1, 113–14).
     [15] Boxer, *Golden Age of Brazil*, 2–7, 138, 165; Robert Southey, *History
of Brazil* (London, 1817–22), II, 644, 674–75; Georges Scelle, *La traite
négrière aux Indes de Castille: contrats et traités d'assiento* (Paris, 1906), I,
504–5; Stein, *Vassouras*, 64, 156–59.

authentic reports of bondsmen being boiled alive, roasted in furnaces, or subjected to other fiendish punishments. More significant than such extreme cases of sadism is the evidence that planters who were successful and were accepted as social leaders equipped their estates with the chambers and instruments of torture; that it was common custom to punish a recalcitrant slave with *novenas*, which meant that he would be tied down and flogged for nine to thirteen consecutive nights, his cuts sometimes being teased with a razor and rubbed with salt and urine. In the mid-eighteenth century, Manuel Ribeiro Rocha attacked the Brazilian "rural theology" which allowed masters to welcome their new slaves with a vicious whipping, to work them in the fields without rest, and to inflict one hundred or more lashes without cause. A century later planters in the Parahyba Valley taught their sons that Negroes were not true men but inferior beings who could only be controlled by continued punishment; and some of the clergy maintained that Africans were the condemned sons of Cain. This widespread conviction of racial inferiority justified a regime of hatred and brutality in which the slave had no right of appeal and even fatal beatings went unpunished.[16]

Obviously much depended on regional differences in economy and social tradition. The recent studies of the extreme southern provinces of Brazil by Octávio Ianni and Fernando Cardoso reveal a picture of harsh chattel slavery and racial prejudice which stands in marked contrast to the familiar images of benign servitude in the north. During the last third of the eighteenth century the southern states developed a

[16] Boxer, *Golden Age of Brazil*, 8-9, 45-47; Williams, "Treatment of Negro Slaves in the Brazilian Empire," 326; Ramos, *Negro in Brazil*, 34-36; Koster, *Travels in Brazil*, 429, 444-55; Boxer, *Race Relations in Portuguese Colonial Empire*, 27, 101, 112; Tarquinio de Sousa, *História dos fundadores do Império do Brasil*, IX, 70; Stein, *Vassouras*, 132-39.

capitalistic economy which was initially stimulated by the export of wheat but which came to rely heavily on the production of jerked beef. Whether engaged in agriculture, stock raising, or the processing of meat or leather, the slaveholding capitalists were bent on maximizing production for commercial profit. Because the economy rested on slave labor and because physical labor was largely associated with the African race, Negroes and mulattoes were regarded as mere instruments of production, wholly lacking in human personality. According to Ianni, the slave was a totally alienated being; able to express himself only through the intermediary of his owner, he was under the complete dominion of a master class which rigidly controlled his movements and held power over his life and death. Though kind and paternalistic masters were to be found in Paraná, Santa Catarina, and Rio Grande do Sul, as elsewhere in the Americas, the overriding fact is that the ideology and judicial framework of southern Brazil were geared to the maintenance of an exploitive system of labor, to the preservation of public security, and to the perpetuation of power in the hands of a white ruling caste. At every point the Negro was forced to shape his behavior in accordance with the actions and expectations of the white man.[17]

Conditions were undoubtedly better in the cities, where protective laws were more often enforced and where Negroes had at least a chance of acquiring money that could purchase freedom. But in colonial Cartagena, Negro slaves were subject to the most repressive police regulations, and to punishments which ranged from death to the cutting off of hands, ears, or

[17] Octávio Ianni, *As metamorfoses do escravo* (São Paulo, 1962), 82, 134-49, 282-85; Fernando Henrique Cardoso, *Capitalismo e escravidão no Brasil meridional* (São Paulo, 1962), 35-81, 133-67, 310-13; Cardoso and Ianni, *Côr e mobilidade social em Florianopólis: aspectos das relações entre negros e brancos numa comunidade do Brasil meridional* (São Paulo, 1960), 125-35.

the penis. In Mariana the city councilors demanded in 1755 that the right to purchase freedom be withdrawn and that slaves who tried to escape be crippled for life. While both proposals aroused the indignation of the viceroy at Bahia, they indicate the state of mind of a master class which, in Minas Gerais, posted the heads of fugitive slaves along the roadsides. And men who accepted such brutality as a necessary part of life could not always be expected to abandon their fields or shut down their sugar mills on thirty-five religious holidays, in addition to fifty-two Sundays.[18] It was not an idyllic, semifeudal servitude that made colonial Brazil widely known as "the hell for Negroes," and as a place where their lives would be "nasty, brutish, and short"; or that drove countless bondsmen to suicide or revolt, and reduced others to a state of psychic shock, of flat apathy and depression, which was common enough in Brazil to acquire the special name of *banzo*.[19]

[18] Southey, *History of Brazil*, III, 780–84; Uribe, "Esclavos y señores en la sociedad colombiana," 21–23; Boxer, *Golden Age of Brazil*, 171–72. According to Boxer, in Brazil's "Golden Age" slaves on sugar plantations were worked around the clock when the mills were grinding cane, and some planters successfully evaded the rules against work on Sundays and religious holidays (*Golden Age of Brazil*, 7). In the nineteenth century, slaves worked on Sundays and saints' days in the Parahyba Valley (Stein, *Vassouras*, 75). Obviously there was more incentive to observe such rules when there were fewer pressures to maximize production. But the laws of many British colonies prohibited Sunday work and provided for religious holidays. Edward Long claimed that Jamaican slaves enjoyed about eighty-six days of leisure a year, counting Sundays and Saturday afternoons. The Jamaican slave code of 1816 prohibited Sunday work and ruled that at least twenty-six extra days a year should be given to slaves to cultivate their own gardens. There is evidence, however, that these regulations were disregarded, especially during crop time ([Edward Long], *The History of Jamaica; or, General Survey of the Antient and Modern State of that Island* . . . [London, 1774], II, 491; *Slave Law of Jamaica: with Proceedings and Documents Relative Thereto* [London, 1828], 2, 63–65, 145–58; Burn, *Emancipation and Apprenticeship*, 44–45).

[19] Boxer, *Golden Age of Brazil*, 7–9; Boxer, *Race Relations in Portuguese Colonial Empire*, 101; Stein, *Vassouras*, 139–41; Pierson, *Negroes in*

In the second half of the eighteenth century Spain and Portugal, like Britain and France, became intensely concerned with the reform of imperial administration. Severe losses in the Seven Years' War forced Spain to re-examine her colonial policy and to consider the best means for increasing the labor force, especially in Cuba. Ideas derived in part from the French Enlightenment encouraged statesmen to centralize administration, draft vast systems of law, and experiment with plans for social and economic progress. In Portugal, the Marquis de Pombal initiated colonial reforms that included a tightening of administration and the enactment of laws for the protection of slaves and the greater equalization of races. It is important to note, however, that Pombal's legislation affirming the civil rights of Indian and Asiatic subjects did not, in the words of C. R. Boxer, extend "in anything like the same measure to persons of Negro blood." And even in Asia there was such racial prejudice among the Portuguese that colonists long resisted the decrees, though they dreaded Pombal's dictatorial methods and usually carried out his orders without delay.[20]

Brazil, 3–7; Ramos, *Negro in Brazil*, 36. It is interesting to note that, according to Elkins, slavery in the United States was so severe and absolute that it molded the Negro's character into a submissive, childlike "Sambo," whose traits resembled those of the victims of Nazi concentration camps. Elkins could find no Sambos in Latin America, and concludes that the character type was unique to the United States (*Slavery*, 81–139). Without debating the merits of this intriguing thesis, we should point out that one source of Sambo, which Elkins ignores, can be found in eighteenth-century English literature. See David Brion Davis, *The Problem of Slavery in Western Culture* (Ithaca, 1966), Chapter Fifteen. In actuality, ship captains and planters of various nationalities agreed that when Negroes were subjected to the harshest treatment, their usual responses were revolt, suicide, flight, or a sullen withdrawal and mental depression. The state which the Portuguese described as *banzo* was clearly the result of severe shock which altered the entire personality.

[20] Raúl Carrancá y Trujillo, "El estatuto jurídico de los esclavos en las postrimerías de la colonización española," in *Revista de historia de América*

Inspired by French ideals and administrative techniques, Charles III of Spain also supported a series of enlightened reforms that were intended to increase the force of reason and humanity in the Spanish Empire. Since Spain intended to stock Cuba with prodigious numbers of new slaves, and since the existing laws were a confused patchwork of ancient statutes and ordinances, it was obviously essential to follow the example of Colbert, and construct a code that would ensure a profitable use of labor without wholly subverting the cardinal precepts of religion and morality. Because the *Real Cédula* was drafted in 1789 and bore the influence of the Enlightenment as well as of Spanish-Catholic tradition, it was an improvement over the *Code Noir* of 1685. Most notably, it included provisions for registering and keeping records of slaves, and machinery for securing information and punishing masters who denied their slaves adequate food or religious instruction. In 1784 a royal edict had also prohibited the branding of Negroes, a protection which had been given to

---

(México, D.F.), No. 3 (Sept., 1938), 28–33; Agostinho Marques Perdigão Malheiro, *A escravidão no Brasil; ensaio historico-juridico-social* (Rio de Janeiro, 1866–67), part iii, 32, 89–129; James Ferguson King, "The Evolution of the Free Slave Trade Principle in Spanish Colonial Administration," *Hispanic American Historical Review*, XXII (Feb., 1942), 34–56; Boxer, *Race Relations in Portuguese Colonial Empire*, 73–74, 98–100. In 1761 Portugal prohibited the introduction of Negro slaves and ruled that all slaves brought to Portugal, the Azores, or Madeira would be emancipated. This law has sometimes been interpreted as humanitarian in motive and has been credited with having abolished slavery in metropolitan Portugal. According to Charles Verlinden, however, slavery remained legal in Portugal, and such legislation was an answer to the protests of free laborers against slave competition. A law of 1773 which provided for the emancipation of imported slaves also prohibited the importation of free colored laborers from Brazil, and in some ways resembled a French law of 1777 excluding all Negroes (see José Antonio Saco, *Historia de la esclavitud desde los tiempos mas remotos hasta nuestros dias* [2nd ed., Habana, 1936–45], III, 345; Charles Verlinden, *L'Esclavage dans l'Europe médiévale; tome premier: Péninsule ibérique, France* [Bruges, 1955], 839; Boxer, *Race Relations in Portuguese Colonial Empire*, 100).

Indians long before. But in spite of laws and traditions in the
Spanish colonies that permitted slaves to buy their own freedom, the *Real Cédula* was silent on the subject of manumission. And it not only ruled that every slave was to work
from dawn to dusk, but made clear that his employment
should be confined to agriculture alone.[21] There are many
indications, moreover, that Spanish planters paid little attention to the law. Certainly the Negro slaves who revolted in
Venezuela in 1795 did not think their grievances could be
expressed through appeals to kindly priests and judges.[22]
Without minimizing the importance of the *Real Cédula* as an
advance in humane legislation, one may observe that by 1789
there were far more enlightened proposals being discussed in
Britain, France, and the United States, and that even British
and American slaveholders were suggesting reforms that went
beyond the Spanish law.

Furthermore, to round out one's picture of Spanish attitudes toward slavery it is well to look at other colonial slave
codes, such as the one written for Santo Domingo in 1785,
which claimed to be in accordance with a recent royal
ordinance. The chief purposes of this detailed code were to
reinvigorate a declining economy, to prevent insurrection, to
put an end to the growing idleness, pride, and thievery of
Negroes, and to preserve a clear-cut division between the
white race and "las clases ínfimas." Since slaves were regarded
as indispensable instruments for the public welfare, their
owners were obliged to provide adequate food and clothing.
Yet slaves were incapable of acting in their own behalf in

[21] The text of the *Real Cédula* is in Carrancá, "Estatuto jurídico de los
esclavos," 51–59; for a detailed discussion of the law, see 34–49.
[22] Uribe, "Esclavos y señores en la sociedad colombiana," 22–35, 42 ff.;
Federico Brito Figueroa, *Las insurrecciónes de los esclavos negros en la
sociedad colonial Venezolana* (Caracas, 1901), xii–xiii, 15–17, 41–42.

court, and could acquire no property except for the benefit and by the permission of their masters. All Negroes, whether slave or free, were barred from public and religious elementary schools; their movements and employment were placed under the strictest regulations; they were required at all times to be submissive and respectful to all white persons, and to treat each one like a master. Any Negro or mulatto who contradicted a white man, or who spoke in a loud or haughty voice, was to be severely whipped. The penalties increased for raising a hand against a white person, but diminished in accordance with the lightness of the offender's skin. The stigma of slavish origin extended even to occupation and dress: Negroes were not to deprive white men of jobs by working in artisan trades, nor were they to wear fine clothes, gold, or precious jewels.[23]

There is evidence that, beginning in the late eighteenth century, Negro bondage became milder and better regulated in certain parts of Latin America. In such areas as New Granada the very survival of the institution was jeopardized by the revolutionary example of Saint Domingue, the outbreak of rebellions and continuing raids by fugitive *cimarrons*, the uncertainty of the African trade in the face of war and British humanitarianism, and the unsettling effects of war on markets and credit. The tumultuous period from the French Revolution to the Spanish American wars for independence brought abrupt changes in economic and political interests which often favored the Negro slave. But even Cuba, which had a long tradition of encouraging manumissions, was the scene of gross cruelty and heavy slave mortality through much of the nineteenth century; and critics of the regime,

[23] Konetzke (ed.), *Colección de documentos*, III, 553-73. If a Negro raised his hand against a white man, the penalty was one hundred lashes and two years in jail.

like the reformer José Antonio Saco, were either silenced or banished from the island.[24]

In 1823, when the British government pledged itself to the amelioration and eventual eradication of colonial slavery, José Bonifácio de Andrada hoped to persuade his fellow Brazilians that the success of their independence and new constitution depended on making a similar commitment. Although Portugal, he charged, was guilty of the initial sin, "we tyrannize over our slaves and reduce them to the state of brutish animals, and they, in return, initiate us in their immorality and teach us all their vices." Calling on Brazil to follow the lead of Wilberforce and Buxton, José Bonifácio's words approached the violence of a Garrison: "Riches, and more riches, do our pseudo-statesmen cry out, and their call is re-echoed by the buyers and sellers of human flesh, by our ecclesiastical blood hounds, by our magistrates." His proposals included the abolition of the African trade, the creation of special councils for the protection of bondsmen, the encouragement of marriage and religious instruction, and the transfer to a new master of any slave who could prove he had been the victim of cruelty or injustice. While we have been told that these moderate provisions were always characteristic of Brazilian slavery, they received no hearing after the General Constituent Assembly was dissolved and José Bonifácio was arrested and banished. His proposal that the sale of slaves be registered so that a price could be fixed for the eventual

[24] Uribe, "Esclavos y señores en la sociedad colombiana," 21–25, 42–51; Figueroa, *Las insurrecciónes de los esclavos negros*, 41–42; Goveia, "West Indian Slave Laws," 79; Friedrich Heinrich Alexander von Humboldt, *The Island of Cuba* (tr. by J. S. Thrasher, New York, 1856), 211–28 and *passim;* Hubert H. S. Aimes, "Coartación: A Spanish Institution for the Advancement of Slaves into Freedom," *Yale Review*, XVII (Feb., 1909), 421; Augustin Cochin, *The Results of Slavery* (tr. by Mary L. Booth, Boston, 1863), 159–85.

purchase of freedom was not guaranteed by statute until 1871, although judges in some areas often enforced such a rule.[25]

In conclusion, it would appear that the image of the warmly human Big House must be balanced by a counterimage of the brutal society of the coffee barons, who even in the 1870s and 1880s governed a world in which there were no gradations between slavery and freedom. In their deep-rooted racial prejudice, their military-like discipline, their bitter resistance to any restrictions on a slaveowner's will, their constant fear of insurrection, and their hostility toward meaningful religious instruction of their Negroes, these planters were hardly superior to their brothers in Mississippi. Even with the approach of inevitable emancipation, they made no effort to prepare their slaves for freedom. It was in the face of this "slave power" that the Brazilian abolitionists resorted to the familiar demands for "immediate" and "unconditional" emancipation, and modeled themselves on the champions of British and American reform. Joaquim Nabuco, the great leader of the Brazilian antislavery movement, adopted the pen name of "Garrison."[26]

[25] José Bonifácio de Andrada, *Memoir Addressed to the General, Constituent and Legislative Assembly*, 14–23, 38–53; José Bonifácio de Andrada, *O patriarcha da independencia* (São Paulo, 1939), 288–316; Tarquinio de Sousa, *História dos fundadores do Império do Brasil*, I, 129–30, 247–49; IX, 71–72. The English translator of José Bonifácio's address wrote a preface presenting a more favorable view of Brazilian slavery; but this was in line with British antislavery doctrine, which held that British slavery was much worse than that in either Latin America or the United States. José Bonifácio, on the other hand, said his reforms had been drawn from Danish, Spanish, and Mosaic legislation, and clearly thought Brazil was lagging behind the more enlightened nations. He was particularly harsh on the clergy, whom he accused of oppressing slaves for profit and sexual gratification.

[26] Stein, *Vassouras*, 67, 132–45, 155–60, 196–99, 290; Ianni, *As metamorfoses do escravo*, 144–49; Cardoso, *Capitalismo e escravidão no Brasil meridional*, 133–67; Carolina Nabuco, *The Life of Joaquim Nabuco* (tr. and ed. by Ronald Hilton, Stanford, 1950), 108–13. One complex question which

With the exception of legal barriers to manumission,[27] the salient traits of North American slavery were to be found among the Spanish and Portuguese. Notwithstanding variations within every colony as a result of environment, economic conditions, social institutions, and the personality of owners, the Negro was everywhere a mobile and transferable possession whose labor and well-being were controlled by another man. Any comparison of slavery in North and South America should take account of the fact that Brazil alone had an area and variety comparable to all British America, and that the privileged artisans, porters, and domestic servants of colonial Brazilian cities can be compared only with their counterparts in New York and Philadelphia. Similarly, conditions in nineteenth-century Alabama and Mississippi must be held against those in the interior coffee-growing areas of south-central Brazil. Given the lack of detailed statistical information, we can only conclude that the subject is too complex and the evidence too contradictory for us to assume that the treatment of slaves was substantially better in Latin America than in the British colonies, taken as a whole.

---

we cannot begin to consider is whether the survival of African cultural patterns in Brazil was the result of a less rigorous system of slavery. It seems possible that this persistence of culture was partly a product of heavy slave mortality and a continuing reliance on the African trade. By 1850 most slaves in the United States were removed by many generations from their African origins; this was certainly not the case in Brazil.

[27] For a discussion of these barriers, see Davis, *The Problem of Slavery in Western Culture*, Chapter Nine.

Anglicanism, Catholicism, and the Negro Slave

HERBERT S. KLEIN

I

In recent years, American scholars have begun to search for the uniqueness of the American institution of Negro slavery, by contrasting it with the experience of the other colonizing nations of Europe in the New World.[1] Even as far back as the seventeenth century, a sharp difference in slave institutions was noted between English, French, and Spanish possessions, yet few historians until recently have attempted to analyze the causes and consequences of these distinctions.

Beginning with the work by Tannenbaum,[2] which was expanded by Elkins, such a preliminary comparative study has been undertaken. Concentrating on the vast structure of the law, these two scholars have relied essentially on a comparative legal analysis. Critics have challenged their generalizations on the grounds that there exists a great distinction between the model of the law and the reality of practice, while re-

[1] Research for this article was made possible by a grant from the Social Science Research Council.

[2] Frank Tannenbaum, *Slave and Citizen: The Negro in the Americas* (New York, 1947).

cently the very distinctness of the legal structure has been
questioned.[3]

But while subjecting these pioneer attempts to internal
textual criticism, few have attempted to challenge their conclusions and generalizations by empirical investigation. The
aim of this paper is to take such an approach, by subjecting
to detailed analysis the slave systems of two colonial powers
in the New World. It studies the operation of one crucial
aspect of the slave system, the relationship between infidel
Negro and Christian Church, in two highly representative
colonies, those of Cuba and Virginia.

The problem of dealing with non-Christian African Negro
slaves was one of the most difficult tasks faced by the churches
of the New World in the colonial period. Whether of the
Roman Catholic or Protestant denomination, each metropolitan church suddenly found its colonial parishes flooded
with human beings held in bondage and ignorant of the
doctrines of Christianity. For each church the question of
the validity of that bondage had to be dealt with, and for
each the human and Christian nature of the African Negro
had to be determined. While the problem might be ignored
in the first hours of establishing a functioning church among
the white colonists, and dealing with the problem of the
evangelization of the American Indians, these questions had
to be eventually resolved before a Christian kingdom could be
established on the shores of the New World.

How the two metropolitan churches dealt with the African
Negro slaves would be determined by a host of considerations,
from the question of organizational differences, to the problem of religious climate. Whatever the cause, however, the

---

[3] Arnold A. Sio, "Interpretations of Slavery: The Slave Status in the
Americas," *Comparative Studies in Society and History*, VII, No. 3 (April,
1965), 289–308.

patterns of dealing with these slaves, which they both evolved, would have a profound impact on the life of the bondsmen. For especially in the Pre-Enlightenment world, when religious thought and action completely pervaded the life of Colonial America, the attitudes and actions of the church did much to create and define the moral, legal, social, and even economic position of the Negro, slave and free, within colonial society.

II

Within colonial Latin American society the Spanish Catholic Church was the prime arbiter in the social and to a considerable extent in the intellectual life of all men. Not only did it define the moral basis of society and determine the limits of its intellectual world view, but it also sanctified and legalized the most basic human relationships. While this was the traditional role of the Church in Catholic Europe, and especially within Spain, the Church in the New World also faced the unique task of dealing with non-European peoples and defining their place within traditional social patterns.

Acutely aware of this problem from the first days of the conquest, the Church conceived of its primary function in the New World as an evangelical one. Putting aside its harsh and negative role as defender of the faith, which dominated its European attitudes against the other "peoples of the book," it adopted a positive role of sympathetic conversion of virgin peoples to the true faith.[4]

[4] The evangelizing mission of the Catholic Church in the New World was in fact a truly novel and powerful departure from previous experience. While the wars of *reconquista* against the Moors had brought the expansion of the faith, this had been through means of the fire and sword. Only in rare instances were attempts made to convert Mohammedans and Jews

While the thrust of this missionary activity was directed toward the American Indians,[5] the evangelical Catholic Church of the New World also intimately concerned itself with the other great religiously primitive peoples, the African Negro slaves. From the beginning of slave importation, in fact, the Church took the position that the African Negroes were to be considered part of the New World Church, on much the same level as the untutored Amerindians. And while the Church was often forced to concede colonists prior claims for the labor of these black and brown races, it never relinquished its position as the guardian of the moral, religious, and even social life of the untutored Indian and Negro races within its New World domain.

This dominant role of the Church in the life of the Negro slaves is well illustrated in the history of the Cuban Church. Because of the virtual extinction of the pre-contact Indians on the island and the subsequent dominance of the slave population, the Cuban Church was forced to give its undivided attention to its Negro communicants, almost from

---

to Christianity peacefully, and thus despite the religious overtones of the centuries-long *reconquista*, the whole concept of evangelization was practically nonexistent. Even when the opening up of virgin territories suddenly brought this great movement to life within Spanish Catholic circles, it was an entirely unique phenomenon, with no parallel in Europe. Thus while the New World church was pacifically preaching a gentle Christ to the Indians, the peninsular church during these same three centuries of colonial rule waged an unrelenting war against Jews, Moors, *mudejares, moriscos, conversos*, judaizers, Lutherans, and Calvinists. Intolerant defender of the faith at home, it proved to be unusually tolerant, patient, and intelligently assimilationist in its encounters with the New World pagans. As one scholar concluded, "Militant Spain guarded its religious purity in the metropolitan territory with the sword, and turned itself into a missionary at the service of the same faith in the New World." Antonio Ybot León, *La iglesia y los eclesiasticos españoles en la empresa de indias*, 2 vols. (Barcelona, 1954–63), I, 347–50.

[5] See e.g., Robert Ricard, *La "conquête spirituelle" du Mexique* (Paris, 1933).

the first years of colonization. Eventually becoming the most heavily populated Negro colony in Spanish America, Cuba, more than any other area, tended to set the pattern of Church-slave relations.

In defining its attitude toward the African slave, the Cuban clergy were of course governed by the ideas which had evolved on the institution of slavery and on African Negroes both in the contemporary mores of Iberians and in the decrees of the Metropolitan Church. In both sets of standards there had been built up in the Iberian peninsula an historic pattern which preceded the creation of the modern Spanish state. The sub-Saharan Negro as well as the North African peoples had had intimate contact with the population of Spain from recorded times to the sixteenth century. Especially important in the armies and slave populations of the Spanish Moslem states, the Iberian peoples had long accepted the individuality, personality, and co-equality of the Negro. In fact, large numbers of Negroes mixed freely in slavery under the Moslem and Christian states, with Iberian Christians, Eastern European Slavs, and other Mediterranean peoples.[6]

Since North African Berbers blended into mulatto and black sub-Saharan Negroes, there was no reason for the white Iberians to conceive of these Africans as anything but normal human beings. As for their position under the slave systems

[6] On the role of the African Negro in medieval Spain, see E. Lévi-Provençal, *Histoire de l'espagne musulmane*, 3 vols. (Paris, 1950–53), III, 72, 74–75, 177–78, 208 ff.; Charles Verlinden, *L'esclavage dans l'Europe médiévale, péninsule ibérique–France* (Bruges, 1955), 225–26, 358–62; José Antonio Saco, *Historia de la esclavitud desde los tiempos mas remotos hasta nuestra dias*, 3 vols. (Barcelona, 1875–77), II, 140–41. African Negro slaves were still a known and recognized element within Iberia's small slave population right up to the opening up of the modern slave trade with West Africa by Portugal in the fifteenth century. *Ibid.*, III, 36; Elizabeth Donnan, *Documents Illustrative of the History of the Slave Trade to America*, 4 vols. (Washington, 1930–35), I, 1.

developed by the Christian kingdoms of the North, they were treated as co-equal to all other non-Christian peoples, with the same obligations, duties, and even rights. For those in the Castilian region, this meant that they were under the modified Roman slave laws elaborated in *Las Siete Partidas* of Alfonso X, a thirteenth-century codification of existing Castilian law and custom, which was the fountainhead for the slave code later to be applied to the New World.

The most fundamental aspect of the slave sections of *Las Siete Partidas* was the initial proposition that the institution of slavery was against natural reason.[7] It declared that "slavery is the most evil and the most despicable thing which can be found among men, because man, who is the most noble, and free creature, among all the creatures that God made, is placed in the power of another. . . ."[8] While recognizing it as an institution of long standing and custom which had to be continued, the code considered it a necessary evil rather than a positive good; thus the slave was to be guaranteed every possible right which he held as a member of the human community, with modification of these rights only where absolutely necessary.

From this position, it followed that the basic legal personality of the slave was to be preserved as much as possible. While the slave was forced to relinquish his natural primary right to liberty, he was guaranteed his other rights to personal security and even the right to property. From the point of view of the Church, his secondary or social rights were even more important. Thus the slave was guaranteed the right of

[7] *Las siete partidas del rey Alfonso el sabio, cotejadas con varios codices antiguos, por la Real Academia de Historia,* 3 vols. (Madrid, 1807), III, 117, Partida IV, titulo xxi, ley 1.

[8] *Ibid.,* 30, Partida IV, titulo v, introdución.

full Christian communion, and through the sanctity of the Church, the right to marriage and parenthood.

To guarantee the sanctity of these sacraments, the Catholic Church, according to these thirteenth-century codes, was made responsible for their fulfillment even in the face of opposition from masters. Thus the Church itself had to pay compensation to masters if slaves married outside their own master's household, so that the couples could be united.[9] It also had to guarantee that no families that were legally bound together could be separated, especially through sale overseas.[10] Finally, the Church was used by the state to encourage the process of manumission as much as possible.[11]

With the opening up of the New World to African slavery, the Castilians transferred these historic codes to the overseas "kingdoms" with little change, adding to them only as local conditions warranted. In the first years, this meant dealing with the background of the African immigrants. When raw blacks (*bozales*) were heavily imported directly from Africa after the granting of the *asientos*, it was suddenly discovered that many of these religiously "primitive" peoples were in fact practicing Moslems. Having as its major aim the religious purity of the Indies, especially in regard to its old enemy, the Crown quickly suppressed all such importations, and thenceforth only "primitive" *bozales* were allowed to enter, and they, like the Indians, fell into the same tutorial status as regards the Church.[12] While this meant exclusion of

[9] *Ibid.*, 31–32, Partida IV, titulo v, ley 2.
[10] *Ibid.*, ley 1.
[11] Among the numerous laws on manumission see *ibid.*, 121–22, Partida IV, titulo xxii, ley 1.
[12] Fernando Ortiz, *Hampa afro-cubana: los negros esclavos, estudio sociologico y de derecho público* (La Habana, 1916), 343 n; also José Antonio Saco, *Historia de la esclavitud de la raza africana en el nuevo mundo y en especial en los paises americo-hispanos*, 2 vols. (Barcelona, 1879), I, 69.

Indians and Negroes from the priesthood for this period, it also meant that they were exempt from the jurisdiction of the Inquisition.

Although the majority of the Catholic Church both in Spain and the New World had early and successfully attacked the legality and practice of enslaving the Indians,[13] only a few exceptional clerics contested the right to Negro slavery.[14] For the Negro was not originally a subject of the Crown of Castile and his enslavement had occurred prior to his entrance into the Spanish realms. This left the clerics no legal grounds and less moral will for denying the practice, since it was initiated, according to the thinking of the day, by the heathens themselves. But while the Church never officially opposed the institution of Negro slavery, it deliberately interfered in the direct relationship between master and slave on

[13] Silvio Zavala, *La filosofía política en la conquista de América* (Mexico City, 1947), chap. iv. For the ending of Indian slavery in Cuba, see Irene Aloha Wright, *The Early History of Cuba, 1492-1586* (New York, 1916), 229, 232.

[14] Las Casas, who had stood at first for the introduction of Negro slaves, later held that the Negroes were injustly enslaved, "for the same reasoning," he claimed, "applies to them as to the Indians." Alonso de Montufar, archbishop of Mexico, in 1560 questioned the enslavement of the Negroes, while Fray Tomas de Mercado in his work *Tratos y contractos de mercaderes* (1569) attacked the right of procuring and enslaving Negroes in Africa itself. Bartolome de Albornoz in his *Arte de contratos* (1573) approved of the slave trade in Moors from Berber, Tripoli, and Cyrenaica, but rejected entirely the trade in Negroes from Ethiopia and the Portuguese traffic in it. Perhaps the most outstanding figures in the evangelical mission to the African Negro slave in the New World were two seventeenth-century friars: Pedro Claver, who worked among the Negro slaves arriving at Cartagena, for which he was later canonized, and the American Jesuit Alonso de Sandoval, who wrote the famous evangelical tract, *De instaurada aethiopum salute* (1627). Silvio Zavala, *New Viewpoints on the Spanish Colonization of America* (Philadelphia, 1943), 65; Zavala, "Relaciones históricas entre indios y negros en Iberoamerica," *Revista de las Indias*, XXVIII, No. 88 (1946), 55-65; Saco, *Historia de la esclavitud de la raza africana*, I, 252-55; Rafael Altamira, *Historia de España y de la civilización española*, 5 vols. (Barcelona, 1900-1930), III, 242.

the grounds that both were communicants in the Church and that nothing must challenge this primary Christian right to salvation and the sacraments.

This responsibility of the Church to care for its Negro communicants, as well as to guarantee that no subject of the Crown was not a practicing Christian, was specifically laid on the New World clergy by the Crown itself. In the very opening book of the *Leyes de Indias,* the famous compilation of colonial legislation, the Crown demanded that the Church take especial care in dealing with Negro slaves. It stated that:

> We order and command to all those persons who have Slaves, Negroes and Mulattoes, that they send them to the Church or Monastery at the hour which the Prelate has designated,[15] and there the Christian Doctrine be taught to them; and the Archbishops and Bishops of our Indies have very particular care for their conversion and endoctrination, in order that they live Christianly, and they give to it the same order and care that is prepared and entrusted by the laws of this Book for the Conversion and Endoctrination of the Indians; so that they be instructed in our Holy Roman Catholic Faith, living in the service of God our Master.[16]

Nor was the Church itself slow in meeting these demands, and in its earliest colonial synods it dealt long and extensively with the problems of its Negro members. Given the close tie which existed between civil and canonical law, the legislation

[15] "We order that in each one of the towns of Christians a determined hour each day, be designated by the prelate in which all the Indians, Negroes and Mulattoes, free as well as slave, that there are within the towns, are brought together to hear the Christian Doctrine." This same law also provided a similar arrangement for those who worked and lived in the countryside. *Recopilación de leyes de los reynos de las Indias,* 3 vols. (Madrid, 1791), I, 4–5, Libro I, titulo i, ley 12.
[16] *Ibid.,* 5, Libro I, titulo i, ley 13.

issuing from these synods became an essential part of the
Cuban slave legislation.[17]
  The first of these colonial Church synods to meet in the
Caribbean was the Dominican provincial synod which met
early in the seventeenth century on the island of Española.
Held under the auspices of the Archbishopric of Española,
which included all of the West Indies, Cuba, Florida, and
Venezuela,[18] this first Caribbean Church synod spent a good
part of its time considering the problem of its Negro communicants. With strong royal representation, in the person of
the Governor and President of the Audiencia of Santo
Domingo,[19] the leading bishops and clerics prepared, after
much discussion, a series of laws and ordinances known as
sanctiones.[20] Because of royal representation and support,
these Latin codes were later translated into Spanish and became the official civil code with the *audiencia*, as well as being
canonical law for the ecclesiastical province.[21]
  One of the very earliest of these *sanctiones* of the Provincial
Dominican Council and the first dealing with the Negro concerned the very basic task of determining if the Negro had
been properly admitted into the Church:

  Since we learn from a certain experienced leader that
  Negroes have been transported from Africa and brought
  from other parts to these Indies without benefit of baptism,
  so if at some time it is claimed that these were besprinkled
  with holy water by traders when they are put ashore by us

[17] Ortiz, *Los negros esclavos*, 348.
[18] Ybot León, *La iglesia y los eclesiasticos españoles*, II, 55.
[19] Fr. Cipriano de Utrera, "El Concilio Dominicano de 1622, con una
introdución historica," *Boletín eclesiastico de la arquidiócesis de Santo
Domingo* (1938–39), 8–9.
[20] The original Latin ordinances, or *Sanctiones Concilii Dominicani*, are
reprinted in *ibid.*, 23–81.
[21] *Ibid.*, 10–11.

it is recommended that they be questioned concerning their baptism: that is, if they have received the water of baptism before they left from Africa, or on the sea, or in any other place or whether they did not receive it at all? . . . Also one may question them whether at the time they received the baptism they had obtained any knowledge, however imperfect, concerning the performance of this sacrament which was conferred upon them, . . . and also whether they willingly received this holy water at the time it was offered to them. If however, any of these conditions are found to be lacking in their baptism, they must be baptized anew.[22]

In the next section it was stated that redoing the baptism was essential if there were any doubts, because to the Negro "it is thus shown that the privilege of the sacrament is given to them, and the Negroes know themselves to be baptized equal to the others."[23] It followed that no cleric of the province could "confer baptism upon Negro adults unless they have been imbued first with the Christian doctrine,"[24] which education was to be undertaken as soon as they entered the province, by a priest specifically designated for this task.[25] If Negroes refused to be baptized, they were given two to three months "during which the fear of the doctrine must be found." At the end of this time the cleric "may administer baptism to them, provided they are, one and all, sorry for their transgressions, they display the sign of this sorrow, and they realize the power of the sacrament of baptism."[26]

As for the sacrament of confirmation, it was demanded that the "priest even warns the master of Negroes to place

[22] *Sanctiones Concilii Dominicani*, Sessio Secunda, Caput I, Sectio vii.
[23] Sessio Secunda, Caput I, Sectio vii.
[24] Sessio Secunda, Caput I, Sectio ix.
[25] Sessio Secunda, Caput I, Sectio x.
[26] Sessio Secunda, Caput I, Sectio ix.

before these same ones the means and the place to receive this divine sacrament, but if they do otherwise they may be punished with a judgement."[27] In the sacrament of marriage, it was required that at Negro weddings (as in the case of Indian ones) two special benedictions be given instead of the usual one, to impress them with the importance of this sacrament.[28] In the case of an unbaptized Negro contracting marriage with someone already baptized, it was required that a new agreement be made and the marriage ceremony be repeated. And this was to be done as soon as possible, "so that the benefits of marriage may be rightfully enjoyed."[29]

Negroes were not to be granted absolution until they had overcome their ignorance and inexperience and had finally accepted the faith.[30] It was also provided that every qualified confessor could hear the confessions of Negroes.[31] Again, with the administration of extreme unction as with all other sacraments, it was demanded that the Negro be taught its meaning and accept its significance before it could be administered to him.[32]

It was required by these *sanctiones* that Negroes who lived at great distances from the churches and worked in the country should hear mass at least at six festive holy days per year. If the master was not willing to allow his slaves to hear mass at least these six times, then the prelate was to see to his legal chastisement.[33] The Church council also demanded that "no master of Negroes may put slaves to any servile work on the festive days, nor may he hire others; under the penalty of ten

---

[27] Sessio Secunda, Caput II, Sectio iii.
[28] Sessio Secunda, Caput IV, Sectio iii.
[29] Sessio Secunda, Caput IV, Sectio vii.
[30] Sessio Secunda, Caput V, Sectio i.
[31] Sessio Secunda, Caput V, Sectio vi.
[32] Sessio Secunda, Caput VII, Sectio iv.
[33] Sessio Tertia, Caput I, Sectio iv.

silver pounds for the first transgression, for the second he will truly be implicated with excommunication."[34] For the Negroes on these days were to be taught by the priest "so that they may learn the articles of faith and reap the harvest of sacraments."[35]

Largely supporting the declarations and ordinances of the Dominican Provincial Synod of 1622, and also providing further clarifications of the rights of Christian Negroes, were the *Constituciones* published by the Church synod which met for the Cuban diocese in June of 1680. Constitución IV repeated a proviso that had become an essential part of the imperial slave code; that is, that all slaves be instructed in the Roman Catholic faith and be baptized within a year of their admittance into the Indies.[36]

It also provided that *bozales* could not be married by a priest until both parties were baptized.[37] In attempting to deal with this problem, the Diocesan Synod was forced to take into account the African background of the slave and to adjust the Catholic atmosphere to the matrimonial situation brought by the slave from his native land. "Because there come many Indians . . . and Negro *bozales,* married in their infidelity: we order that wanting to live together in this bishopric, after being baptized, their marriage be ratified *in facie ecclesiae* [in the sight of the Church]." If either partner refused the faith, he or she was given up to seven months and six warnings to be baptized. If after this time elapsed they still

---

[34] Sessio Tertia, Caput I, Sectio v.

[35] Sessio Quarta, Caput VII, Sectio ii.

[36] Fernando Ortiz, *Hampa afro-cubana: los negros brujos* (Madrid, 1906), 304. This same command was also contained in the very first chapter of the 1789 Slave Code; see "Real Cedula de Su Magestad sobre la educación, trato y ocupaciones de los esclavos en todos sus dominios de Indias . . . ," reprinted in *Revista de Historia de America,* No. 3 (September, 1938), 50–51.

[37] Constitución III, quoted in Ortiz, *Los negros esclavos,* 348.

refused baptism they could not continue their marital relations. And "if any of the said infidels come married with
many wives" he was required to be baptized and married to
the first one with whom "according to their custom and rites"
he had contracted marriage. If the first one could not be so
ascertained, then the male could marry the one he desired.
And it was also required that if he was married within the
direct parental line (mother, sister, etc.), his marriage was
declared invalid and the couple had to separate before baptism
was administered.[38]

The Diocesan Synod also attempted to eradicate a continuing problem, that of unscrupulous masters who, for either
personal reasons or those of economic expediency, tried to
prevent their slaves from marrying or refused to honor these
marriages. Thus Constitución V established that "marriage
should be free" and ordered that

> no master prohibit his slaves against marriage, nor impede
> those who cohibit in it, because we have experienced that
> many masters with little fear of God and with serious dam-
> age to their consciences, proscribe that their slaves not marry
> or impede their cohibition with their married partners, with
> feigned pretexts; . . .

In this same law, masters were prohibited from taking their
slaves outside of Havana to sell them unless they took husband and wife together. Constitución VI added that masters
could not sell their slaves overseas or in remote parts, in order
to impede marital cohabitation. If this was done, then the slaves
sold in this manner should be brought back with the master
paying the expense.[39]

The local Church did all in its power to carry out the in-

[38] *Ibid.*, 349–50.
[39] *Ibid.*, 349.

tent of the metropolitan slave codes, and to guarantee to their Negro communicants their full rights. They met in powerful synods to deal with local conditions and the unique backgrounds of their particular colored congregants, and always legislated in favor of the fullest freedom and rights that were permissible. While the upper clergy dealt with these problems in law, the lower clergy, especially at the parish level, effectively carried this law into practice.

This correlation between law and practice is abundantly supported by the local parish statistics available on the administration of the sacraments. What these materials indicate is that the slave and free colored population had the same percentage and absolute figures of baptism as the white population. According to the census of 1827, for example, when whites represented 44% and the slaves 41% of the total population,[40] each group respectively had 12,938 and 12,729 baptisms performed on the island in that year.[41]

Not only were slaves and free colored fully admitted into the Church, but they also heavily participated in all the sacraments, and most importantly in that of marriage as well. Thus, for example, in the four years from 1752 to 1755, the Rector of the Cathedral Church at Santiago de Cuba reported 55 slave marriages to 75 free white marriages in his parish.[42] At this time the entire urban population of Santiago de Cuba consisted of 6,525 whites and 5,765 slaves,[43] which means that the slave marriages in that period represented one out of 105 slaves in the city, and the free whites one out of 96.3.

[40] Ramón de la Sagra, *Historia economico-política y estadistica de la isla de Cuba* (Habana, 1831), 7–8.

[41] *Ibid.*, 20. The free colored, who made up 15% of the total population in 1827, had 4,826 baptisms.

[42] Archivo General de Indias [hereafter cited as AGI], Sevilla, Audiencia de Santo Domingo, legajo 516, no. 30, June 14, 1758.

[43] Sagra, *Historia economico-política . . . de la isla de Cuba,* 3.

In short, despite the sharp differences in education, social
status, and wealth, the slave marriage rate was very close to
that of the free whites. This is all the more extraordinary
a figure, given the fact that a large portion of the adult
population, of all colors and social conditions, lived in free
unions because of the high cost of clerical ceremonies.

This same pattern is repeated in the local parish of Santo
Tomas, also in the jurisdiction of the Santiago de Cuba
Church. In the parish census for 1824 there were listed 794
married whites, 855 free colored married persons, and 855
married slaves. This breaks down into a percentage of 44%
for the whites, 42% for the free colored, and 29% for the
slaves of the adult population; that is, of persons seventeen or
older.[44] On the one hand these figures reveal the great extent
of illegal unions among adults of all races, but they also
seriously underrate the slave marriages. For the general statistics of the entire island consistently reveal that the free colored
marriage rate was considerably below that of the colored
slaves.

Thus, in 1827 there were listed a total of 1,868 white marriages, 1,381 slave marriages, and only 385 free colored marriages. The ratios in the total population figures for that year
come to one marriage performed for 166 white persons, for
207 colored slaves, and 236 free mulattoes, the worst being one
out of 347 free Negroes.[45] The reason for the high slave marriage rate as contrasted to the free colored population appears
to be the fact that the slave population was accountable to a
master, and through him to the local church, and was there-

44 AGI, Santo Domingo, leg. 223, February 15, 1824.
45 Sagra, *Historia economico-política* . . . *de la isla de Cuba*, 20, 24. In
France at this time, the figure was one married couple for each 134 persons.
Ibid., 24 n.

fore far more under the influence of the local parish priest. Another remarkable factor is the large number of legal marriages between free and slave persons. Of the 702 colored marriages on record in six selected parishes of Havana between 1825 and 1829, 278 were between slaves, 293 between free persons, and 131 involved a slave and a free person.[46]

All of these baptismal and marriage statistics reinforce the fact that civil and canonical law was the very essence of actual practice, and that the Negro slave enjoyed co-equal status with his masters before the sacraments of the Church. That the Church was so effective in carrying law into practice and constantly guaranteeing these rights is also due to the extraordinarily large number of priests on the island. In the census of 1778, exclusive of nuns, there were listed 1,063 practicing clergy in Cuba. This meant that for the island's total population of 179,484, there was one priest for every 168 persons, a figure not even approached in any country in the Americas today.[47]

Aside from its direct role in the sacraments and the carrying out of Catholic education, the Church also encouraged manumission by impressing on masters that it was a meritorious act in the eyes of God. On his special Saint's day, or in honor of a marriage, a birth, or a recovery from a severe illness, a master would give thanks to God by freeing some of his slaves. The Crown greatly encouraged these procedures

---

[46] *Ibid.*, 65.

[47] For the 1778 census breakdown, see AGI, Indiferente General, leg. 1527, December 31, 1778. For a clerical census of the Americas in 1959, see Donald S. Castro *et al.*, *Statistical Abstract of Latin America, 1963* (UCLA, Center of Latin American Studies, 1964), 22. The lowest figure for any contemporary Latin American country was Chile, with one priest for every 2,750 Catholics. The United States figure in 1965 was one priest to 778 practicing Catholics. *The Official Catholic Directory, 1965*, General Summary, 1–2.

by making it possible to manumit a slave by simple declaration of the master in a church before the local priest.[48] That the work of the clergy in providing a moral climate conducive to manumission was successful can also be seen in the statistics. From the early days of slave importation, a large free colored class began to appear in Cuba, largely as a result of voluntary manumission by their masters. By the 1560s the free colored population on the island was numerous enough to elect its own *aguacil*, or constable, in Havana,[49] and by the end of this century they had already fielded one full company of free colored militia of around 100 men.[50] By the end of the next century the free Negro community was able to sponsor a full battalion of some 800 men,[51] and by the census of 1774 the island listed 30,847 free colored, as opposed to 43,333 Negro slaves, making the free colored some 41% of the total black population on the island.[52] In fact, from this first census until the era of mass illegal importations of African slaves after 1820, the percentage of freedmen to slaves never fell below 36%. Even at its lowest ebb, in 1841, the free colored class still numbered 152,838, 26% of the total colored population. When this mass illegal trade was finally halted in the late 1850s, the temporary disequilibrium was overcome; by 1861 the free colored accounted for 39% of the total colored or 213,167 free persons as against 339,872 slaves.[53]

[48] Tannenbaum, *Slave and Citizen*, 53 ff.
[49] Saco, *Historia de la esclavitud de la raza africana*, I, 221.
[50] For the history of the first company of *pardos libres* (free mulattoes) of Havana, see AGI, Santo Domingo, leg. 418, no. 7, 1714.
[51] AGI, Santo Domingo, leg. 419, no. 8, 1715.
[52] Sagra, *Historia economico-política . . . de la isla de Cuba*, 3.
[53] These figures for the census from 1774 to 1827 can be found in *ibid.*, 3–6; those for the census from 1841 to 1861 are calculated by Julio J. Le Riverend Brusone, in Ramiro Guerra y Sanchez *et al.*, *Historia de la nación cubana*, 10 vols. (La Habana, 1950), IV, 170.

The Church was not only the most important factor in encouraging and maintaining the impetus to voluntary manumission, which accounts for the majority of freedmen; it also encouraged *coartación*. Most fully developed in Cuba, *coartación* was the system whereby a slave had the right to purchase his freedom from his master. The slave was granted the right to appear in court at any time to have his price fixed and to begin to pay his purchase price in agreed installments after the initial down payment, usually a minimum sum of 50 pesos, or something like one-fourth of his value. Once a slave became *coartado* he had a whole range of rights including the right to change masters if he could find a purchaser for his remaining price, and to buy his freedom as soon as he was able. Because of the expense and labor involved, it was only the exceptionally able artisan and urban slave who most benefited from the system, though it was open to rural plantation slaves as well, and it has been estimated that about 4,000 per year took advantage of it.[54]

Throughout the whole practice of *coartación* the Church played a vital role, for it was the prime guarantor of the free time and labor of the Negro outside his master's jurisdiction. To obtain funds, the Negro slave was permitted by custom and the Church to work for himself in his own private truck garden, or *conuco*, on all holy days and Sundays. Income from these *conucos* was also exempted from tithe payments. This was a very unusual privilege in colonial society, where the *diezmos*, or tithes, were the most universal form of production and property taxes.[55] Finally in seeking a reliable third party to hold his savings toward the initial down payment,

[54] For a complete discussion of this system, see Herbert H. S. Aimes, "Coartacion: A Spanish Institution for the Advancement of Slaves into Freedmen," *Yale Review*, XVII (February, 1909), 412–31; and Ortiz, *Los negros esclavos*, 313 ff.

[55] AGI, Santo Domingo, leg. 152, ramo 2, no. 39, September 24, 1680.

and also to help him present his legal case, the Negro slave often relied on the local parish priest.[56]

Although the clergy did not interfere with the actual functioning of the slave regime, they could be critical of it. The Bishop of Santiago de Cuba in the late seventeenth century bitterly complained that the masters were not properly clothing their slaves, so that the latter were often embarrassed to come to Church. He warned the masters that they were under obligation to provide the slaves with decent clothing, and not force them to provide for themselves.

The clergy also criticized the Negroes, especially on matters of laxity in church attendance and disinterest in learning their doctrine. This same Bishop who concerned himself over the poor dress of his Negro communicants also was rather shocked at the indifference of some of the slaves to Church service. He charged that many were not attending mass on holidays and Sundays, before they began to work on their own properties, and that others were not seriously learning their lessons. In both situations he wanted the civil authorities to intervene, and in the latter case even proposed that instead of the present gentle method of instruction, the local clergy should adopt "the method by which the clerical teachers of New Spain and Peru teach their Indians," that is by using the whip on them in front of their fellow communicants if they forgot their lessons.[57]

This stern attitude was the exception rather than the rule, most clergy dealing gently with their Negro churchgoers. One who attempted to mold custom to the Church, and who

---

[56] Such for example was the experience of the parish priest of the copper mining town of Santiago del Cobre in the seventeenth century with his 500 free and slave Negro communicants. AGI, Santo Domingo, leg. 417, no. 15, December, 1709.

[57] AGI, Santo Domingo, leg. 151, ramo 2, no. 22, February 22, 1682.

largely succeeded, was Bishop Pedro Agustin Morel de Santa Cruz, in the middle of the eighteenth century. When he took up residence he found that there were 21 Negro clubs, or *cabildos*, in Havana where Negroes of both sexes gathered on holidays and Sundays to drink, dance "in extremely torrid and provocative dances," and commit other excesses too sinful to mention. Many told the Bishop that it was better to leave these *cabildos* alone, for they provided a reasonable outlet for the slaves and freedmen without causing undue harm. But, he declared, "not being satisfied with similar scruples, I attempted the gentle method of going by turns to each of the *cabildos*, to administer the sacrament of confirmation, and praying the Holy Rosary with those of that organization (*gremio*), before an Image of Our Lady which I carried with me. Concluding this act, I left the image in their houses, charging them to continue with their worship and devotion. . . ." He then named a specific clergyman to each of the *cabildos* to go to them on Sundays and holidays to teach them Christian doctrine. He also placed each *cabildo* in charge of a particular Virgin that it was to venerate under the direction of a clergyman. This unusual and enthusiastic bishop went so far as to propose that his clergymen should learn the various African languages spoken by the slaves so that they might teach them better.[58]

Although this step was never taken, there is no question of the successful syncretization of Catholicism with the African folk religions brought to Cuba by the Negro slaves. Bishop Morel de Santa Cruz's action was only one link in a long chain of effort to construct a *cofradía* (or religious brotherhood) system by the Church. This was so successful that the African *cofradías* came to play a vital role in the social life of both

[58] AGI, Santo Domingo, leg. 515, no. 51, 1755.

slaves and freedmen, with their own saints and special functions in various holy marches and carnivals. Usually organized
along lines of regional African origins, their members coming
from the same *nación*, or geographic location, these were
both religious and benevolent associations. They were not
only normal *cofradías* tied to the local church and carrying
saintly images in religious processions, but cooperated with
the *cabildos* in other activities. Throughout the year the
cabildo acted as a mutual relief association, the chief of the
cabildo aiding his subordinates if they were sick; their general
funds were also used to pay burial expenses and sometimes to
free old and invalided slaves. They also maintained *cabildo*
houses as general meeting places for the members of the
cofradía, available to them at all times. Finally, the *cabildos*
were recognized as legitimate political agents for the slaves
and freedmen in dealing with the local authorities, thus providing outlets for political organization and leadership.

The African *cabildo* was not peculiar to Cuba, but existed
throughout the Spanish and Portuguese Indies wherever
Negroes were congregated. It had its origins in medieval
Seville, whose Negro *cofradías* and *cabildos* were active and
fully recognized from as far back as the fourteenth century. As
early as 1573, the Havana municipal government ordered that
all the Negroes of the city turn out for the Corpus Christi
processions, "the same as they assisted in the famous one of
Seville." In the great religious processions, the Negro *cabildos*
in fact played an increasingly important part. Though outright
African fetishes were quickly prohibited from display, the
local saints and virgins were so entwined with African myth-
ology and even costume that these displays often tended to
perpetuate pre–New World patterns and beliefs.[59]

[59] An excellent study of these *cabildos* is Fernando Ortiz, "Los cabildos
afro-cubanos," *Revista Bimestre Cubana*, XVI (1921), 5–39.

The most important religious processional for these organizations was the famous Christmas festival of the Day of the Kings. This day was recognized throughout the island as a special day for the Negro *cabildos* and *cofradías*, and almost unlimited license was permitted by the white authorities in the great dances, drinkings, and ceremonies. For the Negroes, both slave and free, it was the crowning event in their year, and provided an unparalleled opportunity for individual and community expression for the entire Negro population. Thus, between religious processions, annual *dia de reyes* celebrations, and the daily conduct of their *cofradías* and *cabildos* the Negro masses were provided by the Church with a vast and crucial outlet for social expression and community development.[60]

While providing a rich fabric of social existence for the masses under the canopy of the Church, the Cuban clergy also aided the exceptionally able Negro to break through the rigid class-caste barriers of the white community through their control over the educational processes. Since, at the pre-university level, education was exclusively in the hands of the Church, primary and secondary education was available to the exceptional and upwardly mobile free Negro. Education was the only means by which a colored person could break through from the lower economic classes, at least to the learned professions, and possibly higher. For sons of prosperous colored artisans and successful colored militia officers, both mulattoes and Negroes, the open opportunity of the schools run by the secular and regular clergy was their avenue for mobility of their children.

For example, the mulatto, or *pardo*, Antonio Flores, a militia officer in Havana in the mid-eighteenth century, had

[60] Fernando Ortiz, "La fiesta afro-cubana del 'dia de reyes,'" *Revista Bimestre Cubana*, XV (1920), 5–26.

a son who had graduated with highest distinction from the
courses of theology and grammar offered by the local Jesuit
college of Havana. When his son's right to enter the University was challenged on the grounds of his color, Flores, in
bitter though unsuccessful opposition, pointed out to the
Council of the Indies the innumerable examples of free
Negro and mulatto children who had attended local church
and primary schools in pre-university training courses.[61] And
while the University consistently fought the entrance of
colored persons into its ranks, the large number of petitions
of colored persons to the Crown demanding the right to practice a profession to which they had already been trained indicates that many succeeded in "passing" with little trouble,
through the combination of light skins and the pre-collegiate
training they had received from the clerical schools.[62] And
even given denial of University admission to the majority of
free colored, the very possession of a secondary *colegio*
education in the days of mass illiteracy and nonprofessional
university programs was more than enough to break into
the professional classes and the upper social levels. To read
and write, at least according to the Church, if not the colonial
universities, was a right open to all, and a right which held
out almost unlimited opportunities for the few who could
achieve it.

Concerned for his social existence, his freedom, his family,
and his soul, and even in a minority of cases for the training
of his mind, the Church deeply and vitally committed itself
to its guardian role with its Negro slave communicant. Because it effectively controlled an important part of their lives,

[61] AGI, Santo Domingo, leg. 1455, no. 5, 1760.
[62] For example, see the petition of the mulatto Auditor of War of Cuba,
who was a law graduate of the University, in AGI, Santo Domingo, leg.
2236, October 1, 1791.

the Church was unquestionably the primary intermediary agent between master and slave, and the only institution which daily claimed its rights, as opposed to the property rights of the masters.

Although the Church could not abolish the rigors of harsh plantation servitude, it could modify that life to the extent of guaranteeing minimal periods of rest and independence for the blacks. The Church could also guarantee a degree of self-expression for all slaves, which enabled them to escape the close confines of bondage in many ways and thus to validate their human personality and potential. Finally it could create the panoply of mores and attitudes which permitted the Negro to be treated as a co-equal human being, and allowed him to fully merge into Cuban society when the harsh regime of slavery was destroyed.

III

Like Cuba, Virginia was settled by a dominant established church, in this case the Church of England. Both Spain and England at the times of colonization had a hierarchical metropolitan church which was closely tied to the royal government and was considered one of the major governing institutions of the realm. But while the counter-reformation Church of Spain was able to suppress all opposition to its religious authority, the Anglican Church found itself constantly struggling against Protestant dissenter groups who attempted to challenge its established authority. However, at the time of the initial planting of Virginia, the Crown and the Church were fully united and the Anglican Church was declared the established church of the colony. As early as 1606, the Crown decreed that the Virginia Company ". . . should provide that the true word and service of God should be preached, planted and used, *according to the Rites and Doctrine of the Church of England.*"[63] In the first organization of the Company, there was even a bishop of the realm, John King of the London diocese, who was a leading member.[64] Through these actions, Anglicanism was guaranteed as the religion of the colonists, and from then until the end of the colonial period, the Church of England was overwhelmingly the state church of Virginia, and its membership encompassed the majority of the population.

But while there was never any challenge to the religion of the metropolitan Church in Virginia, the Crown never established the leadership and organization whereby the established church could function in its accustomed manner in the colony. In sharp contrast to Cuba, where this problem was never raised, the Crown and the hierarchy made no attempt to fit the colony into the normal functioning of the Church. Whereas Cuba had its first bishop appointed in 1516 just five years after the conquest, neither the Archbishop of Canterbury nor the Crown saw fit to appoint a native bishop, nor even to place the colony within the jurisdiction of an insular diocese.

The Bishop of London, because of his connection with the Company, originally assisted in providing clergymen and some financial assistance to establishing the Virginia Church, but this tenuous connection was destroyed when the Company was dissolved by the Crown in 1624. While the Company provided land for church income, divided the colony up into parishes, and encouraged the migration of clergy-

[63] Quoted in Arthur Lyon Cross, *The Anglican Episcopate and the American Colonies* (Cambridge, 1924), 10.
[64] George Maclaren Brydon, *Virginia's Mother Church and the Political Conditions under Which It Grew*, 2 vols. (Richmond, 1947–52), I, 40–42.

men,[65] it made no effort to obtain the establishment of a native bishop, primarily because of the cost; nor was the Church or the Crown at this time the least bit interested in subsidizing such a venture, or even in considering it. Because of this amazing and gross neglect, the colonists within a few short years had completely usurped hierarchical authority and had transformed the centuries-old organization of English church government. In traditional English ecclesiastical organization, the local landowner, or other outside body or institution, had the power to nominate ministers for the local parish within their jurisdiction. This meant that the landowner or institution could present his own candidate for the local parish office to the Bishop for investiture. The Bishop then had the power to certify or reject the nominee, but once invested with his office, the clergyman served for life. The local parishioners had no say either in the nomination or investiture process, and had no recourse but to accept their minister on a life basis. The minister, in fact, was accountable only to the Church, and only the Bishop could control him. What duties the local parishioners' vestry and churchwarden performed were all determined by law and were subservient to the local clergymen.[66]

The Church hierarchy also had the task of guaranteeing religious uniformity, and had extensive civil-ecclesiastical functions. Thus the Bishops could appoint special courts to try and condemn heretics; they had full jurisdiction over marriages, the probating of wills, the collation to benefices, the appointment of notaries, and extensive rights over tithes and other ecclesiastical taxes.[67]

Without the hierarchic structure, however, most of these

[65] *Ibid.*, 10-11.
[66] *Ibid.*, 42-44.
[67] *Ibid.*, 67; Cross, *Anglican Episcopate*, 2.

functions could not be maintained; and, in fact, rapid erosion
soon wiped out the complete edifice of the Church as it was
known in England. Although the Company at first appeared
to claim the right of nomination of clergymen to Virginia
parishes, it seems not to have exercised that right, but simply
sent out pre-ordained clergymen, which left open the question
of their initiation into their parishes. With the dissolution of
the Company, and the failure of English authorities to claim
their rights, the local colonists absorbed all power. First the
General Court of Virginia, consisting of the members of the
upper house of the General Assembly, claimed that the right
of nomination, or presentation, devolved on them from the
Company. They also proceeded to absorb a host of other
juridical, administrative, and even ecclesiastical matters which
by tradition belonged to the Bishop. This meant that control
over vital statistics, notaries, wills, etc., the establishment of
parishes, the naming and defining of all ecclesiastical offices,
the collection of tithes, the regulation of church conduct, and
even the maintenance of purity of faith and dogma, was determined not by the Bishop, canonical law courts, and ecclesiastical officials as in England, but by the local General
Assembly of Virginia.[68]

While central authority now came to rest in a popular civil
assembly, the local church came increasingly under the power
of the parishioners themselves, rather than the ministry. Developing new institutions and adapting old practices to local
conditions, the colonists began to establish their own distinctly unique form of Church government, at whose center
stood the all-powerful locally elected board of governing
parishioners known as the Vestry.

With the devolution to the General Assembly of all mat-

[68] Brydon, *Virginia's Mother Church*, I, 67–68, 86 ff.

ters pertaining to the Church, the Assembly in turn gave to each local parish vestry a multitude of civil and ecclesiastical rights and obligations, and made it the prime institution of a new type of established church. As early as the 1620s the Assembly was providing that local churchwardens and leading members of the parish should concern themselves with the maintenance of the church. From this simple maintenance task the evolving vestry organization quickly began to assume ever greater powers. A reflection of this occurred in 1643, when, in a formal legal enactment, the Assembly provided that each parish should have a vestry, and "that the most sufficient and selected men be chosen and joyned to the minister and churchwardens to be of that Vestrie." Among the tasks enumerated for the Vestry was the crucial absorption of the right of nomination. The 1643 Act declared "that the vestrie of evrie parish . . . shall henceforward have power, to elect and make choyce of their ministers. . . ."[69] The vestry was to present the minister candidate for their parish appointment to the governor, not to a bishop, as in England, and the governor then made the formal induction and confirmation of that minister to hold the given office for life.[70]

While creation of the first vestries seems to have been by appointment of the General Court,[71] by the 1640s the Assembly provided that the vestry was to be organized on the basis of election from among the parishioners. By the time of the codification of the laws on the Church by the General Assembly in 1662, it was provided:

That for the makeing and proportioning the levyes and assessments for building and repayring the churches, and

[69] William Waller Hening, *The Statutes at Large, Being a Collection of the Laws of Virginia*, 13 vols. (New York, 1823), I, 241–42.
[70] Brydon, *Virginia's Mother Church*, I, 92.
[71] *Ibid.*, 93.

chappells, provision for the poore, maintenance of the minister, and such other necessary *duties* for the more orderly
manageing all parociall affaires, *Be it enacted* that twelve of
the most able men of each parish be by the major part of
the *said* parish, *chosen* to be vestry-men out of which number the minister and vestry to make choice of two churchwardens yearly, as *alsoe* in the case of death of any vestry
man, or his departure out of the parish, that the said minister and vestry make choice of another to supply his
roome. . . .[72]

By this act, which abolished the electoral system, the vestries
in fact became autocratic local bodies of the leading planters,
who exercised enormous control over social and economic
conditions within the parish. After their initial establishment,
elections never took place, and members usually held their
office till death or resignation. When vacancies occurred, the
vestrymen themselves proceeded to choose leading planters as
members. So oligarchic and powerful did these vestries become that one of the constant themes of colonial Virginian
history was the popular, and continually unsatisfied, demand
for periodic elections and the breakup of this autocratic control.[73]

Given this entrenched self-perpetuating planter leadership
in control of the Church, the role of the transitory minister
could be only a subordinate one at best. In complete contradiction to the entire organization of the Church of England,
the Vestry refused to present their ministers for induction.
Since induction by the Governor would guarantee the minister his parish for life, barring ill conduct, the Vestries simply

[72] Hening, *Statutes*, II, 44–45.
[73] One of the major reforms of Bacon's rebellion was the call for vestry
elections every three years. Brydon, *Virginia's Mother Church*, I, 97.

refused to present their ministers, and by this means made the minister's position completely dependent on the goodwill of his leading parishioners. Though the royal governors had full power to force induction on the Vestries, not one governor in the entire history of the colony saw fit to exercise this right, out of fear of Vestry power.[74]

This entire system was bitterly attacked by regular Church of England clergymen. The mid-seventeenth-century clergyman, Morgan Godwyn, who served in Virginia and the British West Indies, scornfully called this arrangement a "probational tenure" system,[75] while the Bishops' representative in the colony, Commissary James Blair, at the end of the century, was badly disturbed by what he described as this "Custom of making annual Agreements with the Ministers, which they [i.e., the Vestries] call by a Name coarse enough, *viz*. Hiring of the Ministers; so that they seldom present any ministers, that they may by that Means keep them in more Subjection and Dependence."[76] In short, stated the commissary, "they are only in the nature of Chaplains," whose tenure of office was dependent on an annual agreement renewable at the option of a small body of men.[77] Thus any independence on the part of the clergymen was quickly suppressed by the planters, who by the very nature of their positions would naturally be the strongest representatives of the status quo in the community. As Godwyn noted, they "obstruct all designs for the good of those Churches, and to report all

[74] Philip Alexander Bruce, *Institutional History of Virginia in the Seventeenth Century*, 2 vols. (New York, 1910), I, 136–39.

[75] Morgan Godwyn, *The Negro's and Indians Advocate, Suing for Their Admission into the Church* (London, 1680), 168.

[76] Henry Hartwell, James Blair, and Edward Chilton, *The Present State of Virginia*, 2d ed. (Williamsburg, 1940), 66.

[77] *Ibid.*, 67.

things already so well settled as not needing the least amendment or alteration."[78]

Because of these developments, the regular clergy of England by and large refused to come to Virginia. For as Blair lamented, "no good Ministers that were inform'd of it would come into the Country, and if they came ignorant of any such Custom, they quickly felt the Effects of it in the high Hand wherewith most Vestries manag'd their Power, and got out of the Country again as soon as they could."[79] A goodly portion of the practicing clergymen in Virginia, until well into the eighteenth century, were in fact deacons, or as Morgan Godwyn called them, *"Lay-Priests* of the *Vestries ordination."*[80]

Even in his very vocation, the minister was challenged by the Vestry. Thus the Reverend Hugh Jones in 1724 warned that ". . . in several places the clerks [of the parish] are so ingenious or malicious, that they contrive to be liked as well or better than the minister, which created ill-will and disturbance, besides other harm."[81] Given the chance, he charged, they will usurp almost all of the clergymen's functions, even to the giving of sermons, and warned that they should have their functions carefully defined by law to prevent these abuses.

So all-embracing was parishioner influence and control that the clergyman had to win popular endorsement, and constantly keep his congregation happy, which of course ex-

[78] Godwyn, *Negro's and Indians Advocate,* Preface, i. According to Godwyn the Virginia colonists chafed at the cost of Church tithes, and quickly lost their interest in the Anglican creed, because, he charged, Virginians "for the most part do know no other *God* but *Money,* nor *Religion* but *Profit."*

[79] Hartwell, Blair, and Chilton, *Present State of Virginia.*

[80] Godwyn, *Negro's and Indians Advocate,* 170.

[81] Hugh Jones, *The Present State of Virginia,* 2d ed. (Chapel Hill, 1956), 96.

cluded all possibilities of independent thought or challenge to the given moral and social situation, for this was the sure road to ruin. This dependence was so pervasive, in fact, that often parishioners even went so far, in this era of nonconformity, as to question and modify standard Church dogma. Reverend Jones noted in his analysis of contemporary Virginia: "In several respects the clergy are obliged to omit or alter some minute parts of the liturgy, and deviate from the strict discipline and ceremonies of the Church; to avoid giving offence. . . ."[82]

While the mother church soon became deeply aware of the heterodoxy and complete breakdown of the established church in Virginia, it could do little to change the situation. Deeply involved in religious civil wars at home, it was not until after the Restoration that the Church of England could even begin to deal with the situation. It was only with the investiture of Henry Compton as Bishop of London, in 1675, that the Church finally forced the Crown to place the colony within a diocese. For a number of historical reasons, the Bishopric of London was chosen; however, traditions were so entrenched that this brought little real change. The Bishop made no attempt to oppose vestry control, or to retake possession of his normal ecclesiastical or civil functions, or even his right of investiture. His only concern was to maintain some kind of purity of dogma by guaranteeing minimal standards for clergymen. This he did by forcing the colonists to accept only accredited clergymen licensed by himself. Thus in the instruction to Governor Culpeper of Virginia, the Bishop had the Crown declare that "no Minister be prefrr'd by you to any Ecclesiastical Benefice in that our Colony *without a Certificate from the Lord Bp. of London, of his*

[82] *Ibid.,* 98.

being conformable to the Doctrine of the Church of England."[83]

While the Bishop eventually succeeded in sending a representative to the colony, with the title of commissary, or vicar general, this clergyman could only exercise moderating influence, and had to persuade rather than enjoin acceptance of Church rules.[84] The first commissary, James Blair (1689–1743), created much heat but little concrete change,[85] and despite all attempts of several energetic London Bishops, the Vestries could not be forced to induct their ministers, leaving the majority of them to the arbitrary will of their congregations. Through the commissary rule of Blair and his successors, some positive results were attained with the problem of providing a regular ordained clergy for all the parishes, but in the end, the commissaries had little or no effect in reforming the general structure of the Virginia Church. When the metropolitan hierarchy realized this failure, it attempted to establish a resident Bishop for the American colonies. But this was a potentially powerful challenge to local authority, and colonial opposition was so constant and vehement against this idea that the matter was never carried to fruition, despite all the strenuous efforts made by the mother church.[86]

Not only was the Church after the Restoration terribly concerned about the religion of the white colonists, but it also began to take an increasingly involved position on the status of the Negro and Indian heathens within England's American Empire. This concern with the plight of the Negro

[83] Quoted in Cross, *Anglican Episcopate,* 26.

[84] *Ibid.,* 3–4, 44.

[85] *Ibid.,* 78–80.

[86] For the history of this struggle, see Cross, *Anglican Episcopate,* and Carl Bridenbaugh, *Mitre and Sceptre: Transatlantic Faiths, Ideas, Personalities and Politics, 1689–1775* (New York, 1962).

slave, especially, is heavily attested to by the growing movement for conversion, education, and even emancipation among
the lower and upper clergy. This movement began as early
as the end of the seventeenth century, and one of its first
advocates was Morgan Godwyn, the angry clergyman who
served both in the British West Indies and the colony of
Virginia, and whose *The Negro's and Indians Advocate*
(1680) created a good deal of sentiment. This growing
awareness of the complete lack of impact of the Church on
the Negro slaves, in sharp contrast to the Catholic Church in
the Spanish and French islands, as many Church of England
men noted,[87] caused the Bishop of London to put pressure
on the Crown.

In the royal instructions to Governor Culpeper of Virginia
in 1681–82, the Crown proposed that:

> Ye shall endeavour to get a Law passed for the restraining
> of any inhuman severity which by ill masters or overseers
> may be used towards their Christian Servants or Slaves.
> And you are alsoe with the assistance of the Council and
> Assembly, to find out the best means to facilitate and en-
> courage the conversion of Negroes to the Christian Religion,

[87] In his famous denunciation of West Indian slavery, for example, the
Reverend James Ramsay constantly contrasted the British to the French
treatment of slaves. "In the French colonies," he declared, "the public pays
an immediate attention to the treatment and instruction of slaves. The in-
tendants [gov't administrative officers] are charged with their protection,
proper missionaries are appointed for the purpose of training them up to a
certain degree of religious knowledge; and ample estates and funds are
allotted for their maintenance of these ecclesiastics." "The respect in which
marriage is held, brings a farther advantage to French slaves. The ceremony
is solemnized by the priest, and the tie continues for life. This gives them an
attachment to their families, . . . that is seldom seen among English slaves;
where the connection between the sexes is arbitrary, and too frequently
casual." Rev. James Ramsay, *An Essay on the Treatment of African Slaves
in the British Sugar Colonies* (London, 1784), 52, 54.

wherein you are to leave a due caution and regards to ye
property of the Inhabitants and safety of the Colonies.[88]

The unusual restraint of this request indicates the royal government's recognition of the primacy of local law and custom
over the humanitarian demands of the clergymen.

Nevertheless, the English hierarchy was becoming deeply
concerned over the failure of the colonials to Christianize the
Negro slaves. Finding that little could be accomplished directly through regular Church and governmental channels,
despite the establishment relationship of the Church, the
Bishops decided that the only alternative was a missionary
society, completely financed from England. Thus, in 1701
the hierarchy in England founded the famous Society for the
Propagation of the Gospel in Foreign Parts.[89]

That one of the primary aims of the Society was conversion of the slaves was understood by the Bishops from the
very beginning. Thus, in the annual sermon given to the Society in 1710, Bishop William Fleetwood bitterly attacked
the refusal of the masters of slaves to permit their conversion
to Christianity. He claimed the refusal to permit baptism and
Christian education was:

A thing so common in all our *Plantations* abroad, that I
have reason to doubt, whether there be any Exception of
any People of *ours*, who cause their slaves to be Baptized.
What do these people think of Christ? . . . That He who
came from Heaven, to purchase to Himself a Church, with
his own precious Blood, should sit contented, and behold
with unconcern, those who profess themselves his Servants,

[88] *The Virginia Magazine of History and Biography*, XXVIII (1920),
43–44.
[89] H. P. Thompson, *Into All Lands: The History of the Society for the
Propagation of the Gospel in Foreign Parts, 1701–1950* (London, 1951),
chap. 1.

excluding from its Gates those who would gladly enter if
they might, and exercising no less Cruelty to their Souls (as
far as they are able) than to their Bodies?

These People were made to be as Happy as themselves, and
are as capable of being so; and however hard their Condition
be in this World, with respect to their Captivity and Sub-
jugation. . . . They were bought with the same Price,
purchased with the same Blood of Christ, their common
Saviour and Redeemer; and on order to all this, they were
to have the Means of Salvation put into their Hands, they
were to be instructed in the Faith of *Christ*, to have the
Terms and Conditions fairly offered to them.

Not only did Bishop Fleetwood attack the very Christianity
of the masters, but he also considered that this was probably
their greatest sin, for he declared, "no Man living can assign
a better and more justifiable Cause, for God's with-holding
Mercy from a *Christian*, than that *Christian's* with-holding
the Mercy of *Christianity* from an Unbeliever."[90] The radical
Bishop even went so far as to attack slavery itself, holding, as Adam Smith was later to proclaim, that hired labor
was a far superior system and that slavery should be abolished. He attacked the ideas of colonists, which held
that Christianity challenged the slave status, but instead of
proclaiming the docility of slaves under Christian doctrine as
some clerics did, he properly attacked the Christianity of the
colonists who would refuse to treat fellow human beings with
Christian brotherly love. Finally, he proposed that the Society
take up the crucial task of Christianizing the infidels, Negroes,
and slaves, and that this example would have a powerful impact on the masters, who apparently were unimpressed by "the

[90] This sermon is reprinted in its entirety in Frank J. Klingberg, *Anglican Humanitarianism in Colonial New York* (Philadelphia, 1940), 203–4.

Example both of *French* and *Spaniards* . . . , who all along
have brought their Slaves to Baptism."[91]

This call appears to have been heeded, for in the annual
sermon of 1740, Bishop Secker pointed to the work of the
Society in this special area. But the Bishop noted the vast
difficulty still faced by the Church in this work as only a few
had been converted and thousands yet remained outside the
fold.

> For it is not to be expected, that Masters, too commonly
> negligent of Christianity themselves, will take much Pains
> to teach it to their Slaves: whom even the better Part of
> them are in a great measure habituated to consider, as they
> do their Cattle, merely with a View to the Profit arising
> from them. Not a few therefore have openly opposed their
> Instruction, from an Imagination, now indeed proved and
> acknowledged to be groundless, that Baptism would entitle
> them to Freedom. . . . And some, it may be feared, have
> been averse to their becoming Christians, because, after
> that, no Pretence will remain for not treating them like
> Men.[92]

Both within and without the Society, the upper clergy were
beginning, by the middle of the eighteenth century, to put
pressure on the colonies to change their local customs and
laws on these subjects, and to create a new panoply of beliefs that would permit the Church to carry on the work of
conversion in a positive atmosphere.

The Bishop of London in 1742 put great pressure on
Commissary Blair to get the local government to support a
school for Negroes, and to indicate to them his great zeal in

[91] *Ibid.*, 211.
[92] *Ibid.*, 217.

converting Negroes to the Christian faith.[93] But incapable of even fully protecting standard dogma and Church practice, Blair and his successors could accomplish little. As for the SPG, the demands on its resources were so great that it concentrated its efforts on the British West Indies, where the bulk of the New World slaves resided, and on the colonies in which the Church was unestablished.[94]

This meant, in essence, that whatever the feelings of the hierarchy in England as to the desirability of conversion of the slaves to Christianity and their participation in the sacraments, this desire had little if any impact on New World conditions. The religious life of the slave remained wholly dependent upon the will of his master, and this was determined almost exclusively by local custom. With no clergymen capable of opposing these assumptions and customs, the planters felt under no obligation to change their ways.

Unfortunately, custom was indifferent, if not openly hostile, to the conversion of Negro slaves. In the early years of the seventeenth century, there had existed the almost universal belief that conversion for the slave required his freedom, since Christians could not hold Christians in bondage. While the General Assembly eventually declared that this was not so,[95] the idea was hard to uproot, and persisted

[93] *William and Mary Quarterly*, 1st Series, IX (1901), 225.

[94] Thompson, *Into All Lands*, chap. 3.

[95] The Virginia legislature itself seriously accepted the thesis that Christianity was incompatible with slavery, and in its early definitions actually defined slaves as those who were not Christians. Thus in 1670 it enacted a statute which declared that "all servants not being christians imported into this country by shipping shalbe slaves for life." Hening, *Statutes*, II, 283. This was finally rectified in 1682 when the Assembly decreed that: "all servants except Turks and Moores . . . which shall be brought or imported into this country, either by sea or land, whether Negroes, . . . Mulattoes or Indians, who and whose parentage and native country are not christian, although afterwards, and before such their importation . . . they shall be converted to the christian faith; . . . shall be judged, deemed and taken to be slaves. . . ." *Ibid.*, 490–91.

throughout the colonial period. Even when this factor was resolved or admitted by the reluctant master, there was still the key fear of education making the slaves intractable. As the Reverend Hugh Jones reported, he constantly tried to disprove this latter assumption among colonials. "As for baptizing Indians and Negroes," he said, "several of the people disapprove of it, because they say it often makes them proud, and not so good servants: But these, and such objections, are easily refuted, for Christianity encourages and orders them to become more humble and better servants, and not worse, then when they were heathens." He did agree with general opinion, however, which held that Negro slaves should not be taught to read and write, since this "has been found to be dangerous upon several political accounts, especially self-preservation."[96]

While masters could be found who sponsored the baptism of their slaves and encouraged them to learn the catechism, and some who even read to them from the Bible, these were the exception rather than the rule. The pattern, in fact, was quite haphazard, and in the majority of cases conversion was never properly undertaken. This is well revealed in a survey of the colonial Church of Virginia carried out in the early eighteenth century. In 1724 Commissary Blair sent out an extraordinarily revealing and exhaustive questionnaire to all the parishes of Virginia. Among the questions asked was: "Are there any Infidels, bond or free, within your Parish; and what means are used for their conversion?" The 29 clergymen who answered the inquiry give the overwhelming impression of only moderate clerical interest in the problem, and general planter indifference, if not hostility. As the

---

[96] Jones, *Present State of Virginia*, 99.

Reverend George Robertson of Bristol Parish reported, "I have several times exhorted their Masters to send such of them as could speak English to Church to be catechised but they would not. Some masters instruct their Slaves at home and so bring them to baptism, but not many such."[97] The Reverend Henry Collings of St. Peter's Parish reported that of the Negro slaves in his parish "Some . . . are suffered by their respective masters to be baptized and to attend on divine service but others not."[98] The Reverend John Warden reported that in his parish "some masters will have their slaves baptised and others will not, by reason that they will not be surities for them in Baptism,"[99] while Alexander Forbes reported that in his parish the local Negro slaves "as soon as they are capable they are taught and baptised by the care of some Masters, but this too much neglected by many."[100] The clergymen of Henrico and Southwark parishes respectively replied of the slaves in their parishes that "their Masters, do no more than let some of them now and then go to Church for their Conversion," and that "there are some of their Masters on whom I do prevail to have them baptised and taught, but not many."[101] The Reverend John Brunskill of Willmington Parish probably best summed up the problem when he concluded that:

> The Negroes who are slaves to the whites cannot, I think, be said to be of any Religion for as there is no law of the Colony oblidging their Masters or Owners to instruct them

[97] William Stevens Perry (ed.), *Historical Collections Relating to the American Colonial Church*, 5 vols. (Hartford, 1870–78), I, 267.
[98] *Ibid.*, 269.
[99] *Ibid.*, 289.
[100] *Ibid.*, 295.
[101] *Ibid.*, 304, 306.

in the principles of Christianity and so they are hardly to be
persuaded by the Minister to take so much pains with them,
by which means the poor creatures generally live and die
without it.[102]

Even for the minority that were baptized, converted, and
taught the Christian religion, there were no positive rewards.
No matter how Christian, no master allowed his slaves to be
married. For if the sacrament of marriage was not to be made
totally ridiculous, Negro slaves could not be admitted: it
deprived human agencies of the right to separate the couple,
and this was never accepted. Even when the best of masters
died, the constant fluidity of fortunes meant that no slave
community could remain intact beyond a few generations.
Families were not sold together; to do so was uneconomic and
therefore impractical. As the Virginia Baptist chronicler John
Leland noted in 1790, "the marriage of slaves, is a subject not

[102] *Ibid.*, 277–78. Interestingly, the few records which survive of slave
education and conversion carried out by masters come not from Church of
England slave owners, but from Presbyterians and Quakers. Thus Roberts
Pleasants, one of the wealthiest planters of Virginia in the eighteenth century, and a Quaker, not only converted his slaves, but even educated and
eventually freed them. Adair P. Archer, "The Quakers' Attitude towards the
Revolution," *William and Mary Quarterly*, 2d Series, I (1921), 168. For his
part, the Presbyterian planter Colonel James Gordon in his journal in 1761
noted that "Several strange negroes come to Mr. Criswell [the local Presbyterian teacher] to be instructed, in which he takes great pains." *William
and Mary Quarterly*, 1st Series, XI (1903), 223. Nevertheless, despite these
and other efforts, the consensus of historical opinion is best summed up by
Marcus W. Jernegan who declared that throughout the colonial period,
"most of the slaves lived and died strangers to christianity" and that "with
comparatively few exceptions the conversion of negro slaves was not
seriously undertaken by their masters. On the contrary many of them
strenuously and persistently opposed the Church of England, and the Society
for the Propagation of the Gospel in Foreign Parts. . . ." Marcus W. Jernegan, "Slavery and Conversion in the American Colonies," *American Historical Review*, XXI, No. 3 (April, 1916), 504; also see Jerome W. Jones, "The
Established Virginia Church and the Conversion of Negroes and Indians,
1620–1760," *Journal of Negro History*, XLVI, No. 1 (January, 1961), 12–31.

known in our code of laws. What promeses soever they make, their masters may and do part at pleasure."[103]

As for the complex web of social organizations to which the Cuban slave had recourse this simply did not exist under the established Church of Virginia. There were no fraternal brotherhoods, no great processionals and special holidays, and absolutely no syncretization of Christian belief with folk religion of African origin. For the Negro slaves on the frontier of Virginia after 1740 there did exist the possibility of admission into the evangelical movement known as the "Great Awakening." From 1740 and especially after 1760 numbers of Methodist, Baptist, Presbyterian, and a host of other sect preachers began invading the frontier counties of Virginia above the tidewater.[104] For these preachers, most of whom like Wesley himself were bitter opponents of slavery, welcomed the Negroes into the Church. Thus John Leland in his Virginia Chronicle of 1790 reported:

The poor slaves, under all their hardships, discover as great inclination for religion as the free-born do, when they engage in the service of God, they spare no pains. It is nothing strange for them to walk 20 miles on Sunday morning to meeting, and back again at night. They are remarkable for learning a toon soon, and have very melodious voices.

They cannot read, and therefore are more exposed to delusion than the whites are; but many of them give clear, rational accounts of a work of grace in their harts, and evidence of the same by their lives. When religion is lively they are remarkable fond of meeting together, to sing, pray and exhort, and sometimes preach, and seem to be unwearied in the procession. They seem in general to put more con-

---

[103] John Leland, *The Virginia Chronicle* (Norfolk, 1790), 8.
[104] *Ibid.*, 21 ff.; also see Wesley M. Gewehr, *The Great Awakening in Virginia, 1740–1790* (Durham, 1930).

fidence in their own colour, then they do in whites; when they attempt to preach, they seldom fail of being very zealous; their language is broken, but they understand each other, and the whites may gain their ideas. A few of them have undertaken to administer baptism, but it generally ends in confusion; they commonly are more noisy in time of preaching than the whites, and are more subject to bodily exercise, and if they meet with any encouragement in these things, they grow extravagant.[105]

But these camp meetings and nonhierarchical churches were not open to the majority of Virginia Negroes, who lived in the predominantly Church of England areas. Nor were the masters too ready to permit them to go to revivalist gatherings. As Leland himself notes: ". . . many masters and overseers will whip and torture the poor creatures for going to meeting, even at night, when the labor of the day is done."[106] As fear of insurrection developed in the period after independence, such meetings became less and less common, public gatherings of more than a few slaves being prohibited.[107]

Not only was the Church incapable of undertaking a general conversion of the slaves, but it was also unable to promote manumission. Thus the common pattern of church-inspired individual planter manumission, which was accepted custom and practice in Cuba, was unknown in Protestant Virginia. Though the Methodists and Quakers early demanded that their members give up slave trading and emancipate their slaves, and though several revolutionary leaders followed their enlightenment thought to its logical conclusion

[105] Leland, *Virginia Chronicle*, 13.

[106] *Ibid.*, 9.

[107] C. G. Woodson, *The Education of the Negro Prior to 1861* (New York, 1915), chaps. vii, viii.

and freed their Negroes, no powerful undercurrent of emancipation ever occurred. Quaker emancipations were few and of little consequence, and the Methodist leadership was soon forced to condone the existence of slaveholding even among its traveling clergy, and to give up its proposals for emancipation.[108] As for the Anglican hierarchy, while it too developed a powerful commitment to emancipation at the end of the eighteenth century, it took forceful Parliamentary legislation to carry out emancipation even in the West Indies. As for Virginia this emancipation movement never found echo in the local episcopal hierarchy, when the latter was finally established in 1790.[109]

The clergy of Virginia were unable to convince the planters that emancipation was a good act in the sight of God, and was to be considered a common and accepted form of pious action, as in Cuba. Nor could the morally aroused and committed clergy, of whatever denomination, convince the masters that slavery was essentially a moral evil and that on these grounds the slaves should be emancipated as soon as possible. Neither forcing emancipation on moral grounds from above, nor having it become a part of routine common practice from below, the whole emancipation movement in Virginia was at best a haphazard and distinctly minor affair.

[108] On the failure of the Methodists, see Gewehr, *Great Awakening,* 242–49; and for the Quakers see Thomas E. Drake, *Quakers and Slavery in America* (New Haven, 1950).

[109] Though the Anglican Church consecrated native candidates between 1784 and 1790, which enabled the Americans to establish the Protestant Episcopal Church in the United States, the new bishops were subservient to local interests and Vestry government was in no way changed. See Cross, *Anglican Episcopate,* 263 ff.; Clara O. Loveland, *The Critical Years: The Reconstruction of the Anglican Church in the United States of America: 1780–1789* (Greenwich, 1956); Edward Lewis Goodwin, *The Colonial Church in Virginia* (Milwaukee, 1927), 127 ff., for the early bishops of the Diocese of Virginia.

In fact, from the late seventeenth to the late eighteenth century it was to all intents and purposes outlawed by the state. By 1691 the reaction had become so intense that the General Assembly of Virginia declared that "great inconveniences may happen to this countrey by setting of negroes and mulattoes free," and provided under heavy penalty that owners who emancipated their slaves had to pay for their transportation out of the country within six months.[110] Not satisfied with this restriction on the growth of the free Negro class, the legislature next made it impossible for a master to free his slaves even on his own initiative. By a law of 1721 all emancipation was prohibited "except for some meritorious services, to be adjudged and allowed by the governor and council."[111]

By these extreme measures, the free Negro population, which probably numbered around 350 in 1691, was kept for the next century to its natural increase alone; by 1782 there were only some 2,800 freedmen in the state.[112] In this year, however, under the impact of the revolution and the growth of clerical opposition, a new law permitted open emancipation at the discretion of the owner.[113] By the first federal census of 1790, the number of freedmen had increased to 12,866. Even with this increase, the free colored population represented only 4% of the total colored population. Nor did the half-century between the first federal census and the Civil War see any major change. The percentage slowly rose from decade to decade, but with almost the identical number of colored, just over 550,000 in Cuba and Virginia in 1860/1861,

[110] Hening, *Statutes*, III, 87–88.
[111] *Ibid.*, IV, 132.
[112] John H. Russell, *The Free Negro in Virginia, 1619–1865* (Baltimore, 1913), 10–11.
[113] Hening, *Statutes*, XI, 39–40.

Virginia had only 58,042 freedmen (or 11%) to Cuba's 213,167 (or 39%).[114] As for the development of education for the free Negroes, this was informal and haphazard in the extreme, except for one short-lived experiment. In the late 1720s, Dr. Thomas Bray, who had been commissary in the state of Maryland for the Bishop of London, helped found a group of missionaries known as "Bray's Associates" who directed considerable attention to founding schools for Negroes in the American colonies. A leading founder of the SPG, Dr. Bray received a private donation of £900 for this purpose.[115] After setting up a successful school with the aid of Benjamin Franklin in Philadelphia in 1759, Dr. Bray helped establish a Negro school in Williamsburg in 1764. Under the direction of Commissary Dawson, local clerics, and Mrs. Ann Wager, the school soon opened its doors to 24 Negro students, and made major progress in the area.[116] It appears to have won some local support, for a local printer, Mr. William Hunter, left in his will in 1761 some £7 for the support of Mrs. Wager.[117] But despite the initial success and support granted to the school, with the death of Mrs. Wager in 1774, the school ceased to operate. In fact, in the agitation of those years all the Negro and Indian schools on the North American continent founded by Dr. Bray and his associates, as well as by the SPG, collapsed. The Williamsburg school seems to have been the model for another which lasted five years in the 1770s in

114 U.S. Bureau of the Census, *Negro Population 1790–1915* (Washington, 1918), 57, table 6. It should be noted that Virginia had the largest number and percentage of freedmen in its colored population in 1860 of any slave state in the Union except Maryland, which was a unique border state.
115 Thompson, *Into All Lands*, 9–19, 42–43.
116 Mary F. Goodwin, "Christianizing and Educating the Negro in Colonial Virginia," *Historical Magazine of the Protestant Episcopal Church*, I, No. 3 (September, 1932), 148–51.
117 *William and Mary Quarterly*, 1st Series, VII (1899), 13.

Fredericksburg, but with the American Revolution, the source of English enthusiasm and funds for these schools was destroyed and local planter interest seems to have become exhausted.[118] Apparently neither free nor slave Negroes were permitted regular education by the local county schools.

There was some attempt by the Vestries, however, to provide for the free Negroes, orphans, and poor some type of apprenticeship in which they were also taught to read and write by the person to whom they were indentured. The Vestry of Petsworth Parish in 1716 required that for his indenture, Mr. Ralph Bevis was to:

> give George Petsworth, a mulattoe boy of the age of 2 years, 3 years' schooling, and carefully to Instruct him afterwards that he may read well in any part of the Bible, also to instruct and Learn him ye sd mulattoe boy such Lawful way and ways that he may be able after his Indented time expired to gitt his own Liveing, and to allow him sufficient meat, Drink, washing, and apparill, until the expiration of ye sd time &c. . . .[119]

But these indentured and apprenticeship programs were for only a few free Negroes, and aside from the temporary Negro school experiment on the eve of the American Revolution, the Church seems to have made almost no serious or successful effort to educate the Virginia Negro. No Negro was admitted to William and Mary College, and none appears to have been trained by the Church in local parish schools for the liberal professions, as was the case in Cuba, while in

118 Thompson, *Into All Lands*, chap. 4.
119 *William and Mary Quarterly*, 1st Series, V (1897), 219; also see the case of Robert, son of the free Negro woman Cuba, who was bound out in Lancaster County in 1719 till his twenty-first birthday. *William and Mary Quarterly*, 1st Series, VIII (1899), 82.

the harsh reaction which took place by the early nineteenth century, even basic literacy was denied the freedmen.[120]

Thus the Virginia Church, dominated by the planter elite, offered no educational escape opportunities either for free or slave Negroes. It totally denied the right to slave marriages, and by and large in the colonial period did not even Christianize the majority of African Negroes. Finally, the established Church in Virginia did nothing to enrich the community life of the Negroes. The religious brotherhoods, the pageantry and processions, the folk religious syncretization, which were such an important part of the fabric of Catholic Cuba, were alien to Anglicanism. Although the dissenter groups in the "Great Awakening" after 1740 provided some compensation in the evangelical and revivalist meetings (which were to give birth to the future Negro church movement) these were confined to the frontier in the colonial period and involved only a few thousand Negro slaves. For the "Great Awakening" in Virginia was the work of only a handful of ministers and never penetrated into the Tidewater parishes where the overwhelming majority of slaves lived under Anglican masters.

Within the great plantation areas, despite all the efforts of the Bishop of London and his commissaries, the few local clergy were hard pressed to maintain even the established Church among the white colonists. As late as 1774, Virginia had only 104 Church of England clergymen,[121] in a total population of roughly 447,000 persons,[122] just one to over 4,000 colonists. Nor was this ratio unusual, for the Reverend

[120] In 1800 the General Assembly specifically prohibited the local parishes from requiring the masters to teach the indentured free colored children to read or write, and by the 1830s the state legislature was prohibiting all types of schooling and education for even free Negroes who were willing to pay the costs. Russell, *Free Negro in Virginia*, 140, 144–45.
[121] Brydon, *Virginia's Mother Church*, II, 608–14.
[122] Evarts B. Greene and Virginia D. Harrington, *American Population before the Federal Census of 1790* (New York, 1932), 141.

James Ramsay in his attack on slavery in the British West
Indies asked for an ideal of one clergyman per 3,000 in-
habitants to carry out the needed Christianization of the
Negroes.[123]

Few in number, operating on provisional contracts based
on the consent of the congregation, completely subservient
to the planter-dominated Vestry, and working against in-
grained opposition to conversion, it is surprising that the
Church of England accomplished as much as it did. Unfortunately, when moral pressure within the Church finally
brought the metropolitan hierarchy to put pressure on the
Crown and Parliament to override local slave legislation, it
was already too late for Virginia. The antislavery crusade did
not fully get under way, despite the sentiments of such early
leaders as Bishop Fleetwood, until after 1783, when the
colonies were no longer a part of the British Empire. Although it was to have a profound influence on the British
West Indies and on the abolition of the slave trade, the
severance of political ties and the establishment of an independent Episcopalian Church in Virginia rendered the North
American colonies impervious to this great moral crusade.
How differently events might otherwise have turned out is
shown by the impact of the aroused Church on the eventual
education, Christianization, and emancipation of the British
West Indian Negro slave.[124]

Too involved with defense of its very position at home in
the seventeenth century, the Church of England had allowed
the colonists to usurp its power and authority, and to create
for themselves a congregational church organization. While

[123] Ramsay, *Essay on the Treatment of African Slaves*, 265–66.
[124] For the history of this struggle see Reginald Coupland, *The British
Anti-Slavery Movement*, 2d ed. (London, 1964), along with Frank Klingberg, *The Anti-Slavery Movement in England: A Study in English Humanitarianism* (New Haven, 1926).

this allowed more religious liberty for the white colonists, and greater individual expression in this age of religious nonconformity and dissent, it was fatal to the rights of the Negroes and mulattoes, slave and free. When the Church finally turned its attention to the issue, it was too late, and the emancipation of the colonies of the North American continent destroyed the hope of the colored peoples that the Church would protect their rights and liberties as human beings.

IV

Having compared the impact of the Church on the lives of the Negro slaves within two distinct New World colonies, we have a clearer conception of the uniqueness and the consequent differences between the two institutions of Negro slavery. As Elkins and Tannenbaum have properly pointed out, the Church was one of the most crucial institutions which had the power to intervene in the relations between master and slave and to help mold that relationship.

In Cuba, the Church took an immediate daily concern and involvement, and succeeded in molding custom and patterns, as well as commanding obedience to higher authorities. From the beginning the Church viewed its own role toward the slaves as distinct from that of the masters and succeeded in establishing its claim on the mind, soul, and time of the Negroes, free or slave. Not troubled by the belief that Christianity was incompatible with the slave status and working with established Iberian attitudes toward the Negro and his place within the Catholic society, the Cuban clergy were able to mold and modify the conditions of human bondage for the African Negro. Capable of carrying imperial and synodal edicts into immediate effect, the Cuban clergy effectively Christianized the imported slaves and freely admitted them into the Church. For the slaves this admittance provided inestimable social advantages and rights, as well as duties, and a host of concrete immediate advantages, from rest days on Sunday to the full sanctity of the family through the sacrament of marriage. In the syncretization of African religions in folk catholicism, and in the organization of *cofradías, cabildos,* and religious processionals, the Africans were provided with a rich cultural and community existence, which paradoxically eased their assimilation into society. Finally, the Church stood as the great potential benefactor to the exceptionally able, who, through church education, could achieve a new upper-class status within society.

None of these things occurred for the Virginia Negro. Beginning with the planters' open hostility even to the admittance of Negroes into the Church, and faced by usurpation of authority by the parishioners, the fight even for minimal conversion was an uphill struggle for the Church of England. Involved with defense of the Church at home, the Anglican hierarchy allowed the Church abroad to be converted into a democratic congregational organization. It therefore had as much as it could do to guarantee church conformity among the white colonists, and had little energy to spare for the Negro, and even less for the Indian. Fully aware of the progress of the Catholic Church in these two areas, and morally sensitive to the issues, the metropolitan Anglican hierarchy could not develop enough power and unity prior to 1776 to break down the American congregational control and overcome planter hostility toward its conversion and incipient emancipation efforts.

Unlike the Cuban Church, the Church of England could not rely on the Crown for unquestioned support on these matters, for in the organization of the Empire, control over slavery and the Negro was left exclusively to the local government. Thus the Anglican Church could not build up a panoply either of canonical or civil law to guarantee free entry of the Negroes into the Church, and even more importantly to provide them with the full rights to the sacraments. As for the local legislature, the glaring silence of Virginia law as to the religious rights and condition of the Negro slave reflects the totally marginal character of slave Christianity, where it even existed. With such hostility built up in the colonial period against conversion, it was impossible for the Church even to suggest that slaves be legally married before God, or that the family had to be protected against the economic needs of the planter.

Even in the revivalist churches of the upland parishes, the "Great Awakening" and the participation of the Negro slaves was a short-lived affair, and within a few decades of Independence, the Virginia branches of the Baptist, Methodist, and Presbyterian churches had conformed to planter opinion and had, by and large, contained slave conversion and participation to a minimum. As for the Virginia Episcopal Church, the successor after 1790 to the Church of England, its own decay and even greater dependence on planter support, made it take even less of an interest in Negroes, slave or free, than its colonial originator.

Denied the full rights of the Christian, with his family unrecognized by the Church or the state, with his previous religious experience rendered totally useless and destroyed, and his chances for self and community expression severely curtailed if not openly discouraged by the local parish, the Virginia Negro slave faced a harsh world dominated by his master, and with little possibility of protective intervention and support from an outside institution.

While the relationship of the Church to the slave was only one of several relationships, it was probably the most important nonplanter one available. Because of this, the success or failure of the Anglican or Catholic Church to mold the life and soul of the Negro slaves had a profound impact on the personality, social organization, and even eventual assimilation of the Negro into Cuban and Virginian society.

The Myth of the
Friendly Master

MARVIN HARRIS

The argument in the previous chapters has been that differences in race relations within Latin America are at root a matter of the labor systems in which the respective subordinate and superordinate groups became enmeshed. I have already attempted to show how a number of cultural traits and institutions which were permitted to survive, or were deliberately encouraged under one system, were discouraged or suppressed in the other. It remains to be shown how the specific combination of features which characterize lowland race relations more narrowly construed can be accounted for by the same set of principles.

At present, probably the majority of American scholars who have found a moment to ponder the peculiar aspects of the Brazilian interracial "paradise" are devoted to an opposite belief. What could be more obvious than the inadequacy of a materialist explanation of the Brazilian pattern? How can plantation slavery be made to explain anything about the lack of interracial hostility in Brazil? Was it not a plantation system in the United States South which bred a condition contrary in every detail to that of Brazil?

The current vogue of opinion about this contrast derives in large measure from the work of Frank Tannenbaum, a noted United States historian, and Gilberto Freyre, Brazil's best-known sociologist. The theories of these influential scholars overlap at many points. It is their contention that the laws, values, religious precepts, and personalities of the English colonists differed from those of the Iberian colonists. These initial psychological and ideological differences were sufficient to overcome whatever tendency the plantation system may have exerted toward parallel rather than divergent evolution.

Freyre's theories, originally proposed in his classic study of Brazilian plantation life, *Casa grande e senzala*, have remained virtually unchanged for over thirty years. What most impresses Freyre about Brazilian slavery is the alleged easygoing, humanized relations between master and slave, especially between master and female slave. Slaves, while subject to certain disabilities and although sometimes cruelly treated, frequently came to play an emotionally significant role in the intimate life of their white owners. A high rate of miscegenation was one of the hallmarks of this empathy between the races. The Portuguese not only took Negro and mulatto women as mistresses and concubines, but they sometimes spurned their white wives in order to enjoy the favors of duskier beauties. Behind these favorable omens, visible from the very first days of contact, was a fundamental fact of national character, namely, the Portuguese had no color prejudice. On the contrary, their long experience under Moorish tutelage is said to have prepared them to regard people of darker hue as equals, if not superiors:

> The singular predisposition of the Portuguese to the hybrid, slave-exploiting colonization of the tropics is to be

explained in large part by the ethnic or, better, the cultural past of a people existing indeterminately between Europe and Africa and belonging uncompromisingly to neither one nor the other of the two continents.[1]

Other colonizers were not as successful as the Portuguese because their libidos were more conservative. Especially poorly endowed sexually were the "Anglo-Saxon Protestants."

The truth is that in Brazil, contrary to what is to be observed in other American countries and in those parts of Africa that have been recently colonized by Europeans, the primitive culture—the Amerindian as well as the African— has not been isolated into hard, dry indigestible lumps. . . . Neither did the social relations between the two races, the conquering and the indigenous one, ever reach that point of sharp antipathy or hatred, the grating sound of which reaches our ears from all the countries that have been colonized by Anglo-Saxon Protestants. The friction here (in Brazil) was smoothed by the lubricating oil of a deep-going miscegenation. . . .[2]

The next and fatal step in this line of reasoning is to assert that the special psychological equipment of the Portuguese, not only in Brazil but everywhere in "The World the Portuguese Created,"[3] yields hybrids and interracial harmony. In 1952, after a tour of Portuguese colonies as an honored guest of the Salazar government, Freyre declared that the Portuguese were surrounded in the Orient, America, and Africa with half-caste "luso-populations" and "a sympathy on the

[1] Gilberto Freyre, *The Masters and the Slaves* (New York, 1956), 4.
[2] *Ibid.*, 181–82.
[3] Gilberto Freyre, *O mundo que o português criou* (Rio de Janeiro, 1940).

part of the native which contrasts with the veiled or open hatred directed toward the other Europeans."[4] How Freyre could have been hoodwinked into finding resemblances between race relations in Angola and Mozambique and Brazil is hard to imagine. My own findings, based on a year of field work in Mozambique, have since been supported by the field and library research of James Duffy.[5] If any reasonable doubts remained about the falsity of Freyre's luso-tropical theory, tragic events in Angola should by now have swept them away. The fact is that the Portuguese are responsible for setting off the bloodiest of all of the recent engagements between the whites and Negroes in Africa (including the Mau Mau). And the Portuguese, alone of all the former African colonial powers, now stand shoulder to shoulder with the citizens of that incorrigible citadel of white supremacy, the Republic of South Africa, baited and damned from Zanzibar to Lagos.

It is true that the Portuguese *in Portugal* tend to be rather neutral on the subject of color differences, if they ever think about such things at all. But this datum can only be significant to those who believe that discrimination is caused by prejudice, when the true relationship is quite the opposite. When the innocent Portuguese emigrants get to Africa, they find

[4] Gilberto Freyre, *Um brasileiro em terras portuguêsas* (Lisbon, 1952), 39.
[5] Marvin Harris, *Portugal's African "Wards"* (New York, 1958); Harris, "Labor Emigration among the Mozambique Thonga," *Africa* 29 (1959), 50–66; James Duffy, *Portugal in Africa* (Cambridge, 1962); Duffy, *Portuguese Africa* (Cambridge, 1959). "Colonial authorities speak of Portugal's civilizing mission, but the realities of life for the Africans in the Colonies are grim. They are subject to an abusive contract labor system. . . . The standard of wages is among the lowest in Africa. . . . Social services for Africans are either minimal or nonexistent. *And, perhaps, most important of all, Africans have become the object of a growing racial prejudice created by the rapid influx of white settlers.*" (Duffy, "Portugal's Colonies in Africa," *Foreign Policy Bulletin* 40 (1961), 90. Italics are mine.)

that legally, economically, and socially, white men can take advantage of black men, and it doesn't take long for them to join in the act. Within a year after his arrival, the Portuguese learns that blacks are inferior to whites, that the Africans have to be kept in their place, and that they are indolent by nature and have to be forced to work. What we call prejudices are merely the rationalizations which we acquire in order to prove to ourselves that the human beings whom we harm are not worthy of better treatment.

Actually the whole issue of the alleged lack of racial or color prejudice among the Portuguese (and by extension among the Spanish as well) is totally irrelevant to the main question. If, as asserted, the Iberians initially lacked any color prejudice, what light does this shed upon the Brazilian and other Latin American lowland interracial systems? The distinguishing feature of these systems is not that whites have no color prejudices. On the contrary, color prejudice as we have seen is a conspicuous and regular feature in all the plantation areas. The parts of the system which need explaining are the absence of a descent rule; the absence of distinct socially significant racial groups; and the ambiguity of racial identity. In Portuguese Africa none of these features are present. The state rules on who is a native and who is a white and the condition of being a native is hereditary:

> Individuals of the Negro race or their descendants who were born or habitually reside in the said Provinces and who do not yet possess the learning and the social and individual habits presupposed for the integral application of the public and private law of Portuguese citizens are considered to be "natives."[6]

[6] Estatuto Indigena, May 1954, quoted in Harris, *Portugal's African "Wards,"* 7.

As for miscegenation, the supposedly color-blind Portuguese libido had managed by 1950 to produce slightly more than 50,000 officially recognized mixed types in an African population of 10 million after 400 years of contact.[7] This record should be compared with the product of the monochromatic libidos of the Dutch invaders of South Africa—in Freyre's terms Anglo-Saxon Protestants to the hilt—a million and a half official hybrids (coloreds).[8] It is time that grown men stopped talking about racially prejudiced sexuality. In general, when human beings have the power, the opportunity, and the need, they will mate with members of the opposite sex regardless of color or the identity of grandfather. Whenever free breeding in a human population is restricted, it is because a larger system of social relations is menaced by such freedom.

This is one of the points about which Tannenbaum and Freyre disagree. Tannenbaum quite correctly observes that "the process of miscegenation was part of the system of slavery, and not just of Brazilian slavery. . . . The dynamics of race contact and sex interests were stronger than prejudice. . . . This same mingling of the races and classes occurred in the United States. The record is replete with the occurrence, in spite of law, doctrine, and belief. Every traveler in the South before the Civil War comments on the widespread miscegenation. . . ."[9] But it should also be pointed out that there is no concrete evidence to indicate that the rank and file of English colonists were initially any more or less prejudiced than the Latins. It is true that the English

---

[7] Homer Jack, *Angola: Repression and Revolt in Portuguese Africa* (New York, 1960), 7; *Recenseamento Geral* (Província de Moçambique, 1953), xxxi.

[8] Absolom Vilakazi, "Race Relations in South Africa," in *Race Relations in World Perspective*, ed. Andrew W. Lind (Honolulu, 1955), 313.

[9] Frank Tannenbaum, *Slave and Citizen* (New York, 1947), 121–23.

colonists very early enacted laws intended to prevent marriage between white women and Negro men and between white men and Negro women. Far from indicating a heritage of anti-Negro prejudices, however, these laws confirm the presence of strong attraction between the males and females of both races. The need for legal restriction certainly suggests that miscegenation was not at all odious to many of the English colonists.

The idea of assigning differential statuses to white indentured servants and Negro workers was definitely not a significant part of the ideological baggage brought over by the earliest colonists, at least not to an extent demonstrably greater than among the Latin colonists. It is true, as Carl Degler has shown, that the differentiation between white indentured servants and Negro indentured servants had become conspicuous before the middle of the seventeenth century even though the legal formulation was not completed until the end of the century. But who would want to suggest that there was absolutely no prejudice against the Negroes immediately after contact? Ethnocentrism is a universal feature of inter-group relations and obviously both the English and the Iberians were prejudiced against foreigners, white and black. The facts of life in the New World were such, however, that Negroes, being the most defenseless of all the immigrant groups, were discriminated against and exploited more than any others. Thus the Negroes were not enslaved because the British colonists specifically despised dark-skinned people and regarded them alone as properly suited to slavery; the Negroes came to be the object of the virulent prejudices because they and they alone could be enslaved. Judging from the very nasty treatment suffered by white indentured servants, it was obviously not sentiment which prevented the Virginia planters from enslaving their fellow Englishmen.

They undoubtedly would have done so had they been able to get away with it. But such a policy was out of the question as long as there was a King and a Parliament in England. The absence of preconceived notions about what ought to be the treatment of enslaved peoples forms a central theme in Tannenbaum's explanation of United States race relations. According to Tannenbaum, since the English had gotten rid of slavery long before the Discovery, they had no body of laws or traditions which regulated and humanized the slave status. Why this legal lacuna should have been significant for the course run by slavery in the United States is quite obscure. Even Degler, who accepts the Freyre-Tannenbaum approach, points out that it was "possible for almost any kind of status to be worked out."[10] One might reasonably conclude

[10] Carl Degler, "Slavery and the Genesis of American Race Prejudice," *Comparative Studies in Society and History* 2 (1960), 51. This article is an attack on Oscar and Mary Handlin's theory (in "The Origins of the Southern Labor System," *William and Mary Quarterly* 7 (1950), 199–222) that the differentiation between Negro and white indentured servants developed gradually during the seventeenth century and that initially there was little specifically anti-Negro discrimination or prejudice. Degler contends that "the status of the Negro in the English colonies was worked out within a framework of discrimination; that from the outset, as far as the available evidence tells us, the Negro was treated as an inferior to the white man, servant or free" (52). Degler suffers from the illusion that early examples of discriminatory treatment of Negroes in the English colonies are relevant to the Tannenbaum (-Freyre) explanation of Latin American race relations. Somehow or other Degler has received the impression that in Latin America there was not an equally early display of discrimination. But of course, in both cases, slavery was reserved for Negroes, Indians, and half-castes. Neither English nor Iberian whites were ever enslaved in the New World; surely this is an instance of discriminatory treatment. Degler explicitly accepts the Tannenbaum (-Freyre) point of view, despite the fact that his article really amounts to a denial of the significance of ideological and psychological factors in the explanation of race relations. The early *de facto* enslavement of Negroes, even when there was no body of law sanctioning slavery, is certainly a rather negative comment on Tannenbaum's use of law as evidence of behavior. To conclude that slavery ". . . was molded by the early colonists' discrimination against the outlander" (66) is to confirm that prejudice followed discrimination, whereas it is essential for the Tannenbaum (-Freyre) point of view that the causality be reversed.

that the first settlers were not overly concerned with race differences, and that they might have remained that way (as many Englishmen have) had they not been brought into contact with Negroes under conditions wholly dictated by the implacable demands of a noxious and "peculiar" institution. Let us turn now to the main substance of Tannenbaum's theory. Tannenbaum correctly believes that the critical difference between race relations in the United States and in Latin America resides in the physical and psychological (he says "moral") separation of the Negro from the rest of society. "In spite of his adaptability, his willingness, and his competence, in spite of his complete identification with the *mores* of the United States, he is excluded and denied. . . ." Also, quite correctly, Tannenbaum stresses the critical role of the free Negro and mulatto in Latin America. Manumission appears to have been much more common, and the position of the freed man was much more secure than elsewhere. Free Negroes and mulattoes quickly came to outnumber the slaves. However, according to Tannenbaum, this phenomenon came about because the slave was endowed with "a moral personality before emancipation . . . which . . . made the transition from slavery to freedom easy and his incorporation into the free community natural."[11] The Negro and mulatto were never sharply cut off from the rest of society because the Latin slave was never cut off from the rest of humanity. This was because slavery in southern Europe and Latin America was embedded in a legal, ethical, moral, and religious matrix which conspired to preserve the slave's individual integrity as the possessor of an immortal human soul. The "definition" of the slave as merely an unfortunate human being, primarily according to state and canonical code, is given most weight:

[11] Tannenbaum, *Slave and Citizen*, 42, 100.

For if one thing stands out clearly from the study of slavery, it is that the definition of man as a moral being proved the most important influence both in the treatment of the slave and in the final abolition of slavery.[12]

Note that it is not merely being claimed that there was a critical difference between Latin American and United States race relations during and after slavery, but that the very institution of slavery itself was one thing in the United States and the British West Indies and another thing in Latin America:

There were, briefly speaking, three slave systems in the Western Hemisphere. The British, American, Dutch, and Danish were at one extreme, and the Spanish and Portuguese at the other. In between these two fell the French. . . . If one were forced to arrange these systems of slavery in order of severity, the Dutch would seem to stand as the harshest, the Portuguese as the mildest, and the French in between. . . .[13]

The contention that the condition of the average slave in the English colonies was worse than that of the average slave in the Latin colonies obscures the main task which confronts us, which is to explain why the treatment of the free mulatto and free Negro were and are so different. To try to explain why the slaves were treated better in Latin America than in the United States is a waste of time, for there is no conceivable way in which we can now be certain that they were indeed treated better in one place than the other. It is true that a large number of travelers can be cited, especially from the nineteenth century, who were convinced that the slaves were happier under Spanish and Portuguese masters than

[12] *Ibid.*, vii.
[13] *Ibid.*, 65n.

under United States masters. But there was plenty of dissenting opinion. Tannenbaum makes no provision for the fact that the English planters had what we would today call a very bad press, since thousands of intellectuals among their own countrymen were in the vanguard of the abolitionist movement. The West Indian and Southern planters, of course, were in total disagreement with those who preferred slavery under foreign masters. Actually all of the distinctions between the Anglo-American and Latin slave systems which Tannenbaum proposes were already the subject of debate at the beginning of the eighteenth century between Anglo-American abolitionists and Anglo-American planters. For example, in 1827, the Jamaican planter Alexander Barclay responded to the English critics of his island's slave system as follows:

> According to Mr. Stephen [author of *Slavery of the British West India Colonies*] there exists among his countrymen in the West Indies, an universal feeling of hatred and contempt of the Negroes. . . . It is by this assumed hatred and contempt, that he strives to give probability to the most incredible charges of cruelty and oppression; and indeed, in many cases, this alleged feeling of aversion and abhorrence on the part of the whites, is the sole ground for supposing that the charges should be made, and the sole proof of them. Such things must have happened, because the colonists hate the Negroes. Now, I most solemnly affirm, not only that I am unconscious of any such surely unnatural feelings having place in my own breast, but that I have never seen proof of its existence in the breasts of others.[14]

All slave owners of whatever nationality always seem to have been convinced that "their" slaves were the happiest of

[14] Alexander Barclay, *A Practical View of the Present State of Slavery in the West Indies* (London, 1827), xi–xii.

earthly beings. Barclay claims that the Jamaican slaves celebrated the cane harvest with an interracial dance:

> In the evening, they assemble in their master's or man-
> ager's house, and, as a matter of course, take possession of
> the largest room, bringing with them a fiddle and tambourine.
> Here all authority and all distinction of colour ceases; black
> and white, overseer and book-keeper, mingle together in
> the dance.[15]

At Christmas time the same thing happens. The slaves

> . . . proceed to the neighbouring plantation villages, and
> always visit the master's or manager's house, into which they
> enter without ceremony, and where they are joined by the
> white people in a dance.[16]

Concludes Barclay: "All is life and joy, and certainly it is
one of the most pleasing sights that can be imagined."[17] In
the United States, equally rapturous descriptions of the slave's
lot were a conspicuous part of the ideological war between
North and South. Many planters felt that their slaves were
better off than the mass of Northern whites, and Southern
poets did not hesitate to cap their comparisons of free and
slave labor with panegyrics

> . . . on the happy life of the slave, with all his needs
> provided, working happily in the fields by day, enjoying
> the warm society of his family in the cabin at night, idling
> through life in "the summer shade, the winter sun," and
> without fear of the poorhouse at its close . . . until we

[15] *Ibid.,* 10.
[16] *Ibid.,* 11.
[17] *Ibid.*

finally find the slave "luxuriating" in a "lotus-bearing paradise."[18]

If one were so inclined by lack of an understanding of the nature of sociological evidence, it would not be difficult to paint a picture in which the position of the Anglo-American slave system was promoted from last to first place. Freyre himself provides enough material on cruelty in the Brazilian plantations to fill at least a corner in a chamber of horrors:

> And how, in truth, are the hearts of us Brazilians to acquire the social virtues if from the moment we open our eyes we see about us the cruel distinction between master and slave, and behold the former, at the slightest provocation or sometimes out of mere whim, mercilessly rending the flesh of our own kind with lashes?[19]
>
> There are not two or three but many instances of the cruelties of the ladies of the big house toward their helpless blacks. There are tales of *sinhámoças* who had the eyes of pretty *mucamas* gouged out and then had them served to their husband for dessert, in a jelly-dish, floating in blood that was still fresh. . . . There were others who kicked out the teeth of their women slaves with their boots, or who had their breasts cut off, their nails drawn, or their faces and ears burned.[20]

Another Brazilian observer, Arthur Ramos, goes even further:

> During the period of slavery, suppression and punishment prevented almost any spontaneous activity. . . . The number of instruments of torture employed was numerous and profoundly odious. . . . There was the *tronco*, of

[18] Bernard Mandel, *Labor: Slave and Free* (New York, 1955), 99.
[19] Freyre, *The Masters and the Slaves*, 392, quoting Lopes Gomes.
[20] *Ibid.*, 351.

wood or of iron, an instrument which held the slave fast
at the ankles and in the grip of which he was often kept
for days on end; the *libambo* which gripped the unfortunate
victim fast at the neck; the *algemas* and the *anjinhos*, which
held the hands tightly, crushing the thumbs. . . . Some
plantation owners of more perverted inclinations used the
so-called *novenas* and *trezenas*. . . . The Negroes tied face
down on the ground, were beaten with the rawhide whip
on from nine to thirteen consecutive nights. . . .[21]

The testimony of the travelers, poets, planters, abolitionists,
and scholars in this matter, however, is worthless. Better to
dispute the number of angels on a pinhead than to argue that
one country's slavery is superior to another's. The slaves,
wherever they were, didn't like it; they killed themselves and
they killed their masters; over and over again they risked
being torn apart by hounds and the most despicable tortures
in order to escape the life to which they were condemned.
It is a well-known fact that Brazil was second to none in the
number of its fugitive slaves and its slave revolts. In the seventeenth century one successful group held out in the famous
quilombo of Palmares for sixty-seven years and in the nineteenth century scarcely a year went by without an actual or
intended revolt.[22]

The historian Stanley M. Elkins attempts to save Tannenbaum's theory by admitting that slavery in the United States
(at least by 1850) "in a 'physical' sense was in general, probably, quite mild" and that there were very "severe" sides to
the Spanish and Portuguese systems (78). Elkins assures us,
however, that even if slavery had been milder here than any-
where else in the Western Hemisphere, "it would still be

[21] Arthur Ramos, *The Negro in Brazil* (Washington, 1939), 34–35.
[22] *Ibid.*, 43 ff.

missing the point to make the comparison in terms of physical comfort. In one case we would be dealing with cruelty of man to man, and, in the other, with the care, maintenance, and indulgence of men toward creatures who were legally and morally *not* men—not in the sense that Christendom had traditionally defined man's nature" (78). It is devoutly to be hoped that Elkins shall never be able to test his exquisite sense of equity by experiencing first thirty lashes dealt out by some-one who calls him a black man and then a second thirty from someone who calls him a black devil. But if there be such talents as Elkins' among us, we had better take a closer look at the proposition that the Negro was regarded as a human being by the Latin colonists but not by the Anglo-Saxons. The principal source of evidence for this resides in the law codes by which the respective slave systems were theoretically regulated. Admittedly, these codes do show a considerable difference of legal opinion as to the definition of a slave. The Spanish and Portuguese codes were essentially continuations of medieval regulations stretching back ultimately to Roman law. The British and American colonial codes were the orig-inal creations of the New World planter class, developed first in the West Indies (Barbados) and then copied throughout the South.[23] Although the Constitution of the United States said that slaves were persons, state laws said they were chattels —mere property. "Slaveholders, legislators, and judges were forever trying to make property out of them. . . . They sim-ply did not regard them as human beings."[24] On the other hand, Spanish and Portuguese slave laws did, as Tannenbaum claims, specifically preserve the human identity of the slave: "The distinction between slavery and freedom is a product of accident and misfortune, and the free man might have been

[23] Dwight Lowell Dumond, *Antislavery* (Ann Arbor, 1961), 8.
[24] *Ibid.*, 251.

a slave."[25] From this there flowed a number of rights, of which Fernando Ortiz identifies four as most significant: (1) the right to marry freely; (2) the right to seek out another master if any were too severe; (3) the right of owning property; and (4) the right to buy freedom.[26] Tannenbaum shows how all of the U.S. slave states denied these rights. He goes further and shows how the U.S. slaves were virtually left without legal remedy for harms committed upon them, and he emphasizes the casual fines which protected the life of a slave under the early laws,[27] and the total lack of legal recognition given to the slave's affinal or consanguine family. Indeed, for every favorable section in the Spanish law, both Elkins and Tannenbaum readily find an unfavorable section in the Anglo-Saxon codes.

What the laws of the Spanish and Portuguese kings had to do with the attitudes and values of the Spanish and Portuguese planters, however, baffles one's imagination. The Crown could publish all the laws it wanted, but in the lowlands, sugar was king. If there were any Portuguese or Spanish planters who were aware of their legal obligations toward the slaves, it would require systematic misreading of colonialism, past and present, to suppose that these laws psychologically represented anything more than the flatus of a pack of ill-informed Colonel Blimps who didn't even know what a proper cane field looked like. Ortiz leaves no room for doubt in the case of Cuba. Yes, the slave had legal rights, "But these rights were not viable . . . if they contrast with the barbaric laws of the French and above all, of the English colonies, it was no less certain that all of these rights were illusory, especially in

---

[25] Tannenbaum, *Slave and Citizen*, 46.

[26] Fernando Ortiz, *Los negros esclavos* (Havana, 1916), 303.

[27] Actually, quite severe laws regulating punishment of the slaves were eventually passed by the slave states. (Cf. Kenneth Stampp, *The Peculiar Institution* (New York, 1956), 217–21.)

earlier times. . . ." Sanctity of the family? "Man and wife were permanently separated, sold in separate places, and separated from their children."[28] "How many times was a son sold by his father!" and "Pregnant or nursing slaves were sold with or without their actual or future offspring."[29] Protection of the law? "The sugar and coffee plantations were in fact feudal domains where the only authority recognized was that of the master. . . . Could the Negroes hope in these circumstances to change masters? The rawhide would quiet their voices. . . ." Rights to property? "From what I have said in relation to the work of the rural slave, to speak of his right to hold property and to buy freedom, is futile. . . ." "But I repeat, the plantation slave was treated like a beast, like a being to whom human character was denied. . . ."[30]

Tannenbaum makes much of the fact that there was no set of ancient slave laws to which the Anglo-Saxon planters or the slaves could turn for guidance. He prominently displays the meager penalties attached to murder of slaves as examples of their sub-human status in the eyes of the Anglo-Saxon colonists. But Ortiz informs us that "it was not until 1842 that there was any specific legal regulation of the form of punishment which a Cuban master could give his slave."[31] Actually it turns out that "the state did not concern itself with the limitation of the arbitrary power of the master in relation to the punishment of his slave until after the abolition of slavery [1880]."[32]

In Brazil, as everywhere in the colonial world, law and reality bore an equally small resemblance to each other. Stanley Stein's recent historical study of slavery in the county

[28] Ortiz, *Los negros esclavos*, 303–4.
[29] *Ibid.*, 173.
[30] *Ibid.*, 303–4.
[31] *Ibid.*, 265.
[32] *Ibid.*, 267.

of Vassouras during the last century yields a picture almost totally at variance with that drawn by Gilberto Freyre for the earlier plantations. The Vassouras planters went about their business, methodically buying, working, beating, and selling their slaves, in whatever fashion yielded the most coffee with the least expense. The master's will was supreme. "It was difficult to apply legal restraints to the planter's use of the lash."[33]

> Typical is an eyewitness account of a beating told by an ex-slave. On order from the master, two drivers bound and beat a slave while the slave folk stood in line, free folk watching from further back. The slave died that night and his corpse, dumped into a wicker basket, was borne by night to the slave cemetery of the plantation and dropped into a hastily dug grave. "*Slaves could not complain to the police, only another fazendeiro* [master] *could do that*," explained the eyewitness.[34] [Italics are mine.]

If Stein's picture of nineteenth-century Vassouras is accurate —and it is the most carefully documented study of its kind in existence—then the following recent pronouncement from Charles Boxer will have to be accepted minus the time restriction:

> The common belief that the Brazilian was an exceptionally kind master is applicable only to the 19th century under the Empire, and it is contradicted for the colonial period by the testimony of numerous reliable eyewitnesses from Vieira to Vilhena, to say nothing of the official correspondence between the colonial authorities and the Crown.[35]

---

[33] Stanley Stein, *Vassouras* (Cambridge, 1957), 135.
[34] *Ibid.*, 136.
[35] Charles Boxer, *The Golden Age of Brazil* (Berkeley, 1962), 173.

Of special interest in Boxer's refutation of the myth of the friendly master is the evidence which shows that Brazilian planters and miners did not accept the legal decisions which awarded human souls and human personalities to the slaves. The Brazilian slave owners were convinced that Negroes were descended from Cain, black and "therefore not people like ourselves." Making due allowance for exceptions and the special circumstances of household slaves, Boxer concludes that "it remains true that by and large colonial Brazil was indeed a 'hell for blacks.' "[36]

[36] Boxer, *Race Relations in the Portuguese Colonial Empire, 1415–1825* (Oxford, 1963), 114.

Quashee

ORLANDO PATTERSON

The various traits of the personality of the Negro slave fell into a general pattern that has been recognized all over the New World. Stanley Elkins has recently analyzed what he termed the "Sambo" personality. His descriptions bear a remarkable resemblance to those which existed in Jamaica. The term used in Jamaica to designate this personality pattern was Quashee. This term came originally from the Twi day-name meaning "Sunday."[1] In addition to being a popular name for slaves, Edward Long's own use of the term demonstrates that by the beginning of the second half of the eighteenth century at the latest it came to designate peculiarly Negro character traits. Writing at the beginning of the nineteenth

---

[1] Long gives these day-names, commonly used among the slaves, as follows:

Male	Female	Day
Cudjoe	Juba	Monday
Cubbenah	Beneba	Tuesday
Quaco	Cuba	Wednesday
Quao	Abba	Thursday
Cuffee	Phibba	Friday
Quamin	Mimba	Saturday
Quashee	Quasheba	Sunday

[Edward Long], *The History of Jamaica* (London, 1774), III, 427.

century, Stewart, speaking of the illiteracy of the creole white women, remarked that many of them exhibit much of the "Quasheba" (the feminine of Quashee). Cassidy has pointed out that today "Quashie simply means a peasant, but one also finds it glossed as 'fool.' "[2] From my own experience as a Jamaican I have often heard the word used in the hyphenated manner "quashie-fool." It is clear, however, that during slavery the term related specifically to Negro personality traits.

Perhaps the best comment on Quashee was made by Stewart, who wrote that: It is not an easy matter to trace with an unerring pencil the true character and disposition of the Negro, they are often so ambiguous and disguised.[3] This evasive, indefinable, somewhat disguised, and ambiguous quality was the most essential element of Quashee. Stewart also remarked: "The Negroes are crafty, artful, plausible; not often grateful for small services; but, frequently deceitful and over-reaching."[4] The evasiveness of Quashee manifested itself in various ways. It was evident, first, in what appeared to have been a compulsion to lie. Cooper speaks of his "low cunning and contempt of truth."[5] The editors of the *Jamaica Journal* who, though pro-slavery, were liberal-minded within the context of Jamaican slave society, wrote:

There is in the Negro character such an inherent sense of falsehood, and so ready a talent for the perversion of truth, that we fear even the dread of capital punishment would not effectually eradicate this favourite and habitual vice.

[2] F. G. Cassidy, *Jamaica Talk* (1961), 157.
[3] John Stewart, *A View of the Past and Present State of the Island of Jamaica* (1808), 234.
[4] *Ibid.*
[5] Cooper, *Facts Illustrative of the Condition of the Negro Slaves in Jamaica* (1824), 14. According to R. Bicknell, "As soon as they are born they go away and speak lies"; *The West Indies as They Are* (1825), 94.

We know of no mortal torture that would prevent or deter them from indulging this propensity; indeed, so strong is the predilection in some Negroes for the perversion of facts, that even where they expect reward for a "plain un-varnished tale," they generally find more difficulty in re-lating the real truth, than in uttering a lie. Those who have had the longest and most frequent intercourse with Negroes are aware that theft and lying are amongst their most be-setting sins: And that to discover the truth through means of Negro evidence is one of the most hopeless tasks any manager can undertake. The most clever and intelligent Negro is usually the most deceitful and we have seen some with art enough to baffle the most expert lawyer that ever put question. . . .[6]

Lewis, after detecting one of his slaves lying for no apparent reason, remarked that "I am assured that unless a Negro has an interest in telling the truth, he always lies—in order to 'keep his tongue in practice.' "[7] Even R. R. Madden, an anti-slavery writer and strong sympathizer of the slave, had to admit that they were pathological liars.

The evasiveness of the slave was also expressed in his peculiar mode of arguing, the essence of which seemed to have been to stray from the point as far as possible. It was this quality which was partly referred to as "congo saw." It could be one of the most exasperating experiences that a white per-son might have with a slave and one strongly suspects that its primary purpose was deliberate annoyance. Edwards has a detailed account of this trait[8] and Lewis gives several amus-ing instances. McNeill acidly remarked that:

[6] *Jamaica Journal & Kingston Chronicle*, Vol. 2, No. 32.
[7] M. G. Lewis, *Journal of a West-India Proprietor* (London, 1834), 129.
[8] Bryan Edwards, *The History of the British Colonies in the West Indies* (London, 1801–7), Book 4, 100.

. . . a Negro, without much violence of metaphor, may be compared to a bad pump, the working of which exhausts your strength before you can produce a drop of water.[9]

Another frequently noted trait of Quashee was distrustfulness, allied to which was a strong grain of conservatism. "They are so accustomed to be the subject of exaction," wrote Mathison, "that every innovation, though intended for their benefit, gives rise to a suspicion that it is intended for their oppression."[10] Quashee was also extremely capricious, a quality noted by many writers. Beckford observed that:

> Negroes are capricious, the recurrence of everyday life will evince. Give them a house ready built, they will not inhabit it—a ground ready cleared, they will not work it— if you study their convenience, their ease, and happiness, they will be discontented—they must have everything their own way; and would sooner complain of a good overseer, than not covet an exchange by the risk of one who is bad.[11]

The laziness of Quashee became proverbial and hardly needs any documentation here.[12] Quashee was, in addition, extremely childlike, a quality which Lady Nugent, among others, often remarked on.[13] Quashee was also, from all reports, gay, happy-go-lucky, frivolous, and cheerful. To Stewart, "He is patient, cheerful, and commonly submissive,

[9] Hector McNeill, *Observations on . . . the Negroes in Jamaica*, 15.
[10] G. Mathison, *Notices Respecting Jamaica* (1805–10), 101.
[11] W. Beckford, *Situation of the Negroes in Jamaica* (1788), 90.
[12] The classic exposition of the stereotyped view of Quashee's laziness was written several years after slavery by Thomas Carlyle in his *An Occasional Discourse on the Nigger Question.*
[13] Frank Cundall (ed.), *Lady Nugent's Journal, Jamaica One Hundred Years Ago* (London, 1907); see for example p. 288.

capable at times of grateful attachments where uniformly well
treated, and kind and affectionate toward his kindred and off-
springs."[14] And Sir John Keane found it "a most extraordinary
thing that they are always singing, and seem excessively delighted."[15] But Quashee's darker traits were stressed just as
often. He was revengeful, harboring grudges for a long time;
when placed in positions of authority he was likely to be
extremely cruel and tyrannical; he was "possessed of passions
not only strong but ungovernable . . . a temper extremely
irascible; a disposition indolent, selfish and deceitful; fond of
joyous sociality; riotous mirth and extravagant show."[16]

In addition, the contemporary accounts almost all attribute
an element of stupefaction to Quashee, and an almost complete lack of judgment. Quashee somehow managed to do
everything wrongly. Repeated attempts at correction were
doomed to failure. Lewis, despite his fondness for his slaves,
wrote toward the end of his journal that "Somehow or
other, they never can manage to do anything quite as it
should be done. If they correct themselves in one respect
today, they are sure of making a blunder in some other manner tomorrow."[17] This stupidity was often quite consciously
feigned, as Madden makes clear:

It is a difficult thing to get a Negro to understand anything which he does not wish to hear; the more you try to
explain a matter that is disagreeable to him, the more incapable he appears of comprehension; or if he finds this
plan ineffectual, he endeavours to render the matter ridic-

[14] Stewart, *Past and Present State*, 234–35.
[15] Evidence of Sir John Keane, House of Lords Committee on Slavery,
1832, 179.
[16] McNeill, *Negroes in Jamaica*, 28.
[17] Lewis, *Journal of a West-India Proprietor*, 392.

ulous; and his talent at rendering ridicule sarcastic is really surprising.[18]

On the other hand, several penetrating observers did not fail to notice the acuteness of the slave in judging the character of those about him. Phillippo noted, for example, that "so far from being more deficient in acuteness and discrimination than other men, none can penetrate more deeply than the Negro into the character, or form an opinion of strangers with greater correctness and precision."[19]

That Quashee existed there can be no doubt. The problem is to ascertain how real, how meaningful, this psychological complex was in the life of the slave. A full answer to this question would involve a digression into existential and role psychology which is outside the confines of this work.[20] We may, however, make a few tentative observations.

Quashee may be said to have existed on three levels. First, as a stereotyped conception held by the whites of their slaves; second, as a response on the part of the slave to this stereotype; and third, as a psychological function of the real life situation of the slave. All three levels of Quashee's existence were closely related and mutually reinforced each other.

Let us begin with the third level. The real life situation of the slave, as we have shown, was one in which there was a complete breakdown of all major institutions—the family,

[18] R. R. Madden, *A Twelvemonths' Residence in the West Indies during the Transition from Slavery to Apprenticement* (London, 1835), II, 155–56.

[19] J. M. Phillippo, *Jamaica: Its Past and Present State* (1843), 204. Similarly, it was often remarked by American slave owners that "a Negro understands a white man better than the white man understands the Negro"; U. B. Phillips, *American Negro Slavery* (New York, 1918), 327.

[20] For an extremely suggestive analysis of similar personality complexes, see R. D. Laing's discussion of "The False-Self System" in Chapter 6 of his book *The Divided Self*. See also J.-P. Sartre's analysis of "bad faith" in his *Being and Nothingness*.

marriage, religion, organized morality. This situation was made worse by the fact that the white group offered no alternate mores and institutions, but were just as disorganized socially as they were. There could be no kind of guiding principle, then, in the socialization of the slave, except that of evasion, which he learned from hard experience. The habitual laziness of the slave was also largely the function of his work situation. From early childhood he was stimulated to work, not by the expectations of reward, but entirely by the threat of punishment. Naturally, he grew to hate work and could only be industrious if forced to. The happy-go-lucky irresponsibility of the slave could also be explained in terms of his upbringing, especially with regard to males when we recall the demoralizing effect of slavery on them.

But the complexity of Quashee cannot be completely explained in situational terms. The explanation of the element of evasiveness and dissemblance, the pathological lying, must be sought elsewhere. To some extent this was to be found in the stereotype the whites had of Quashee.[21] This stereotype undoubtedly possessed what Prothro and Milikian have called a "kernel of truth" about the real situation. But stereotypes, as the above writers pointed out, also reflect the "characteristics of the individuals holding stereotype or the state of politico-economic relations between groups."[22] The same principle holds for the plantocrats of Jamaican slave society. The outright brutality and unrestrained exploitation of the

[21] "Stereotyping may be defined as the tendency to attribute generalized and simplified characteristics to groups of people in the form of verbal labels and to act towards the members of these groups in terms of these labels"; W. E. Vinacke, "Stereotyping among National-Racial Groups in Hawaii: A Study in Ethnocentricism," in *The Journal of Social Psychology*, Vol. 30, 1949.
[22] Prothro & Milikian, "Studies in Stereotype: Familiarity and the Kernel of Truth," in *The Journal of Social Psychology*, Vol. 41, 1955.

system made even the most hardened plantocrat desirous of a system of rationalization. Certain aspects—usually either those which were the worst, or the most easily patronized—of the personality traits of the slaves were therefore seized upon and elaborated into a generalized body of "truths" about the Negro.

At this point, Merton's concept of the "self-fulfilling prophecy" becomes useful. As he wrote: "The systematic condemnation of the outgrouper continues largely irrespective of what he does; more; through a freakish exercise of capricious judicial logic, the victim is punished for the crime."[23] Since masters had absolute control over their slaves, it was not difficult for them to create the conditions that would actualize the stereotypes they had of these slaves.

The self-fulfilling prophecy, however, has a further dimension which Merton failed to point out. It is the fact that the subordinate group, in addition to being forced into situations which fulfill the stereotype of the superordinate group, also responds directly to these stereotypes by either appearing to or actually internalizing them. The slave, in fact, played upon the master's stereotype for his own ends. Playing the stereotype had three broad functions.

First, with his acute sensitivity, the slave easily saw that although the master might consciously protest at his stupidity or frivolity or whatever Quashee trait he was playing up, he was nonetheless inwardly pleased by the slave offering further proof of his rationalizations. From the slaves' point of view, this was a direct appeal to, and exploitation of, the inevitable see-what-I-mean mentality of their masters.[24]

---

[23] R. K. Merton, *Social Theory and Social Structure* (New York, 1956), 186.
[24] The American psychologist Gordon Allport identified this kind of behavior as "clowning." He wrote: "And if the master wants to be amused, the slave sometimes obligingly plays the clown. . . . Richard Wright in

Second, by playing the stereotype, the slave both disguised his true feelings (which it was his cardinal principle never to reveal since no one, least of all the master, could be trusted)[25] and had the psychological satisfaction of duping the master. The well-known Jamaican Negro proverb, "Play fool to catch wise," well sums up this form of stereotype playing.[26]

Third, if the slaves strongly resented an overseer or bookkeeper and wanted to get rid of him, in the majority of cases they could achieve their objective by simply being the perfect Quashee—stupid, bungling, exasperating, and completely inefficient. Long has left us a penetrating account of the overseer-slave relationship which illustrates all three types of stereotype playing:

> . . . Their principal address is shown in finding out their master's temper, and playing upon it so artfully as to bend it with most convenience to their own purposes. They are not less studious in sifting their master's representative, the overseer; if he is not too cunning for them, which they soon discover after one or two experiments, they will easily find means to over-reach him on every occasion, and make his

---

Black Boy describes the colored elevator man who wins his way by exaggerating his Negro accent, and affecting the traits ascribed to his racial group: begging, laziness, and tall tales. His passengers give him coins and make him a pet." Allport also speaks of "protective clowning," a perfect example of which was the "spook" personality among Negro soldiers, of whom he writes: "A spook can't be hurt; he can't be downed; he doesn't talk back, but he can't be coerced. He will come right through doors and walls whatever you do; he has a sassy if silent invulnerability"; *The Nature of Prejudice* (New York, 1958), 144.

[25] There is the problem, however, of deciding exactly what the true feelings of the slave were. This goes to the heart of the problem of deciding where the difference lies between *conscious* role playing and *natural* role playing. See Elkins' discussion in *Slavery*, 131–33.

[26] See also Izett Anderson and Frank Cundall, *Jamaica Negro Proverbs and Sayings* (1927), Nos. 263–68, 536, and 544.

indolence, his weakness, or sottishness, a sure prognostic of some comfortable term of idleness to them; but if they find him too intelligent, wary and active, they leave no expedient untried, by thwarting his plans, misunderstanding his orders, and reiterating complaints against him, to ferret him out of his post; if this will not succeed, they perplex and worry him, especially if he is of an impatient, fretful turn, till he grows heartily sick of his charge, and voluntarily resigns it. An overseer therefore, like a prime minister, must always expect to meet with a faction, ready to oppose his administration, right or wrong; unless he will give the reins out of his hands, and suffer the mob to have things their own way; which if he complies with, they will extol him to his face, condemn him in their hearts, and very soon bring his government to disgrace.[27]

[27] [Long], *History of Jamaica*, III, 405.

PART THREE

BEYOND THE THESIS: EXTENSIONS AND ALTERNATIVES

Resistance to Slavery

GEORGE M. FREDRICKSON AND CHRISTOPHER LASCH

The issues involved in the study of "resistance" to slavery are badly in need of clarification. The problem, one would suppose, is not whether the plantation slave was happy with his lot but whether he actively resisted it. But even this initial clarification does not come easily. Too many writers have assumed that the problem of resistance consists mainly of deciding whether slaves were docile or discontented and whether their masters were cruel or kind. In this respect and in others, as Elkins has noted, the discussion of slavery has locked itself into the terms of an old debate. The pro-slavery stereotype of the contented slave, which was taken over without much conceptual refinement by U. B. Phillips and others, has been attacked by recent historians in language much the same as that employed by the abolitionists more than a hundred years ago, according to which slaves hated bondage and longed to be free. "That they had no understanding of freedom," Kenneth Stampp argues, ". . . is hard to believe." A few pages later, and without any intervening evidence, Stampp progresses from this cautious thought to a fullblown statement of the case for "resistance." "Slave resistance, whether bold and persistent or mild and sporadic, created for all slaveholders a serious problem of discipline." He concludes, in a burst of rhetoric, that "the record of slave resistance forms a chapter in the story of the endless struggle to give dignity to human life."[1]

It should be apparent that the traditional terms of reference, on either side of the dispute, are not sufficiently precise to serve as instruments of analysis. One of the faults of Phillips' work is his consistent failure to distinguish between cruelty and coercion. By compiling instances of the kindness and benevolence of masters, Phillips proved to his own satisfaction that slavery was a mild and permissive institution, the primary function of which was not so much to produce a marketable surplus as to ease the accommodation of the lower race into the culture of the higher. The critics of Phillips have tried to meet him on his own ground. Where he compiled lists of indulgences and benefactions, they have assembled lists of atrocities. Both methods suffer from the same defect: they attempt to solve a conceptual problem—what did slavery do to the slave—by accumulating quantitative evidence. Both methods assert that plantations conformed to one of two patterns, terror or indulgence, and then seek to prove these assertions by accumulating evidence from plantation diaries, manuals of discipline, letters, and other traditional sources for the study of slavery. But for every instance of physical cruelty on the one side an enterprising historian can find an instance of indulgence on the other. The only conclusion that one can legitimately draw from this debate is that great variations in treatment existed from plantation to plantation. (But as we shall see, this conclusion, barren in itself, can be made to yield important results if one knows how to use it.)

Even if we could make valid generalizations about the

<hr>

[1] Kenneth Stampp, *The Peculiar Institution* (New York, 1956), 88, 91.

severity of the regime, these statements would not automatically answer the question of whether or not widespread resistance took place. If we are to accept the testimony of Frederick Douglass, resistance was more likely to result from indulgence and rising expectations than from brutalizing severity.[2] A recent study of the geographical distribution of authentic slave revolts shows that most of them occurred in cities and in areas of slavebreeding and diversified agriculture, where, according to all accounts, the regime was more indulgent than in the productive plantation districts of the Cotton Kingdom.[3] Open resistance cannot be inferred from the extreme physical cruelty of the slave system, even if the system's cruelty could be demonstrated statistically.

II

There is the further question of what constitutes resistance. When Kenneth Stampp uses the term he means much more than open and flagrant defiance of the system. To him resistance is all noncooperation on the part of the slaves. And it cannot be denied that the annals of slavery abound in examples of this kind of behavior. Slaves avoided work by pretending to be sick or by inventing a hundred other plausible pretexts. They worked so inefficiently as to give rise to the suspicion that they were deliberately sabotaging the crop. They stole from their masters without compunction, a fact which gave rise to the complaint that slaves had no moral sense, but which is better interpreted as evidence of a double

[2] Frederick Douglass, *The Narrative of the Life of Frederick Douglass, an American Slave* (Cambridge, 1960), 132–33.
[3] Martin D. de B. Kilson, "Towards Freedom: An Analysis of Slave Revolts in the United States," *Phylon*, XXV (1964), 179–83.

standard—cheating the master while dealing honorably with other slaves. Nor was this all. Their grievances or frustrations led at times to the willful destruction of the master's property by destroying tools, mistreating animals, and setting fire to plantation buildings. Less frequently, they took the ultimate step of violent attack on the master himself. Perhaps the most common form of obvious noncooperation was running away; every large plantation had its share of fugitives.[4]

The question which inevitably arises, as Stampp piles up incident after incident in order to show that slaves were "a troublesome property," is whether this pattern of noncooperation constitutes resistance. Resistance is a political concept. Political activity, in the strictest sense, is organized collective action which aims at affecting the distribution of power in a community; more broadly, it might be said to consist of any activity, either of individuals or of groups, which is designed to create a consciousness of collective interest, such consciousness being the prerequisite for effective action in the realm of power. Organized resistance is of course only one form of political action. Others include interest-group politics; coalitions of interest groups organized as factions or parties; reform movements; or, at an international level, diplomacy and war. In total institutions, however, conventional politics are necessarily nonexistent.[5] Politics, if they exist at all, must take the form of resistance: collective action designed to subvert the system, to facilitate and regularize escape from it, or, at the very least, to force important changes in it.

[4] Stampp, *Peculiar Institution*, Ch. III.

[5] Total institutions are distinguished not by the absolute power of the authorities—a definition which, as will become clear, prejudges an important issue—but by the fact that they are self-contained, so that every detail of life is regulated in accordance with the dominant purpose of the institution. Whether that purpose is defined as healing, punishment, forced labor, or (in the case of the concentration camps) terror, all total institutions are set up in such a way as to preclude any form of politics based on consent.

Among despised and downtrodden people in general, the most rudimentary form of political action is violence; sporadic and usually short-lived outbursts of destruction, based on a common sense of outrage and sometimes inspired by a millennialistic ideology. Peasant revolts, all over the world, have usually conformed to this type.[6] In total institutions, prison riots are perhaps the nearest equivalent. In American slavery, the few documented slave rebellions fall into the same pattern.[7] What makes these upheavals political at all is that they rest on some sense, however primitive, of collective victimization. They require, moreover, at least a minimum of organization and planning. What makes them rudimentary is that they do not aim so much at changing the balance of power as at giving expression on the one hand to apocalyptic visions of retribution, and on the other to an immediate thirst for vengeance directed more at particular individuals than at larger systems of authority. In the one case, the sense of grievance finds an outlet in indiscriminate violence (as against Jews); in the other, it attaches itself to a particular embodiment of authority (as in prisons, where a specific departure from established routine may set off a strike or riot demanding the authority's dismissal and a return to the previous regime). But in neither case does collective action rest on a realistic perception of the institutional structure as a whole and the collective interest of its victims in subverting it. That

[6] See E. J. Hobsbawm, *Primitive Rebels: Studies in Archaic Forms of Social Movement in the 19th and 20th Centuries* (Manchester, 1959); Norman Cohn, *The Pursuit of the Millennium* (New York, 1957).

[7] Nat Turner's rebellion in 1831, the only significant slave uprising in the period 1820–60 that got beyond the plotting stage, would seem to be comparable to a millennialist peasants' revolt. Turner was a preacher who, according to his own testimony, received the visitation of a spirit commanding him to "fight against the serpent, for the time was fast approaching when the first should be last and the last should be first." Quoted in Herbert Aptheker, *American Negro Slave Revolts* (New York, 1943), 296. See also Aptheker, *Nat Turner's Slave Rebellion* (New York, 1966).

explains why such outbreaks of violence tend to subside very quickly, leaving the exploitive structure intact. Underground resistance to the Nazis in western Europe, on the other hand, precisely because it expressed itself in an organized underground instead of in futile outbreaks of indiscriminate violence, had a continuous existence which testifies to the highly political character of its objectives.

It is easy to show that Negro slaves did not always cooperate with the system of slavery. It is another matter to ⚡ prove that noncooperation amounted to political resistance. Malingering may have reflected no more than a disinclination to work, especially when the rewards were so meager. Likewise, what is taken for sabotage may have originated in apathy and indifference. Acts of violence are subject to varying interpretations. If there is something undeniably political about an organized, premeditated rebellion, an isolated act of violence could arise from a purely personal grievance. Even the motive of flight is obscure: was it an impulse, prompted by some special and immediate affront, or was it desertion, a sort of separate peace? These acts in themselves tell us very little. We begin to understand them only when we understand the conceptual distinction between resistance and noncooperation; and even then, we still feel the need of a more general set of conceptions, derived from recorded experience, to which slavery—an unrecorded experience, except from the masters' point of view—can be compared; some general model which will enable us to grasp imaginatively the system as a whole.

III

Only the testimony of the slaves could tell us, once and for all, whether slaves resisted slavery. In the absence of their testimony, it is tempting to resort to analogies. Indeed it is almost impossible to avoid them. Those who condemn analogies, pretending to argue from the documentary evidence alone, delude themselves. Resistance to slavery cannot be established (any more than any other general conception of the institution can be established) without making an implicit analogy between Negro slavery and the struggles of free men, in our own time, "to give dignity to human life" by resisting oppression. The question, in the case of slavery, is not whether historians should argue from analogy but whether they are willing to make their analogies explicit.

Elkins compares slavery to the Nazi concentration camps and concludes that the effect of slavery was to break down the slave's adult personality and to reduce him to a state of infantile dependence, comparable to the condition observed by survivors of the concentration camps. In evaluating this particular analogy, we are entitled to ask how well it explains what we actually know about slavery. In one respect, it explains too much. It explains the fact that there were no slave rebellions in the United States comparable to those which took place in Latin America, but it also rules out the possibility of noncooperation. Elkins' analogy suggests a state of internalized dependency that does not fit the facts of widespread intransigence, insubordination, and mischief-making. Stampp may not adequately explain this pattern of behavior, but he convinces us that it existed. Elkins is open to criticism on empirical grounds for failing to take into account a vast amount of evidence that does not fit his theory of slave behavior. Many of Elkins' critics, however, have not concerned themselves with the substance of his analogy. Raising neither empirical nor theoretical objections against it, they have seized on its mere existence as a means of discrediting Elkins' work. He should rather be congratulated for having made the analogy explicit, thereby introducing into the study of slavery the kinds of questions that modern studies of total institutions have dealt with far more systematically than conventional studies of slavery.

Elkins was careful to emphasize the limits of the comparison. He did not argue that the plantation resembled a concentration camp with respect to intentions or motives; "even 'cruelty,' " he added, "was not indispensable as an item in my equation" (226). His "essentially limited purpose" in bringing the two institutions together was to show the psychological effects of closed systems of control; and the objections to the analogy may after all derive not from the analogy itself but from a tendency, among Elkins' critics, to take it too literally. As Elkins observes, the "very vividness and particularity [of analogies] are coercive: they are almost too concrete. One's impulse is thus to reach for extremes. The thing is either taken whole hog . . . ; or it is rejected out of hand on the ground that not all of the parts fit" (226). It is precisely because all the parts don't fit that an analogy is an analogy rather than a literal correspondence, and it ought to be enough, therefore, if just one of the parts demonstrably fits.

The real objection to Elkins' analogy is not that analogies in themselves are pernicious but that there is no compelling theoretical reason, in this case, to stop with one. The concentration camp is only one of many total institutions with which slavery might have been compared; a total institution being defined, in Erving Goffman's words, as "a place of residence and work where a large number of like-situated individuals, cut off from the wider society for an appreciable period of time, together lead an enclosed, formally administered round of life."[8] An excellent example—the one, indeed, that springs

---

[8] Erving Goffman, *Asylums: Essays on the Social Situation of Mental Patients and Other Inmates* (Garden City, 1961; Chicago, 1962), xiii.

immediately to mind—is the prison, "providing," Goffman says, that "we appreciate that what is prison-like about prisons is found in institutions whose members have broken no laws."[9] In several respects, prisons, especially penitentiaries, are more analogous to plantation slavery than concentration camps. Prisons are not, like the concentration camps, designed as experiments in deliberate dehumanization, although they often have dehumanizing effects; in this respect the motive behind the system more nearly approximates that of slavery than of the concentration camp. More important, the problem of control is more nearly analogous. The disproportion between the authority of the guards and the impotence of the inmates is not absolute, as it was at Dachau and Buchenwald, but subject, as it seems to have been under slavery, to a number of variables—the temperament of the guard or master, the composition of the prisoners or slaves, the immediate history of the institutions involved.

Prison officials, like slaveowners and overseers, face a constant problem of noncooperation. "Far from being omnipotent rulers who have crushed all signs of rebellion against their regime, the custodians are engaged in a continuous struggle to maintain order—and it is a struggle in which the custodians frequently fail."[10] This situation occurs, according to the sociologist Gresham Sykes, because although the custodians enjoy an absolute monopoly of the means of violence, their enormous power does not rest on authority; that is, on "a rightful or legitimate effort to exercise control," which inspires in the governed an internalized sense of obligation to obey. In the absence of a sense of duty among the prisoners, the guards have to rely on a system of rewards, incentives, punishments,

[9] *Ibid.*
[10] Gresham M. Sykes, *The Society of Captives: A Study of a Maximum Security Prison* (Princeton, 1958), 42.

and coercion. But none of these methods can be carried too far without reaching dangerous extremes of laxity or demoralization. As in most total institutions—the concentration camp being a conspicuous exception—rigid standards of discipline tend to give way before the need to keep things running smoothly without undue effort on the part of the custodians. An absolute monopoly of violence can be used to achieve a state of total terror, but it cannot persuade men to work at their jobs or move "more than 1,200 inmates through the mess hall in a routine and orderly fashion."[11] The result, in the maximum-security prison, is a system of compromises, an uneasy give-and-take which gives prisoners a limited leverage within the system. To the extent that this adjustment limits the power of the guards, a corruption of authority takes place.[12]

Plantation literature produces numerous parallels. We can read the masters' incessant and heartfelt complaints about the laziness, the inefficiency, and the intractability of slaves; the difficulty of getting them to work; the difficulty of enlisting their cooperation in any activity that had to be sustained over a period of time. We can read about the system of rewards and punishments, spelled out by the master in such detail, the significance of which, we can now see, was that it had had to be resorted to precisely in the degree to which a sense of internalized obedience had failed. We see the same limitation on terror and physical coercion as has been observed in the prison; for even less than the prison authorities could the planter tolerate the demoralization resulting from an excess of violence. We can even see the same "corruption of authority"

[11] *Ibid.*, 49.
[12] *Ibid.*, 52–58.

in the fact that illicit slave behavior, especially minor theft, was often tolerated by the masters in order to avoid unnecessary friction.

One of the most curious features of the "society of captives," as described by Sykes, is this: that while most of the prisoners recognize the legitimacy of their imprisonment and the controls to which they are subjected, they lack any internalized sense of obligation to obey them. "The bond between recognition of the legitimacy of control and the sense of duty has been torn apart."[13] This fact about prisons makes it possible to understand a puzzling feature of the contemporary literature on slavery, which neither the model of submission nor that of resistance explains—the curious contradiction between the difficulty of discipline and the slaves' professed devotion to their masters. Those who argue that the slaves resisted slavery have to explain away their devotion as pure hypocrisy. But it is possible to accept it as sincere without endorsing the opposite view—even in the sophisticated form in which it has been cast by Stanley Elkins—that slaves were children. The sociology of total institutions provides a theory with which to reconcile the contradiction. "The custodial institution," Sykes argues, "is valuable for a theory of human behavior because it makes us realize that men need not be motivated to conform to a regime which they define as rightful."[14] It is theoretically possible, in short, that slaves could have accepted the legitimacy of their masters' authority without feeling any sense of obligation to obey it. The evidence of the masters themselves makes this conclusion seem not only possible but highly probable. Logic, moreover, supports this view. For how could a system that rigorously defined the

[13] *Ibid.*, 46.
[14] *Ibid.*, 48.

Negro slave not merely as an inferior but as an alien, a separate order of being, inspire him with the sense of belonging on which internalized obedience necessarily has to rest?

IV

It might be argued, however, that slaves developed a sense of obedience by default, having had no taste of life outside slavery which would have made them dissatisfied, by contrast, with their treatment as slaves. It might be argued that the convict's dissatisfaction with prison conditions and the insubordination that results derive from his sense of the outside world and the satisfactions it normally provides; and that such a perspective must have been lacking on the plantation. Elkins, in denying the possibility of any sort of accommodation to slavery short of the complete assimilation of the master's authority by the slave, contends that a consciously defensive posture could not exist, given the total authority of the master and the lack of "alternative forces for moral and psychological orientation" (133n). This objection loses its force, however, if it can be shown that the slave did in fact have chances to develop independent standards of personal satisfaction and fair treatment within the system of slavery itself. Such standards would have made possible a hedonistic strategy of accommodation and, in cases where such a strategy failed, strong feelings of personal grievance.

It is true that the plantation sealed itself off from the world, depriving the slave of nearly every influence that would have lifted him out of himself into a larger awareness of slavery as an oppressive social system which, by its very nature, denied him normal satisfaction. In order to understand why slaves did not, as Elkins suggests, become totally submissive and ready to accept any form of cruelty and humiliation, it is necessary to focus on an aspect of slavery which has been almost totally ignored in discussion of slave personality. The typical slave, although born into slavery, was not likely to spend his entire life, or indeed any considerable part of it, under a single regime. The slave child could anticipate many changes of situation. It would appear likely, from what we know of the extent of the slave trade, that most slaves changed hands at least once in their lives; slave narratives and recollections suggest that it was not at all uncommon for a single slave to belong to several masters in the course of his lifetime of servitude. In addition, the prevalence of slave-hiring, especially in the upper South, meant that many slaves experienced a temporary change of regime. Even if a slave remained on the same plantation, things could change drastically, as the result of death and the accession of an heir, or from a change of overseer (especially significant in cases of absentee ownership).[15] Given the wide variation in standards of treatment and management techniques—a variation which, we suggested earlier, seems the one inescapable conclusion to be drawn from the traditional scholarship on the management of slaves—we are left with a situation that must have had important

[15] Frederic Bancroft, in *Slave Trading in the Old South* (New York, 1959), concludes (382–406) that more than 700,000 slaves were transported from the upper South to the cotton kingdom in the years 1830–60, and that most went by way of the slave trade. He also estimates (405) that in the decade 1850–60 an annual average of approximately 140,000 slaves were sold, interstate or *intra-state*, or hired out by their masters. This meant that one slave in twenty-five changed his *de facto* master in a given year. When we add to these regular exchanges the informal transfers that went on within families, we get some idea of the instability which characterized the slave's situation in an expansive and dynamic agricultural economy. The way slaves were sometimes shuttled about is reflected in several of the slave narratives, especially Frederick Douglass, *Narrative;* Solomon Northrop, *Twelve Years a Slave* (Auburn, Buffalo, and London, 1853); and [Charles Ball], *Fifty Years in Chains: Or the Life of an American Slave* (New York, 1858).

psychological implications. An individual slave might—like Harriet Beecher Stowe's Uncle Tom—experience slavery both at its mildest and at its harshest. He might be sold from an indulgent master to a cruel one or vice versa. He might go from a farm where he maintained a close and intimate relationship with his master to a huge impersonal "factory in the fields," where his actual master would be only a dim presence. These changes in situation led many slaves to develop standards of their own about how they ought to be treated and even to diffuse these standards among the stationary slave population. By comparing his less onerous lot under a previous master to his present hard one, a slave could develop a real sense of grievance and communicate it to others.[16] Similarly,

[16] Positive evidence of this development of internal standards and of the vacillation between contentment and dissatisfaction to which it gave rise is as difficult to find as evidence on any other aspect of slave psychology. As we have indicated, adequate records of personal slave response simply do not exist. There is, however, some indication of this process in the slave narratives and recollections. One of the most revealing of the slave narratives is Charles Ball, *Fifty Years in Chains*. Ball's account seems truer than most to the reality of slavery because, unlike most fugitives, he escaped from servitude at an age when it was difficult for him to acquire new habits of thought from his free status and association with abolitionists. Ball recounts the common experience of being sold from the upper South with its relatively mild and permissive regime into the more rigorous plantation slavery farther south. Upon his arrival on a large South Carolina cotton plantation, Ball, who was from Maryland, makes the acquaintance of a slave from northern Virginia who tells him what he can now expect. "He gave me such an account of the suffering of the slaves, on the cotton and indigo plantations—of whom I now regarded myself as one—that I was unable to sleep this night" (103–4). Later, he describes himself as "far from the place of my nativity, in a land of strangers, with no one to care for me beyond the care that a master bestows upon his ox . . ." (115). The regime is indeed a harsh one, and he feels very dissatisfied, except on Sunday when he is taken up by the general hilarity that prevails in the slave quarters on the holiday. Eventually, however, he experiences a temporary improvement in his situation when he is given to his master's new son-in-law, who seems kindly and permissive. In a remarkable description of slave hedonism, Ball recalls his state of mind. "I now felt assured that all my troubles in this world were ended, and that, in future, I might look forward to a life of happiness and ease, for I did not consider labor any hardship,

slaves were quick to take advantage of any new leniency or
laxity in control.[17] Hence it is quite possible to account for
widespread noncooperation among slaves as resulting from a
rudimentary sense of justice acquired entirely within the
system of slavery itself. These standards would have served
the same function as the standards convicts bring from the
outside world into the prison. At the same time it is necessary
to insist once again that they give rise to a pattern of intransigence which is hedonistic rather than political, accom-
modationist rather than revolutionary.

   If this picture of slave motivation is less morally sublime
than contemporary liberals and radicals would like, it should
not be construed as constituting, in any sense, a moral judgment on the Negro slave. Sporadic noncooperation within a

---

if I was well provided with good food and clothes, and my other wants
properly regarded" (266). This is too good to last, however; and Ball's new
master dies, leaving him in the hands of another man, "of whom, when I
considered the part of the country from whence he came, which had always
been represented to me as distinguished for the cruelty with which slaves
were treated, I had no reason to expect much that was good" (271–72). His
new master turns out to be much less harsh than anticipated, but the master's wife, a woman with sadistic tendencies, takes a positive dislike to Ball
and resents her husband's paternal attitude toward him. When the master
dies, Ball recognizes his situation as intolerable and resolves upon flight
(307). Ball's narrative reveals the way in which a slave could evaluate his
changes of condition by standards of comfort and accommodation derived
from experience within the system itself. In desperate situations, this evaluation could lead to extreme forms of noncooperation.

   Despite the fact that he was recalling his experience after having escaped
from slavery and, presumably, after coming under the influence of Northern
anti-slavery sentiment, Ball's general attitude remained remarkably accom-
modationist, at least in respect to slavery at its best. In a revealing passage,
he notes that the typical slave lacks a real sense of identity of interest with
his master, is jealous of his prerogatives, and steals from him without qualms.
Yet, Ball concludes, there "is in fact, a mutual dependence between the
master and his slave. The former could not acquire anything without the
labor of the latter, and the latter would always remain in poverty without
the judgment of the former in directing labor to a definite and profitable
result" (219).

[17] See Stampp, *Peculiar Institution*, 104–8.

broad framework of accommodation was the natural and
inevitable response to plantation slavery. It should go without saying that white men born into the same system would
have acted in the same way. Indeed, this is the way they have
been observed to act in modern situations analogous to
slavery. In total institutions, the conditions for sustained resistance are generally wanting—a fact that is insufficiently
appreciated by those armchair moralists who like to make
judgments at a safe distance about the possibilities of resistance
to totalitarianism. Rebellions and mutinies "seem to be the
exception," Erving Goffman observes, "not the rule." Group
loyalty is very tenuous, even though "the expectation that
group loyalty should prevail forms part of the inmate culture
and underlies the hostility accorded to those who break inmate solidarity."[18]

Instead of banding together, inmates of total institutions
typically pursue various personal strategies of accommodation.
Goffman describes four lines of adaptation, but it is important
to note that although these are analytically distinguishable,
"the same inmate will employ different personal lines of
adaptation at different phases in his moral career and may
even alternate among different tacks at the same time." "Situational withdrawal," a fatalistic apathy, is the condition into
which many inmates of concentration camps rapidly descended, with disastrous psychic consequences to themselves;

[18] Goffman, *Asylums*, 18–19. Cf. Donald Clemmer, *The Prison Community* (New York, 1958), 297–98: "The prisoner's world is an atomized
world. . . . There are no definite communal objectives. There is no consensus for a common goal. The inmates' conflict with officialdom and opposition toward society is only slightly greater in degree than conflict and
opposition among themselves. Trickery and dishonesty overshadow sympathy and cooperation. . . . It is a world of 'I,' 'me,' and 'mine,' rather than
'ours,' 'theirs,' and 'his.' " Clemmer adds, p. 293: "Such collective action of
protest as does arise, comes out of an immediate situation in which they
themselves are involved, and not as protest to an idea."

it undoubtedly took its toll among slaves newly arrived from Africa during the colonial period. "Colonization," which in some cases can be regarded as another type of institutional neurosis, rests on a conscious decision that life in the institution is preferable to life in the outside world. Colonization, in turn, must be distinguished from "conversion," the inmate's internalization of the view of himself held by those in power. In Negro slavery, this is the Sambo role and is accompanied, as in the concentration camp, by an infantile sense of dependence. Colonization, on the other hand, would apply to the very small number of slaves who agreed to reenslavement after a period as free Negroes.[19]

The fourth type of accommodation is "intransigence," which should not be confused with resistance. The latter presupposes a sense of solidarity and an underground organization of inmates. Intransigence is a personal strategy of survival, and although it can sometimes help to sustain a high morale, it can just as easily lead to futile and even self-destructive acts of defiance. In slavery, there was a substantial minority who were written off by their masters as chronic trouble-makers, "bad niggers," and an even larger group who indulged in occasional insubordination. It is precisely the pervasiveness of "intransigence" that made slaves, like convicts, so difficult to manage, leading to the corruption of authority analyzed above. But as we have already tried to show, there is nothing about intransigence that precludes a partial ac-

[19] Colonization, while uncommon among slaves, is frequently encountered in prisons and particularly in mental institutions. The high rate of recidivism among convicts and the frequency with which mental patients are sent back to asylums reflect not simply a relapse into a former sickness which the institution did not cure, but in many cases, a sickness which the institution itself created—an institutional neurosis which has its own peculiar characteristics, the most outstanding of which is the inability to function outside systems of total control.

ceptance of the values of the institution. In fact, Goffman observes that the most defiant of inmates are paradoxically those who are most completely caught up in the daily round of institutional life. "Sustained rejection of a total institution often requires sustained orientation to its formal organization, and hence, paradoxically, a deep kind of involvement in the establishment."[20] The same immersion in the institutional routine that makes some inmates so easy to manage makes others peculiarly sensitive to disruptions of the routine, jealous of their "rights" under the system. Indeed, periods of intransigence can alternate, in the same person, with colonization, conversion, and even with periods of withdrawal.

The concentration camp was unique among total institutions in confronting the typical prisoner with a choice between situational withdrawal, which meant death, and conversion, which, in the absence of alternatives, came to dominate the personality as a fully internalized role. In other total institutions, however, all four roles can be played to some extent, and "few inmates seem to pursue any one of them very far. In most total institutions most inmates take the tack of what some of them call 'playing it cool.' This involves a somewhat opportunistic combination of secondary adjustments, conversion, colonization, and loyalty to the inmate group, so that the inmate will have a maximum chance, in the particular circumstances, of eventually getting out physically and psychologically undamaged."[21] The slave had no real prospect of "getting out," but unless he was infantilized—a hypothesis that now seems quite untenable—he had a powerful stake in psychic survival. He had every reason to play it cool; and what is more, slavery gave him plenty of opportunities.

20 Goffman, *Asylums*, 62.
21 *Ibid.*, 64–65.

But the most compelling consideration in favor of this interpretation of slavery is that the very ways in which slavery differed from other total institutions would have actually reinforced and stabilized the pattern of opportunistic response that we have described. The most obvious objection to an analogy between slavery and the prison, the mental hospital, or any other institution of this kind is that slaves for the most part were born into slavery rather than coming in from the outside as adults; nor did most of them have any hope of getting out. We have answered these objections in various ways, but before leaving the matter we should point out that there is, in fact, a class of people in modern asylums—a minority, to be sure—who spend the better part of their lives in institutions of one kind or another. "Lower class mental hospital patients," for instance, "who have lived all their previous lives in orphanages, reformatories, and jails," are people whose experience in this respect approximates the slave's, especially the slave who served a series of masters. As a result of their continuous confinement, such patients have developed a kind of institutional personality. But they are not, as one might expect, Sambos—genuine converts to the institutional view of themselves. Quite the contrary; these people are the master-opportunists, for whom "no particular scheme of adaptation need be carried very far."[22] They have "perfected their adaptive techniques," experience having taught them a supreme versatility; and they are therefore likely to play it cool with more success than those brought in from the outside and incarcerated for the first time. These are the virtuosos of the system, neither docile nor rebellious, who spend their lives in skillful and somewhat cynical attempts to beat the system at its own game.

[22] *Ibid.*, 65–66.

V

There is a passage in Frederick Douglass' *Narrative* that suggests how difficult it was even for an ex-slave—an unusually
perceptive observer, in this case—to understand his former
victimization without resorting to categories derived from
experiences quite alien to slavery, categories that reflected the
consciousness not of the slaves themselves but, in one way or
another, the consciousness of the master-class. Douglass described how eagerly the slaves on Colonel Lloyd's Maryland
plantations vied for the privilege of running errands to the
Great House Farm, the master's residence and home plantation. The slaves "regarded it as evidence of great confidence
reposed in them by the overseers; and it was on this account,
as well as a constant desire to be out of the field from under
the driver's lash, that they esteemed it a high privilege, one
worth careful living for. He was called the smartest and most
trusty fellow, who had this honor conferred upon him the
most frequently."

Then follows a passage of unusual vividness and poignancy:

> The slaves selected to go to the Great House Farm, for
> the monthly allowance for themselves and their fellow-
> slaves, were peculiarly enthusiastic. While on their way,
> they would make the dense old woods, for miles around,
> reverberate with their wild songs, revealing at once the
> highest joy and the deepest sadness. . . . They would some-
> times sing the most pathetic sentiment in the most rapturous
> tone, and the most rapturous sentiment in the most pathetic
> tone. Into all of their songs they would manage to weave
> something of the Great House Farm. Especially would they
> do this, when leaving home. They would then sing most
> exultingly the following words: —

'I am going away to the Great House Farm!
O, yea! O, yea! O!'

This they would sing, as a chorus, to words which to many
would seem unmeaning jargon, but which, nevertheless,
were full of meaning to themselves. I have sometimes thought
that the mere hearing of those songs would do more to impress some minds with the horrible character of slavery,
than the reading of whole volumes of philosophy on the
subject could do.

But as these passages so clearly show, the "horrible character
of slavery" did not lie, as the abolitionists tended to think,
in the deprivations to which the slaves were forcibly subjected—deprivations which, resenting, they resisted with whatever means came to hand—but in the degree to which the
slaves (even in their "intransigence") inevitably identified
themselves with the system that bound and confined them,
lending themselves to their own degradation. In vying for
favors they "sought as diligently to please their overseers,"
Douglass says, "as the office-seekers in the political parties
seek to please and deceive the people."[23]

Even more revealing are the reflections that follow. "I did
not, when a slave, understand the deep meaning of those rude
and apparently incoherent songs. I was myself within the
circle; so that I neither saw nor heard as those without might
see and hear." It was only from without that the slave songs
revealed themselves as "the prayer and complaint of souls
boiling over with the bitterest anguish"—anguish, it should
be noted, which expressed itself disjointedly, "the most
pathetic sentiment" being set to "the most rapturous tone."
It was only from without that the "dehumanizing character
of slavery" showed itself precisely in the slave's incapacity to

[23] Douglass, *Narrative*, 35–37.

resist; but this perception, once gained, immediately distorted the reality to which it was applied. Douglass slides imperceptibly from these unforgettable evocations of slavery to an abolitionist polemic. It is a great mistake, he argued, to listen to slaves' songs "as evidence of their contentment and happiness." On the contrary, "slaves sing most when they are most unhappy." Yet the slaves whose "wild songs" he has just described were those who were "peculiarly enthusiastic," by his own account, to be sent to the Great House Farm, and who sang "exultingly" along the way. The ambiguity of the reality begins to fade when seen through the filter of liberal humanitarianism, and whereas the songs revealed "at once the highest joy and the deepest sadness," in Douglass' own words, as an abolitionist he feels it necessary to insist that "crying for joy, and singing for joy, were alike uncommon to me while in the jaws of slavery."[24]

If the abolitionist lens distorted the "horrible character" of slavery, the picture of the docile and apparently contented bondsman was no more faithful to the reality it purported to depict. But this should not surprise us. It is not often that men understand, or even truly see, those whom in charity they would uplift. How much less often do they understand those they exploit?

[24] *Ibid.*, 37–38.

Through the Prism of Folklore:
The Black Ethos in Slavery

STERLING STUCKEY

It is not excessive to advance the view that some historians, because they have been so preoccupied with demonstrating the absence of significant slave revolts, conspiracies, and "day to day" resistance among slaves, have presented information on slave behavior and thought which is incomplete indeed. They have, in short, devoted very little attention to trying to get "inside" slaves to discover what bondsmen thought about their condition. Small wonder we have been saddled with so many stereotypical treatments of slave thought and behavior.[1]

Though we do not know enough about the institution of slavery or the slave experience to state with great precision how slaves felt about their condition, it is reasonably clear that slavery, however draconic and well supervised, was not the hermetically sealed monolith—destructive to the majority of slave personalities—that some historians would have us believe. The works of Herbert Aptheker, Kenneth Stampp,

[1] Historians, in addition to Elkins, who have provided stereotypical treatments of slave thought and personality are Ulrich B. Phillips, *American Negro Slavery* (New York, 1918); and Samuel Eliot Morrison and Henry Steele Commager, *The Growth of the American Republic* (New York, 1950).

Richard Wade, and the Bauers, allowing for differences in
approach and purpose, indicate that slavery, despite its brutality, was not so "closed" that it robbed most of the slaves of
their humanity.[2]

It should, nevertheless, be asserted at the outset that blacks
could not have survived the grim experience of slavery un-
scathed. Those historians who, for example, point to the
dependency complex which slavery engendered in many
Afro-Americans offer us an important insight into one of the
most harmful effects of that institution upon its victims. That
slavery caused not a few bondsmen to question their worth as
human beings—this much, I believe, we can posit with certi-
tude. We can also safely assume that such self-doubt would
rend one's sense of humanity, establishing an uneasy balance
between affirming and negating aspects of one's being. What
is at issue is not whether American slavery was harmful to
slaves but whether, in their struggle to control self-lacerating
tendencies, the scales were tipped toward a despair so con-
suming that most slaves, in time, became reduced to the level
of Sambos.[3]

My thesis, which rests on an examination of folk songs and
tales, is that slaves were able to fashion a life style and set of
values—an ethos—which prevented them from being imprisoned

[2] See Herbert Aptheker, *American Negro Slave Revolts* (New York,
1943); Kenneth M. Stampp, *The Peculiar Institution* (New York, 1956);
Richard Wade, *Slavery in the Cities* (New York, 1964); and Alice and
Raymond Bauer, "Day to Day Resistance to Slavery," *Journal of Negro
History*, XXVII, No. 4 (October, 1942).

[3] I am here concerned with the Stanley Elkins version of "Sambo," that
is, the inference that the overwhelming majority of slaves, as a result of
their struggle to survive under the brutal system of American slavery,
became so callous and indifferent to their status that they gave survival
primacy over all other considerations. See Chapters III through VI of *Slavery* for a discussion of the process by which blacks allegedly were reduced
to the "good humor of everlasting childhood" (132).

altogether by the definitions which the larger society sought
to impose. This ethos was an amalgam of Africanisms and
New World elements which helped slaves, in Guy Johnson's
words, "feel their way along the course of American slavery,
enabling them to endure. . . ."[4] As Sterling Brown, that wise
student of Afro-American culture, has remarked, the values
expressed in folklore acted as a "wellspring to which slaves"
trapped in the wasteland of American slavery "could return
in times of doubt to be refreshed."[5] In short, I shall contend
that the process of dehumanization was not nearly as pervasive
as Stanley Elkins would have us believe; that a very large
number of slaves, guided by this ethos, were able to maintain
their essential humanity. I make this contention because folklore in its natural setting is of, by, and for those who create
and respond to it, depending for its survival upon the accuracy with which it speaks to needs and reflects sentiments.
I therefore consider it safe to assume that the attitudes of a
very large number of slaves are represented by the themes of
folklore.[6]

[4] I am indebted to Guy Johnson of the University of North Carolina for
suggesting the use of the term "ethos" in this piece, and for helpful commentary on the original paper which was read before the Association for
the Study of Negro Life and History at Greensboro, North Carolina, on
October 13, 1967.

[5] Professor Brown made this remark in a paper delivered before the
Amistad Society in Chicago, Spring, 1964. Distinguished poet, literary critic,
folklorist, and teacher, Brown has long contended that an awareness of
Negro folklore is essential to an understanding of slave personality and
thought.

[6] I subscribe to Alan Lomax's observation that folk songs "can be taken
as the signposts of persistent patterns of community feeling and can throw
light into many dark corners of our past and our present." His view that
Afro-American music, despite its regional peculiarities, "expresses the same
feelings and speaks the same basic language everywhere" is also accepted as
a working principle in this paper. For an extended treatment of these points
of view, see Alan Lomax, *Folk Songs of North America* (New York, 1960),
Introduction, xx.

II

Frederick Douglass, commenting on slave songs, remarked his utter astonishment, on coming to the North, "to find persons who could speak of the singing among slaves as evidence of their contentment and happiness."[7] The young Du Bois, among the first knowledgeable critics of the spirituals, found white Americans as late as 1903 still telling Afro-Americans that "life was joyous to the black slave, careless and happy." "I can easily believe this of some," he wrote, "of many. But not all the past South, though it rose from the dead, can gainsay the heart-touching witness of these songs."

> They are the music of an unhappy people, of the children of disappointment; they tell of death and suffering and unvoiced longing toward a truer world, of misty wanderings and hidden ways.[8]

Though few historians have been interested in such wanderings and ways, Frederick Douglass, probably referring to the spirituals, said the songs of slaves represented the sorrows of the slave's heart, serving to relieve the slave "only as an aching heart is relieved by its tears." "I have often sung," he continued, "to drown my sorrow, but seldom to express my happiness. Crying for joy, and singing for joy, were alike uncommon to me while in the jaws of slavery."[9]

[7] Frederick Douglass, *Narrative of the Life of Frederick Douglass* (Cambridge, Mass., 1960), 38. Originally published in 1845.

[8] John Hope Franklin (ed.), *Souls of Black Folk* in *Three Negro Classics* (New York, 1965), 380. Originally published in 1903.

[9] Douglass, *Narrative*, 38. Douglass' view adumbrated John and Alan Lomax's theory that the songs of the folk singer are deeply rooted "in his life and have functioned there as enzymes to assist in the digestion of hardship, solitude, violence [and] hunger." John A. and Alan Lomax, *Our Singing Country* (New York, 1941), Preface, xiii.

Sterling Brown, who has much to tell us about the poetry and meaning of these songs, has observed: "As the best expression of the slave's deepest thoughts and yearnings, they [the spirituals] speak with convincing finality against the legend of contented slavery."[10] Rejecting the formulation that the spirituals are mainly otherworldly, Brown states that though the creators of the spirituals looked toward heaven and "found their triumphs there, they did not blink their eyes to trouble here." The spirituals, in his view, "never tell of joy in the 'good old days.' . . . The only joy in the spirituals is in dreams of escape."[11]

Rather than being essentially otherworldly, these songs, in Brown's opinion, "tell of this life, of 'rollin' through an unfriendly world!" To substantiate this view, he points to numerous lines from spirituals: "Oh, bye and bye, bye and bye, I'm going to lay down this heavy load"; "My way is cloudy"; "Oh, stand the storm, it won't be long, we'll anchor by and by"; "Lord help me from sinking down"; and "Don't know what my mother wants to stay here fuh, Dis ole world ain't been no friend to huh."[12] To those scholars who "would have us believe that when the Negro sang of freedom, he meant only what the whites meant, namely freedom from sin," Brown rejoins:

> Free individualistic whites on the make in a prospering civilization, nursing the American dream, could well have felt their only bondage to be that of sin, and freedom to be religious salvation. But with the drudgery, the hardships, the auction block, the slave-mart, the shackles, and the lash so literally present in the Negro's experience, it is hard to

[10] Sterling Brown, "Negro Folk Expression," *Phylon* (October, 1953), 47.
[11] Brown, "Folk Expression," 48.
[12] *Ibid.*, 47.

imagine why for the Negro they would remain figurative. The scholars certainly did not make this clear, but rather take refuge in such dicta as "the slave never contemplated his low condition."[13]

"Are we to believe," asks Brown, "that the slave singing 'I been rebuked, I been scorned, done had a hard time sho's you bawn,' referred to his being outside the true religion?" A reading of additional spirituals indicates that they contained distinctions in meaning which placed them outside the confines of the "true religion." Sometimes, in these songs, we hear slaves relating to divinities on terms more West African than American. The easy intimacy and argumentation, which come out of a West African frame of reference, can be heard in "Hold the Wind."[14]

> When I get to heaven, gwine be at ease,
> Me and my God *gonna do as we please.*

> Gonna chatter with the Father, argue with the Son,
> *Tell um 'bout the world I just come from.*[15] (Italics added.)

If there is a tie with heaven in those lines from "Hold the Wind," there is also a clear indication of dislike for the restrictions imposed by slavery. And at least one high heavenly authority might have a few questions to answer. *Tell um 'bout the world I just come from* makes it abundantly clear that

---

[13] *Ibid.*, 48.

[14] Addressing himself to the slave's posture toward God, and the attitudes toward the gods which the slave's African ancestors had, Lomax has written: "The West African lives with his gods on terms of intimacy. He appeals to them, reviles them, tricks them, laughs at their follies. In this spirit the Negro slave humanized the stern religion of his masters by adopting the figures of the Bible as his intimates." Lomax, *Folk Songs of North America*, 463.

[15] Quoted from Lomax, *Folk Songs of North America*, 475.

some slaves—even when released from the burdens of the world—would keep alive painful memories of their oppression. If slaves could argue with the son of God, then surely, when on their knees in prayer, they would not hesitate to speak to God of the treatment being received at the hands of their oppressors.

> Talk about me much as you please, (2)
> Chillun, talk about me much as you please,
> Gonna talk about you when I get on my knees.[16]

That slaves could spend time complaining about treatment received from other slaves is conceivable, but that this was their only complaint, or even the principal one, is hardly conceivable. To be sure, there is a certain ambiguity in the use of the word "chillun" in this context. The reference appears to apply to slaveholders.

The spiritual, *Samson*, as Vincent Harding has pointed out, probably contained much more (for some slaves) than mere biblical implications. Some who sang these lines from *Samson*, Harding suggests, might well have meant tearing down the edifice of slavery. If so, it was the antebellum equivalent of today's "burn baby burn."

> He said, 'An' if I had-'n my way,'
> He said, 'An' if I had-'n my way,'
> He said, 'An' if I had-'n my way,
> I'd tear the build-in' down!'
>
> He said, 'And now I got my way, (3)
> And I'll tear this buildin' down.'[17]

[16] Quoted from Sterling A. Brown, Arthur P. Davis, and Ulysses Lee, *The Negro Caravan* (New York, 1941), 436.
[17] Vincent Harding, *Black Radicalism in America*. An unpublished work which Dr. Harding recently completed.

Both Harriet Tubman and Frederick Douglass have reported that some of the spirituals carried double meanings. Whether most of the slaves who sang those spirituals could decode them is another matter. Harold Courlander has made a persuasive case against widespread understanding of any given "loaded" song,[18] but it seems to me that he fails to recognize sufficiently a further aspect of the subject: slaves, as their folk tales make eminently clear, used irony repeatedly, especially with animal stories. Their symbolic world was rich. Indeed, the various masks which many put on were not unrelated to this symbolic process. It seems logical to infer that it would occur to more than a few to seize upon some songs, even though created originally for religious purposes, assign another meaning to certain words, and use these songs for a variety of purposes and situations.

At times slave bards created great poetry as well as great music. One genius among the slaves couched his (and their) desire for freedom in a magnificent line of verse. After God's powerful voice had "Rung through Heaven and down in Hell," he sang, "My dungeon shook and my chains, they fell."[19]

In some spirituals, Alan Lomax has written, Afro-Americans turned sharp irony and "healing laughter" toward heaven, again like their West African ancestors, relating on terms of intimacy with God. In one, the slaves have God engaged in a dialogue with Adam:

[18] See Harold Courlander, *Negro Folk Music, U.S.A.* (New York, 1963), 42, 43. If a great many slaves did not consider Harriet Tubman the "Moses" of her people, it is unlikely that most failed to grasp the relationship between themselves and the Israelites, Egypt and the South, and Pharaoh and slavemasters in such lines as: "Didn't my Lord deliver Daniel / And why not every man"; "Oh Mary don't you weep, don't you moan / Pharaoh's army got drowned / Oh Mary don't you weep"; and "Go down Moses / Way down in Egypt-land / Tell old Pharaoh / To let my people go."

[19] Quoted from Lomax, *Folk Songs of North America*, 471.

'Stole my apples, I believe.'
'No, marse Lord, I spec it was Eve.'
Of this tale there is no mo'
Eve et the apple and Adam de co'.[20]

Douglass informs us that slaves also sang ironic seculars about the institution of slavery. He reports having heard them sing: "We raise de wheat, dey gib us de corn; We sift de meal, dey gib us de huss; We peel de meat, dey gib us de skin; An dat's de way dey take us in."[21] Slaves would often stand back and see the tragicomic aspects of their situation, sometimes admiring the swiftness of blacks:

> Run, nigger, run, de patrollers will ketch you,
> Run, nigger, run, its almost day.
> Dat nigger run, dat nigger flew;
> Dat nigger tore his shirt in two.[22]

And there is:

> My ole mistiss promise me
> W'en she died, she'd set me free,
> She lived so long dat 'er head got bal'
> An' she give out'n de notion a-dyin' at all.[23]

In the antebellum days, work songs were of crucial import to slaves. As they cleared and cultivated land, piled levees along rivers, piled loads on steamboats, screwed cotton bales into the holds of ships, and cut roads and railroads through forest, mountain, and flat, slaves sang while the white man,

[20] *Ibid.*, 476.
[21] Frederick Douglass, *The Life and Times of Frederick Douglass* (New York, 1962), 146.
[22] Brown, "Folk Expression," 51.
[23] Brown, Davis, and Lee, *Caravan*, 447.

armed and standing in the shade, shouted his orders.[24] Through
the sense of timing and coordination which characterized
work songs well sung, especially by the leaders, slaves sometimes quite literally created works of art. These songs not
only militated against injuries but enabled the bondsmen to
get difficult jobs done more easily by not having to concentrate on the dead level of their work. "In a very real sense the
chants of Negro labor," writes Alan Lomax, "may be considered the most profoundly American of all our folk songs, for
they were created by our people as they tore at American
rock and earth and reshaped it with their bare hands, while
rivers of sweat ran down and darkened the dust."

> Long summer day makes a white man lazy,
>   Long summer day.
> Long summer day makes a nigger run away, sir,
>   Long summer day.[25]

Other slaves sang lines indicating their distaste for slave labor:

> Ol' massa an' ol' missis,
> Sittin' in the parlour,
> Jus' fig'in' an' a-plannin'
> How to work a nigger harder.[26]

And there are these bitter lines, the meaning of which is clear:

> Missus in the big house,
> Mammy in the yard,
> Missus holdin' her white hands,
> Mammy workin' hard, (3)

---

[24] Lomax, *Folk Songs of North America*, 514.
[25] *Ibid.*, 515.
[26] *Ibid.*, 527.

Missus holdin' her white hands,
Mammy workin' hard.

Old Marse ridin' all time,
Niggers workin' round,
Marse sleepin' day time,
Niggers diggin' in the ground, (3)
Marse sleepin' day time,
Niggers diggin' in the ground.[27]

Courlander tells us that the substance of the work songs "ranges from the humorous to the sad, from the gentle to the biting, and from the tolerant to the unforgiving." The statement in a given song can be metaphoric, tangent, or direct, the meaning personal or impersonal. "As throughout Negro singing generally, there is an incidence of social criticism, ridicule, gossip, and protest."[28] Pride in their strength rang with the downward thrust of axe—

When I was young and in my prime, (hah!)
Sunk my axe deep every time, (hah!)

Blacks later found their greatest symbol of manhood in John Henry, descendant of Trickster John of slave folk tales:

A man ain't nothing but a man,
But before I'll let that steam driver beat me down
I'll die with my hammer in my hand.[29]

[27] Courlander, *Negro Folk Music*, 117.
[28] *Ibid.*, 89.
[29] Brown, "Folk Expression," 54. Steel-driving John Henry is obviously in the tradition of the axe-wielding blacks of the antebellum period. The ballad of John Henry helped spawn John Henry work songs:

Dis ole hammer—hunh
Ring like silver—hunh (3)
Shine like gold, baby—hunh
Shine like gold—hunh

Though Frances Kemble, an appreciative and sensitive listener to work songs, felt that "one or two barbaric chants would make the fortune of an opera," she was on one occasion "displeased not a little" by a self-deprecating song, one which "embodied the opinion that 'twenty-six black girls not make mulatto yellow girl,' and as I told them I did not like it, they have since omitted it."[30] What is pivotal here is not the presence of self-laceration in folklore, but its extent and meaning. While folklore contained some self-hatred, on balance it gives no indication whatever that blacks, as a group, liked or were indifferent to slavery, which is the issue.[31]

To be sure, only the most fugitive of songs sung by slaves contained direct attacks upon the system. Two of these were associated with slave rebellions. The first, possibly written by ex-slave Denmark Vesey himself, was sung by slaves on at least one island off the coast of Charleston, S.C., and at meet-

---

Dis ole hammer—hunh
Killt John Henry—hunh (3)
Twont kill me baby, hunh
Twon't kill me. (Quoted from Brown, "Folk Expression," 57.)

[30] Frances Anne Kemble, *Journal of a Residence on a Georgia Plantation, 1838–1839* (New York, 1961), 260–61. Miss Kemble heard slaves use the epithet "nigger": "And I assure you no contemptuous intonation ever equalled the prepotenza (arrogance) of the despotic insolence of this address of these poor wretches to each other." Kemble, *Journal*, 281. Here she is on solid ground, but the slaves also used the word with glowing affection, as seen in the "Run, Nigger, Run" secular. At other times they leaned toward self-laceration but refused to go the whole route: "My name's Ran, I wuks in de sand, I'd rather be a nigger dan a po' white man." Brown, "Folk Expression," 51. Some blacks also sang, "It takes a long, lean, black-skinned gal, to make a preacher lay his Bible down." Newman I. White, *American Negro Folk Songs* (Cambridge, 1928), 411.

[31] Elkins, who believes Southern white lore on slavery should be taken seriously, does not subject it to serious scrutiny. For a penetrating—and devastating—analysis of "the richest layers of Southern lore" which, according to Elkins, resulted from "an exquisitely rounded collective creativity," see Sterling A. Brown, "A Century of Negro Portraiture in American Literature," *The Massachusetts Review* (Winter, 1966).

ings convened by Vesey in Charleston. Though obviously not
a folk song, it was sung by the folk.

> Hail! all hail! ye Afric clan,
> Hail! ye oppressed, ye Afric band,
> Who toil and sweat in slavery bound
> And when your health and strength are gone
> Are left to hunger and to mourn,
> Let independence be your aim,
> Ever mindful what 'tis worth.
> Pledge your bodies for the prize,
> Pile them even to the skies![32]

The second, a popular song derived from a concrete reality,
bears the marks of a conscious authority:

> You mought be rich as cream
> And drive you coach and four-horse team,
> But you can't keep de world from moverin' round
> Nor Nat Turner from gainin' ground.
>
> And your name it mought be Caesar sure,
> And got you cannon can shoot a mile or more,
> But you can't keep de world from moverin' round
> Nor Nat Turner from gainin' ground.[33]

The introduction of Denmark Vesey, class leader in the
A.M.E. Church, and Nat Turner, slave preacher, serves to
remind us that some slaves and ex-slaves were violent as well
as humble, impatient as well as patient.

It is also well to recall that the religious David Walker,
who had lived close to slavery in North Carolina, and Henry

---

[32] Quoted from Archie Epps, "A Negro Separatist Movement," *The
Harvard Review*, IV, No. 1 (Summer–Fall, 1956), 75.

[33] Quoted in William Styron, "This Quiet Dust," *Harpers* (April, 1965),
135.

Highland Garnett, ex-slave and Presbyterian minister, produced two of the most inflammatory, vitriolic, and doom-
bespeaking polemics America has yet seen.[34] There was
theological tension here, loudly proclaimed, a tension which
emanated from and was perpetuated by American slavery and
race prejudice. This dimension of ambiguity must be kept in
mind, if for no other reason than to place in bolder relief the
possibility that a great many slaves and free Afro-Americans
could have interpreted Christianity in a way quite different
from white Christians.

Even those songs which seemed most otherworldly, those
which expressed profound weariness of spirit and even faith
in death, through their unmistakable sadness, were accusa-
tory, and God was not their object. If one accepts as a given
that some of these appear to be almost wholly escapist, the
indictment is no less real. Thomas Wentworth Higginson
came across one—". . . a flower of poetry in that dark soil,"
he called it.[35]

> I'll walk in de graveyard, I'll walk through de graveyard,
>   To lay dis body down.
> I'll lie in de grave and stretch out my arms,
>   Lay dis body down.

Reflecting on "I'll lie in de grave and stretch out my arms,"
Higginson said that "Never, it seems to me, since man first
lived and suffered, was his infinite longing for peace uttered
more plaintively than in that line."[36]

[34] For excerpts from David Walker's *Appeal* and Henry H. Garnett's
Call to Rebellion, see Herbert Aptheker (ed.), *A Documentary History of
the Negro People in the United States*, 2 vols. (New York, 1965). Originally
published in 1951.
[35] Thomas Wentworth Higginson, *Army Life in a Black Regiment* (New
York, 1962), 199.
[36] *Ibid.*

There seems to be small doubt that Christianity contributed
in large measure to a spirit of patience which militated against
open rebellion among the bondsmen. Yet to overemphasize
this point leads one to obscure a no less important reality:
Christianity, after being reinterpreted and recast by slave
bards, also contributed to that spirit of endurance which
powered generations of bondsmen, bringing them to that
decisive moment when for the first time a real choice was
available to scores of thousands of them.

When that moment came, some slaves who were in a position to decide for themselves did so. W. E. B. Du Bois
recreated their mood and the atmosphere in which they lived.

> There came the slow looming of emancipation. Crowds
> and armies of the unknown, inscrutable, unfathomable
> Yankees; cruelty behind and before; rumors of a new slave
> trade, but slowly, continuously, the wild truth, the bitter
> truth, the magic truth, came surging through. There was
> to be a new freedom! And a black nation went tramping
> after the armies no matter what it suffered; no matter how
> it was treated, no matter how it died.[37]

The gifted bards, by creating songs with an unmistakable
freedom ring, songs which would have been met with swift,
brutal repression in the antebellum days, probably voiced the
sentiments of all but the most degraded and dehumanized.
Perhaps not even the incredulous slavemaster could deny the
intent of the new lyrics. "In the wake of the Union Army and
in the contraband camps," remarked Sterling Brown, "spirituals of freedom sprang up suddenly. . . . Some celebrated
the days of Jubilo: 'O Freedom; O Freedom!' and 'Before I'll

---

[37] W. E. B. Du Bois, *Black Reconstruction in America* (Philadelphia,
1935), 122. Originally published in 1935 by Harcourt, Brace and Company.

be a slave, I'll be buried in my grave!,' and 'Go home to my
lord and be free.' " And there was: " 'No more driver's lash
for me. . . . Many thousand go.' "[38]
Du Bois brought together the insights of the poet and historian to get inside the slaves:

> There was joy in the South. It rose like perfume—like a
> prayer. Men stood quivering. Slim dark girls, wild and
> beautiful with wrinkled hair, wept silently; young women,
> black, tawny, white and golden, lifted shivering hands, and
> old and broken mothers, black and gray, raised great voices
> and shouted to God across the fields, and up to the rocks
> and the mountains.[39]

Some sang:

> Slavery chain done broke at last, broke at last, broke at last,
> Slavery chain done broke at last,
> Going to praise God till I die.

> I did tell him how I suffer,
> In de dungeon and de chain,
> *And de days I went with head bowed down,*
> And my broken flesh and pain,
> Slavery chain done broke at last, broke at last, broke at last.[40]

Whatever the nature of the shocks generated by the war,
among those vibrations felt were some that had come from
Afro-American singing ever since the first Africans were

---

[38] Brown, "Folk Expression," 49.
[39] Du Bois, *Reconstruction*, 124.
[40] Quoted in Brown, Davis, and Lee, *Caravan*, 440–41. One of the most
tragic scenes of the Civil War period occurred when a group of Sea Island
freedmen, told by a brigadier-general that they would not receive land
from the government, sang, "Nobody knows the trouble I've seen." Du
Bois, *Souls*, 381.

forcibly brought to these shores. Du Bois was correct when he said that the new freedom song had not come from Africa, but that "the dark throb and beat of that Ancient of Days was in and through it."[41] Thus, the psyches of those who gave rise to and provided widespread support for folk songs had not been reduced to *tabula rasas* on which a slave-holding society could at pleasure sketch out its wish fulfillment fantasies.

We have already seen the acute degree to which some slaves realized they were being exploited. Their sense of the injustice of slavery made it so much easier for them to act out their aggression against whites (by engaging in various forms of "day to day" resistance) without being overcome by a sense of guilt, or a feeling of being ill-mannered. To call this nihilistic thrashing about would be as erroneous as to refer to their use of folklore as esthetic thrashing about.[42]

---

[41] Du Bois, *Reconstruction*, 124.

[42] If some slavemasters encouraged slaves to steal or simply winked at thefts, then slaves who obliged them were most assuredly *not acting against their own interests*, whatever the motivation of the masters. Had more fruitful options been available to them, then and only then could we say that slaves were playing into the hands of their masters. Whatever the masters thought of slaves who stole from them—and there is little reason to doubt that most slaves considered it almost obligatory to steal from white people—the slaves, it is reasonable to assume, were aware of the unparalleled looting in which masters themselves were engaged. To speak therefore of slaves undermining their sense of self-respect as a result of stealing from whites—and this argument has been advanced by Eugene Genovese—is wide of the mark. Indeed, it appears more likely that those who engaged in stealing were, in the context of an oppressor-oppressed situation, on the way to realizing a larger measure of self-respect. Moreover, Genovese, in charging that certain forms of "day to day" resistance, in the absence of general conditions of rebellion, "amounted to individual and essentially nihilistic thrashing about," fails to recognize that that which was possible, that which conditions permitted, was pursued by slaves in preference to the path which led to passivity or annihilation. Those engaging in "day to day" resistance were moving along meaningful rather than nihilistic lines, for their activities were designed to frustrate the demands of the authority-system. For a very suggestive discussion of the dependency complex engendered by slavery and

For if they did not regard themselves as the equals of whites in many ways, their folklore indicates that the generality of slaves must have at least felt superior to whites morally. And that, in the context of oppression, could make the difference between a viable human spirit and one crippled by the belief that the interests of the master are those of the slave.

When it is borne in mind that slaves created a large number of extraordinary songs and greatly improved a considerable proportion of the songs of others, it is not at all difficult to believe that they were conscious of the fact that they were leaders in the vital area of art—giving protagonists rather than receiving pawns. And there is some evidence that slaves were aware of the special talent which they brought to music. Higginson has described how reluctantly they sang from hymnals—"even on Sunday"—and how "gladly" they yielded "to the more potent excitement of their own 'spirituals.' "[43] It is highly unlikely that the slaves' preference for their own music went unremarked among them, or that this preference did not affect their estimate of themselves. "They soon found," commented Alan Lomax, "that when they sang, the whites recognized their superiority as singers, and listened with respect."[44] He might have added that those antebellum whites who listened probably seldom understood.

---

highly provocative views on the significance of "day to day" resistance among slaves, see Eugene Genovese, "The Legacy of Slavery and the Roots of Black Nationalism," *Studies on the Left*, VI, No. 6 (Nov.–Dec., 1966), especially p. 8.

[43] Higginson, *Black Regiment*, 212. Alan Lomax reminds us that the slaves sang "in leader-chorus style, with a more relaxed throat than the whites, and in deeper-pitched, mellower voices, which blended richly." "A strong, surging beat underlay most of their American creations . . . words and tunes were intimately and playfully united, and 'sense' was often subordinated to the demands of rhythm and melody." Lomax, *Folk Songs of North America*, Introduction, xx.

[44] Lomax, *Folk Songs of North America*, 460.

What is of pivotal import, however, is that the esthetic realm was the one area in which slaves knew they were not inferior to whites. Small wonder that they borrowed many songs from the larger community, then quickly invested them with their own economy of statement and power of imagery rather than yield to the temptation of merely repeating what they had heard. Since they were essentially group rather than solo performances, the values inherent in and given affirmation by the music served to strengthen bondsmen in a way that solo music could not have done.[45] In a word, slave singing often provided a form of group therapy, a way in which a slave, in concert with others, could fend off some of the debilitating effects of slavery.

The field of inquiry would hardly be complete without some mention of slave tales. Rich in quantity and often subtle in conception, these tales further illumine the inner world of the bondsmen, disclosing moods and interests almost as various as those found in folk songs. That folk tales, like the songs, indicate an African presence, should not astonish; for the telling of tales, closely related to the African griot's vocation of providing oral histories of families and dynasties, was deeply rooted in West African tradition. Hughes and Bontemps have written that the slaves brought to America the

[45] Commenting on the group nature of much of slave singing, Alan Lomax points out that the majority of the bondsmen "came from West Africa, where music-making was largely a group activity, the creation of a many-voiced, dancing throng. . . . Community songs of labour and worship (in America) and dance songs far outnumbered narrative pieces, and the emotion of the songs was, on the whole, joyfully erotic, deeply tragic, allusive, playful, or ironic rather than nostalgic, withdrawn, factual, or aggressively comic—as among white folk singers." Lomax, *Folk Songs of North America*, xix and xx of Introduction. For treatments of the more technical aspects of Afro-American music, see Courlander, *Negro Folk Music*, especially Chapter II; and Richard A. Waterman, "African Influences on the Music of the Americas," in *Acculturation in the Americas*, edited by Sol Tax (New York, 1967).

"habit of storytelling as pastime, together with a rich bestiary."
Moreover, they point out that the folk tales of slaves "were
actually projections of personal experiences and hopes and
defeats, in terms of symbols," and that this important dimension of the tales "appears to have gone unnoticed."[46]
Possessing a repertoire which ranged over a great many
areas, perhaps the most memorable tales are those of Brer
Rabbit and John.[47] Brer Rabbit, now trickster, ladies' man, and
braggart, now wit, joker, and glutton, possessed the resourcefulness, despite his size and lack of strength, to outsmart
stronger, larger animals. "To the slave in his condition," according to Hughes and Bontemps, "the theme of weakness
overcoming strength through cunning proved endlessly fascinating."[48] John, characterized by a spiritual resilience born
of an ironic sense of life, was a secular high priest of mischief
and guile who delighted in matching wits with Ole Marster,
the "patterollers," Ole Missy, and the devil himself. He was
clever enough to sense the absurdity of his predicament and
that of white people, smart enough to know the limits of his
powers and the boundaries of those of the master class. While

[46] Arna Bontemps and Langston Hughes (eds.), *The Book of Negro
Folklore* (New York, 1965), Introduction, viii. Of course if one regards
each humorous thrust of the bondsmen as so much comic nonsense, then
there is no basis for understanding, to use Sterling Brown's phrase, the
slave's "laughter out of hell." Without understanding what humor meant to
slaves themselves, one is not likely to rise above the superficiality of a
Stephen Foster or a Joel Chandler Harris. But once an effort has been made
to see the world from the slave's point of view, then perhaps one can understand Ralph Ellison's reference to Afro-Americans, in their folklore, "back-
ing away from the chaos of experience and from ourselves," in order to
"depict the humor as well as the horror of our living." Ralph Ellison, "A
Very Stern Discipline," *Harpers* (March, 1967), 80.
[47] For additional discussions of folk tales, see Zora Neale Hurston, *Mules
and Men* (Philadelphia, 1935); Richard Dorson, *American Negro Folktales*
(Greenwich, Conn., 1967); and B. A. Botkin, *Lay My Burden Down* (Chicago, 1945).
[48] Bontemps and Hughes, *Negro Folklore*, Introduction, ix.

not always victorious, even on the spacious plane of the imagination, he could hardly be described as a slave with an inferiority complex. And in this regard it is important to note that his varieties of triumphs, though they sometimes included winning freedom, often realistically cluster about ways of coping with everyday negatives of the system.[49]

Slaves were adept in the art of storytelling, as at home in this area as they were in the field of music. But further discussion of the scope of folklore would be uneconomical, for we have already seen a depth and variety of thought among bondsmen which embarrasses stereotypical theories of slave personality. Moreover, it should be clear by now that there are no secure grounds on which to erect the old, painfully constricted Sambo structure.[50] For the personalities which lay beneath the plastic exteriors which slaves turned on and off for white people were too manifold to be contained by cheerful, childlike images. When it is argued, then, that "too much of the Negro's own lore" has gone into the making of the Sambo picture "to entitle one in good conscience to con-

---

[49] The fact that slaveowners sometimes took pleasure in being outwitted by slaves in no way diminishes from the importance of the trickster tales, for what is essential here is how these tales affected the slave's attitude toward himself, not whether his thinking or behavior would impress a society which considered black people little better than animals. Du Bois' words in this regard should never be forgotten: "Everything Negroes did was wrong. If they fought for freedom, they were beasts; if they did not fight, they were born slaves. If they cowered on the plantation, they loved slavery; if they ran away, they were lazy loafers. If they sang, they were silly; if they scowled, they were impudent. . . . And they were funny, funny—ridiculous baboons, aping men." Du Bois, *Reconstruction*, 125.

[50] Ralph Ellison offers illuminating insight into the group experience of the slave: "Any people who could endure all of that brutalization and keep together, who could undergo such dismemberment and resuscitate itself, and endure until it could take the initiative in achieving its own freedom is obviously more than the sum of its brutalization. Seen in this perspective, theirs has been one of the great human experiences and one of the great triumphs of the human spirit in modern times, in fact, in the history of the world." Ellison, "A Very Stern Discipline," 84.

demn it as 'conspiracy,' "[51] one must rejoin: Only if you strip
the masks from black faces while refusing to read the irony
and ambiguity and cunning which called the masks into
existence. Slave folklore, on balance, decisively repudiates the
thesis that Negroes *as a group* had internalized Sambo traits,
committing them, as it were, to psychological marriage.

III

It is one of the curiosities of American historiography that a
people who were as productive esthetically as American slaves
could be studied as if they had moved in a cultural cyclotron,
continually bombarded by devastating, atomizing forces which
denuded them of meaningful Africanisms while destroying
any and all impulses toward creativity. Elkins, for example,
has been tempted to wonder how it was ever possible that
"*all* this [West African] native resourcefulness and vitality
could have been brought to such a point of *utter* stultification
in America" (93; italics added). This sadly misguided view is,
of course, not grounded in any recognition or understanding
of the Afro-American dimension of American culture. In any
event, there is a great need for students of American slavery
to attempt what Gilberto Freyre tried to do for Brazilian
civilization—an effort at discovering the contributions of
slaves toward the shaping of the Brazilian national character.[52]
When such a study has been made of the American slave we
shall probably discover that, though he did not rival his
Brazilian brother in staging bloody revolutions, the quality
and place of art in his life compared favorably. Now this sug-

---

[51] Elkins sets forth this argument in *Slavery*, 84.
[52] Gilberto Freyre, *The Masters and the Slaves* (New York, 1956).
Originally published by Jose Olympio, Rio de Janeiro, Brazil.

gests that the humanity of people can be asserted through means other than open and widespread rebellion, a consideration that has not been appreciated in violence-prone America. We would do well to recall the words of F. S. C. Northrop who has observed:

> During the pre-Civil War period shipowners and southern landowners brought to the United States a considerable body of people with a color of skin and cultural values different from those of its other inhabitants. . . . Their values are more emotive, esthetic and intuitive. . . . [These] characteristics can become an asset for our culture. For these are values with respect to which Anglo-American culture is weak.[53]

These values were expressed on the highest level in the folklore of slaves. Through their folklore black slaves affirmed their humanity and left a lasting imprint on American culture. No study of the institutional aspects of American slavery can be complete, nor can the larger dimensions of slave personality and style be adequately explored, as long as historians continue to avoid that realm in which, as Du Bois has said, "the soul of the black slave spoke to man."[54]

In its nearly two and one half centuries of existence, the grim system of American slavery doubtless broke the spirits of uncounted numbers of slaves. Nevertheless, if we look through the prism of folklore, we can see others transcending their plight, appreciating the tragic irony of their condition, then seizing upon and putting to use those aspects of their

[53] F. S. C. Northrop, *The Meeting of East and West* (New York, 1952), 159–60.
[54] Du Bois, *Souls*, 378. Kenneth M. Stampp in *The Peculiar Institution* employs to a limited extent some of the materials of slave folklore. Willie Lee Rose, in *Rehearsal for Reconstruction* (New York, 1964), makes brief but highly informed use of folk material.

experience which sustain in the present and renew in the future. We can see them opposing their own angle of vision to that of their oppressor, fashioning their own techniques of defense and aggression in accordance with their own reading of reality, and doing those things well enough to avoid having their sense of humanity destroyed.

Slave folklore, then, affirms the existence of a large number of vital, tough-minded human beings who, though severely limited and abused by slavery, had found a way both to endure and preserve their humanity in the face of insuperable odds. What they learned about handling misfortune was not only a major factor in their survival as a people, but many of the lessons learned and esthetic standards established would be used by future generations of Afro-Americans in coping with a hostile world. What a splendid affirmation of the hopes and dreams of their slave ancestors that some of the songs being sung in antebellum days are the ones Afro-Americans are singing in the freedom movement today: "Michael, row the boat ashore"; "Just like a tree planted by the water, I shall not be moved."

Slaves as Inmates, Slaves as Men: A Sociological Discussion of Elkins' Thesis

ROY SIMON BRYCE-LAPORTE

Repeatedly, it has been implied that some aspects of the behavioral patterns of the Afro-American people can be attributed to the slave plantation background. Just as frequently, this notion has been challenged. This discussion, then, deals with material which is considered controversial by students of the Black American people.[1]

SLAVES AS INMATES

We have no argument with Elkins regarding the general nature of the slave plantation, the ideology and conception promoted about the African or "Negro" as man or member, or the requirements the slave plantation imposed upon the slave. We do challenge, however, his assertion or his need to have asserted that the impact reached the dimensions of

[1] This paper is drawn from the author's Ph.D. dissertation, "The Conceptualization of the American Slave Plantation as a Total Institution" (University of California, Los Angeles, 1968), a revision of which is forthcoming from Allyn & Bacon entitled *A Sociology of Black Captivity*.

creating a prevailing and crystallized *personality*. We challenge his reluctance to conceive of apparently childish, obedient manifestations as parts of an acquired repertoire of mechanisms in ecstatic role play, bicultural behavior, and, perhaps, as flight or fantasy projections. We challenge his failure to accentuate the presence of elusive, expressive, or escapist forms as much as he did the absence of openly defiant or aggressively resistive efforts. We concur that the duration of confinement, breadth of control, and extent of pervasiveness of the slave plantation must have had intense mortifying and dehumanizing impact on the slaves and their offspring. However, had slaves *fully* succumbed to those conditions they would have been all zombiefied or psychologically dead, and to have *fully* resisted they would have all been physically dead or absent by way of escape, exodus, or revolution. Slave literature indicates many cases which fell on both these extremes. Slave literature also illustrates and implies that many more fell somewhere between the two extremes.

It is our thesis that the impact of the slave plantation is more appropriately understood in terms of alternative and varied behavioral mechanisms used by slaves rather than prevalence of a fixed personality type derived from the contrived dichotomy of choices between killing or being killed. Even if every slave may at some time have engaged in submissive behavior it is unfair to suggest that inasmuch as he was not a "successful" revolutionary he was a Sambo. Situation variation and choice were characteristic of all levels of behavior within the contextual limitation of the slave plantation.

Most students of American slavery agree that large-scale, open, collective resistance by the slaves was unusual, those cases that occurred being largely unsuccessful. Even Aptheker,[2] who perhaps makes the claim for the largest number of such revolts by American slaves, does not deny their abortive nature and limited revolutionary success. On the other hand, rather than portraying zombiefied, emasculated Sambos or Toms, plantation scholars have described and presented the wide variety and unending efforts of slaves to engage in both individual defiance and more subtle collective protest against the system. Among the forms of protest most commonly referred to by plantation scholars were slowing down work, misuse of implements, resistance to acculturation, apologetic and fantasy folklore, religion and exorcism, malingering, running away, suicide, infanticide, stealing, poisoning, murder, and arson.[3] The observation can be made that these forms ranged from intro-punitive to extra-punitive measures, from elusive to openly defiant or resistive actions, and from individual to group behavior. They were largely subversive or expressively rebellious. That is, they were usually not directed to replacement or overthrowing of the estate, region, system, or society. Their effect was generally to create nuisances for the planter or estate, although in some cases they caused widespread fear. Some, the more subtle or intro-punitive, caused no great surprise to planters and Southern whites, inasmuch as many such acts were explainable within the ideology or stereotype that was entertained of the slaves. These actions were often viewed as symptoms of inbred illness, indolence, inferiority, and barbarism. Thus, as Genovese has suggested, when slaves stole (justified as they were) they were not taken seriously (even if punished). Their stealing merely reinforced the stereotype held by their masters about

[2] See Herbert Aptheker, *Negro Slave Revolts* (New York, 1943).
[3] Raymond Bauer and Alice Bauer, "Day to Day Resistance to Slavery," *Journal of Negro History*, 27 (October, 1962), 388–419; Melville Herskovits, *Myth of the Negro Past* (New York, 1941).

them.[4] Other forms of protest, even though extra-punitive, were individual or small-scale, i.e., murder, robbery, and rape, and were often considered criminal rather than rebellious.[5] Others, the extra-punitive but collective forms, caused great awe in the slaveholding population, particularly in the light of the successes of Caribbean and Latin American slave revolts and the increasing number of short-lived slave revolts and alleged mass slave crimes in the United States.

Elkins' suggestion that slavery in general and the large plan-

[4] Eugene D. Genovese, "The Legacy of Slavery and the Roots of Black Nationalism," *Studies on the Left*, 6, No. 6 (1966), 7–8. Parenthetical phrases added by this writer. Even so, we must agree with Sterling Stuckey ("Through the Prism of Folklore") with regard to the inappropriate need of the notion of "nihilistic thrashing about" to which Genovese relegates the rebellious behavior of the slaves. Such a notion presupposes a break between the insinuations of the spirituals and folk tales and the heightening of awareness and discontent among the slaves and another break between the more simplistic gestures of defiance by individual slaves and the sophistication of the underground railroad. Genovese really does not speak from the world view of the slaves as *actors*, but from an *objective*-Marxist analytic stance. In fact, he seemingly disregards the *subjective*-Marxist analytic stance, where identification and consciousness rather than consequence become the issues of concern. He furthermore does not allow for the structural development of *organization* to take place before discrediting these early "black revolutionaries"–*slaves as they were*. See Genovese's essay "American Slaves and Their History," herein, for a modification of the *objective* stance.

Notwithstanding the distinction between rebellion and revolution as portrayed in Camus' *The Rebel* and in Harold Cruse's *Rebellion or Revolution* (New York, 1969), the Black movement is objectively revolutionary, inasmuch as its basic demand for equality cannot take place without serious institutional rearrangements of the social order. This is true even though the acts of slaves and their contemporary successors may often be acts of rebellion when seen "objectively." But from a "subjective" approach there is no difference between rebellious and revolutionary acts if the actors themselves do not distinguish the motives and purposes behind such acts. In this sense the Black Revolution is an old and real revolution with no reasons for apologies to be made for the "unsuccessful" slave revolutionaries. The Black Revolution is an unending political process of planned and unplanned activities and planned and unplanned consequences, as are all revolutions.

[5] Winthrop D. Jordan, *White over Black: American Attitudes toward the Negro, 1550–1812* (Chapel Hill, 1968), 112–13.

tation system in particular demanded a submissive, dependent, childish, obedient performance of the slave and that it prohibited and punished aggressive independence or assertive resistance may be well taken. It is known that not all plantation slaves complied with the regulations of the plantations. And, it does not necessarily follow that the slaves who complied experienced an *internalization* of their compliant role as part of their selves, nor does it mean such personality traits were inherited by latter-day Blacks.[6] Elkins himself voices his reluctance to see a neat separation of "mere acting" and "true self" but concedes at least the existence of a broad belt of "indeterminacy" between the two (227–29). However, he fails to pursue the point. By so doing he is unable to reconcile observations that the same slaves who were believed to be indolent and irresponsible in their plantation chores would perform competently and competitively in their own lots or when hired out on their own time. By so doing he also is unable to elucidate the variation in slaves, situation, and styles of elusion or escape, e.g., those who tried to escape or elude, those who helped or concealed the effort of others but did not do it themselves, those who entertained the thought but did not try it, those who betrayed, discouraged, or seriously hunted out the escapees or would-be escapees, and those who were ambivalent in these and other situations.

Kardiner and Ovesey reinterpreted historical reports into

[6] For historical treatments of Black culture which go beyond the unidimensional approach utilized by Elkins, see Roger Abrahams, *Positively Black* (Englewood Cliffs, 1970); Houston Baker, "Completely Well: One View of Black American Culture," in Nathan Huggins, Martin Kilson, and Daniel Fox (eds.), *Key Issues in the Afro-American Experience* (New York, 1971); Vincent Harding, "Religion and Resistance among Antebellum Negroes, 1800–1860," in August Meier and Elliott Rudwick (eds.), *The Making of Black America* (New York, 1969), I, 179–97; Sterling Stuckey, "Through the Prism of Folklore: The Black Ethos in Slavery," herein; Okan Uya, "Everyday Life in Slavery," unpublished manuscript.

four basic adaptational patterns among slaves: (1) overt aggression and flight, (2) passivity or submissiveness and the plea for rescue, (3) vicarious aggression in folk tales, and (4) suicide, which was rare and occurred mostly in early days of capture.[7] Thus in addition to open aggressive resistance and passive submission, the two alternatives which Elkins most seriously considered, there were a wide range of elusive-expressive behaviors in the form of fantasy, feigning, or flight. In fact, they were but *forms* of escape, and thus the theme of escape also seemed to underlie both the open revolts as well as the passive submission. There is the old adage: "If you can't beat them, join them." It was suggested that the more aggressive and defiant actions were usually unsuccessful, repressed, and followed by more stringent and savage reprisals. Thus even the submission, identification, ingratiation, and idealization of the master may well have been last recourses of *overdetermination* in the conscious hope of escaping the physical hazards and psychological assaults made on the self by the slave plantation. Given the prohibitions—power, pervasiveness, permeability of the plantation—perhaps these elusive-expressive choices were the most practical, and as such accommodation became a form of resistance, a technique for survival.[8] Accordingly, slave accommodation and so-called Uncle Tomism need to be reevaluated, but in terms of the motives of slaves who practiced them.[9]

[7] See Abraham Kardiner and Lionel Ovesey, *The Mark of Oppression* (Cleveland and New York, 1962), 382.

[8] See William H. Grier and Price M. Cobbs, *Black Rage* (New York, 1968), 60–63.

[9] See Sidney Mintz, "Slavery and the Slaves" [review article], *Caribbean Studies*, 8, No. 4 (1969), 66–70. He points out that some of the so-called forms of accommodation in the West Indies, i.e., agricultural skills, became the mainstay of escaped, manumitted, and emancipated slaves and the economy of their free villages in the hills. Obviously, like many of the interpretative remarks about slavery, this point is *post factum* and must be con-

In the language of Erving Goffman such expressiveness and elusiveness represent an admixture of contained and disruptive secondary adjustments. They were *secondary* because they were illicit as means or in their ends. Some were *contained*, inasmuch as they fell within manageable ranges of anticipated or conceded "deficiencies" of the slave inmates. Others were *disruptive* because they were obvious means to abandon or disturb the system. Nevertheless, they were adjustments. As such they were laden with implicit legitimacy as well as residual submission. Thus, as adjustments, such expressive-elusive actions were cases of camouflage rather than all-out confrontations or contests for freedom, equality, or power.

Flight or escape required a different form of organization and role repertoire than would be required for open defiance. It demanded more invisible and covert bonds and called for

---

sidered with great caution within the context of this essay. It becomes very important to remember that most slaves (even in the West Indies) were not trained for the express purpose of preparing them for competent lives as free citizens. Furthermore, if it *were* so, then the fact that their training for *freedom* was largely limited to menial dependent skills makes for a more sinister conspiracy than their training for continued service as slaves. It is plausible that if these overseas Africans were free, they might have drawn upon their own agricultural heritage or engaged in techno-logical innovation or selective borrowing to adapt to the natural or man-created ecology of the West Indies. Slavery and the plantation denied them the full range of adaptation possibilities. Thus to consider either or both the *necessary* condition through which slaves acquired particular agricultural skills is to be inconsistent and to underplay the basic adaptive feature that anthropologists concede even to the least "civilized" of human groupings.

Thus while Uncle Tomism and other forms of slave accommodation are worthy of reconsideration, they must not be allowed to become part of the *apologia* for slavery, as if it were that slavery was by intention or accident a benevolent experiment. The question is, did the slaves purpose-fully accommodate to the plantation regimen in a conscious or hopeful effort to survive and to prepare themselves (or their offspring) for freedom? This is an empirical question and, as Mintz undoubtedly would agree, it must be directed to the slaves themselves. That task requires bold innova-tions in empirical research—a combination of sociological imagination, oral history, and ethnomethodology to say the least.

cunning and elusive skills rather than confrontation and power. By the same token, however, such escapist actions were not able to accommodate the large numbers desiring freedom. Thus, many slaves found relief in removal activities, e.g., folklore, spirituals, prayers, and work songs, and in institutional ceremonies, e.g., prayer meetings, festive celebrations, etc. Such removal activities and institutional ceremonies had tension-releasing rather than freedom-rendering functions. They represented more means of expression and rebellion than means of strategic revolution. Given the limitations of these expressive and escapist actions, there were occasional sporadic riots and rebellions among the slaves. However, these more aggressive forms of defiance were generally suppressed in vicious public manner and were often followed by the tightening of custodial regulations. The failure of the resistance in part was an indication of the lack of necessary organization and power for successful para-military rebellion. On the other hand, the failure indirectly boosted the *invisible* underground approach or led to penting up of tensions for some other time and sublimation of tensions in some other way.

The absence of a rehabilitative process also meant the absence of official programs for promoting full self-aggrandizement or a release ideology among the slaves. However, such absences did not mean that there were no opportunities for self-aggrandizement and release. Nor do they mean that among the inmates self-aggrandizement and release were not aspired to and actualized. More likely such absence meant that realizing either self-aggrandizement or release in a total sense was limited, improbable, and discouraged, and therefore not usually overt, widespread, or uncontrolled.

Limited aggrandizement and tension release were the anticipated consequences of many activities and processes sponsored by the slave plantation. These took different forms: the granting of permission of different sorts to slaves for good performance and good deportment; the promotion or stratification and instilling of feelings of status differences among the slaves; the sponsoring of various holidays and celebrations where the distance between staff and slaves would be reduced. It should be noted, however, that such practices rarely led to manumission. Even if and when they did, the hegemony of the plantation over the rest of the Southern society made the lot of rural freed men of color often more miserable and less secure than that of the slaves and less exalted than that of most free whites.

Thus the aggrandizement which slaves were to derive from within the plantation regimen was supposedly limited, pathological, and against their own self-interest—a sort of *false consciousness*. Slaves were to gain their feeling of aggrandizement relative to other slaves and not relative to white men, fully free and fully responsible citizens. This aggrandizement was to be gained either in terms of how much they physically, spatially, structurally, or culturally approximated their oppressors or owners or of how much they were different from their peers, whether the latter be newly arrived Africans, field slaves, or roaming runaways. When carried to its logical end, the aggrandizement sponsored among slaves by the slave plantation was against either extreme at which slaves could attain *real* selves and *real* group pride—the free pre-slave African whom they were taught to see as barbaric and the roaming free rural Negro or the runaway ex-slave whom they were taught to see as insecure and often backward or worthless. Thus the status and pride that slaves were taught to gain by conforming to the plantation standards were against their peers and with shame toward themselves and demanded of them loyalty and performance toward the perpetuation of an organizational system oriented against their self-interest. Although this status and pride were to be enjoyed in relation to the proximity they, the individual slaves, enjoyed with their master or his status, they could never become the masters of white men, white women, or white children. They could only remain children themselves to all white men, white women, and white children. Thus it may be concluded that one perpetual dilemma of the American plantation slave was the choice between *dehumanizing comfort* and *inhumane cruelty*.

The attainment of true and equally respectable selves and group pride among slaves by way of white-oriented conformity and emulation was pathological and unrealistic, given the plantation as a social organization and slavery as a system. Yet to believe that slaves as men did not come to aspire to and appreciate a sense of self-respect and group pride on less pathological grounds is to equivocate intended consequences as represented by institutional context and unintended consequences as represented by individual behavior. Frederick Douglass in his *Life and Times* leaves us with two penetrating insights as to the *consciousness* some slaves demonstrated. The first is against a co-opting mistress: "My interests were in a direction opposite to hers, and we both had our private thoughts and plans. She aimed to keep me ignorant, and I resolved to *know*, although knowledge only increased my misery. . . . I saw through the attempt to keep me in ignorance. I saw that slaveholders would have gladly made me believe that, in making a slave of me and in making slaves of others, they were merely acting under the authority of God and I felt to them as robbers and deceivers. The feeding and clothing me well could not atone for taking my liberty from me." The second refers to a cruel master: "Covey was a tyrant and a cowardly one withal. After resisting him, I felt as I had never felt before. It was a resurrection from the dark and pestiferous tomb of slavery, to the heaven of comparative freedom. I was no longer a servile coward. . . . This spirit made me a freeman in *fact*, though I still remained a slave in *form*."

Elkins' thesis of Sambo personality as a consequence of *totalization* is also disputable in terms of growing sociological knowledge on Nazi concentration camps. Passive submission was neither the universal nor the sole behavioral pattern among the Jewish prisoners. Organized resistance and elusiveness were as much a part of the inmates' reaction as submission.[10] In this regard, the question can be asked: If the concentration camp was as total as Elkins interprets Bruno Bettelheim to be suggesting, how does one explain Bettelheim's survival and rather sophisticated, scientific behavior as an inmate? Bettelheim's own answer is as follows:

> The study of these behaviors was a mechanism developed by [me] *ad hoc* in order that [I] might have at least some intellectual interests and in this way be better equipped to endure life in the camp.[11]

Bettelheim considered this as an example of individual behavior. Could it not be that some of the "dehumanized" behavior attributed to his fellow inmates was also individual or collective defense for eluding the system? Or was Bettelheim the exception to the rule? We tend to favor the first

[10] See Ernest Kaiser, "Negro History, a Bibliographic Survey," *Freedomways*, 7, No. 4 (1969), 341–43.
[11] Bruno Bettelheim, "Individual and Mass Behavior in an Extreme Situation," *Journal of Abnormal Psychology*, 38 (1943), 420–27.

interpretation. At any rate, the fact that Bettelheim differed from his colleagues, remained humanized, and eluded the system denies the logic that the only or necessary consequence of totalization is total mortification, dehumanization, infantilization, emasculation—becoming a Sambo or an Uncle Tom.

In reference to the larger range of total institutions, Goffman suggests that despite the assaults made on the self by the establishment, the adaptation of individual inmates differs. Among the forms of individual adaptation are "situational withdrawal," "intransigent line," "colonization," "conversion," "playing it cool," and "immunization."[12] In addition to these obviously astute means of fending off the pressures of the establishment, Goffman also speaks of "overdetermination," which means basically to "overconform."[13] That is, the inmates come to take their new status so seriously that they develop pseudo-selves—pathologically aggrandized self-concepts—and overplay their roles or engage in forms of *removal activities* which are to the detriment or embarrassment of the organization. Given the "belt of indeterminancy between 'mere acting' and 'true self,' " acknowledged by Elkins, it is probable that for some inmates overdetermination became a conscious mechanism for escape, while for others it may have been their true selves or some mixture of the two. Elkins failed to pursue such possibilities, and this led to hasty, incomplete conclusions as well as to serious misinterpretations of his perhaps well-meaning message. Conceptually and empirically the distinctions between role-taking and role-playing are so very complex, not to speak of personality.[14]

---

[12] George M. Fredrickson and Christopher Lasch, "Resistance to Slavery," herein.

[13] Goffman, *Asylums*, 38.

[14] Walter Coutu, "Role Playing vs. Role Taking: An Appeal for Clarification," *American Sociological Review*, 11 (April), 180–87; Ralph H.

The suggestion of the prevalence of the Sambo personality by Elkins was not limited to the slaves but extended to their later-day successors, the Black Americans. Perhaps what Elkins was trying to suggest was that (1) slavery, as a phenomenon, has left its long-run effects and (2) that conditions have not changed sufficiently to eliminate these ill effects. On one level these two statements can be accepted as truths; on another level they are hypotheses worth empirical investigation. Elkins and many other sympathetic liberal scholars evoke rather harsh and unsympathetic reactions from the Black population, not so much because of their intentions, as for the incomplete, distorted, and injurious picture they present of the Black man and their inadvertent proposal of historistic solutions for present-day problems. Ralph Ellison, a noted Black writer not known to be of a nationalistic persuasion, commented on Elkins' work and its influence as follows:

> Contrary to some, I feel our experience as a people involves a great deal of heroism. From one perspective slavery was horrible and brutalizing. . . . And the Negro writer is tempted to agree. . . . And he sometimes agrees to the next step, which holds that slaves had very little humanity because slavery destroyed it for them and their descendants. That's what the Stanley M. Elkins "Sambo" argument implies . . . I am forced to look at these people (my Negro ancestors and brothers) and upon the history of life in the U.S. and conclude that there is another reality behind the appearance of reality which they would force upon us as truth.
>
> Any people who could endure all of that brutalization and keep together, who could undergo such dismemberment

Turner, "Moral Judgment: A Study in Roles," *American Sociological Review*, 17, 70–77, and "Role Taking, Role Standpoint, and Reference Group Behavior," *American Journal of Sociology*, 41, No. 4, 316–28.

and resuscitate itself, and endure until it could take the initiative in achieving its own freedom is obviously more than the sum of its brutalization.[15]

Elkins' thesis fails to explain how some slaves made it then and how some Blacks make it now—without being Toms, Jemimas, house slaves, or Black bourgeoisie, geniuses or gifted. By his conclusion Elkins obscures or overlooks the kinds of *roles played* by slaves and the *careers pursued* by Blacks in "making it." Slave literature identifies music, magic, arts, and religion as activities in which leading blacks were permitted to perform. These activities were permitted because they were perceived as either necessary, legitimate, or harmless. They were not usually perceived as dangerous to the regimen, or at least not seriously so. The fact is that they were all ambivalent and allegorical self- and group-asserting actions and thus subversive of the slave plantation system even if they were also partially legitimate.

Since Emancipation, and among the freedmen of antebellum times, the more conventional careers and roles among "leaders" and "successful" blacks have included these: musicians, minstrels, ministers, composers, comedians, con men, artists, actors, authors, poets, rhythmic, symbolic, and "fictional" prose writers. These roles are much the same as those of their ancestors but of wider range. Kiel has openly criticized the emasculating, ephemeral, and effeminate image of the Black male as a misunderstanding and disservice to the race (notwithstanding the perhaps noble intentions behind such portrayals).[16] In the autobiographical novels such as Richard Wright's *Black Boy*, Claude Brown's *Manchild in the Promised Land*, Robert Peck's (Iceberg Slim) *Pimp, the*

---

[15] Ralph Ellison, "A Very Stern Discipline—An Interview with Ralph Ellison," *Harpers*, March, 1967.
[16] Charles Kiel, *Urban Blues* (Chicago, 1966).

Story of My Life, and Henry Williamson's *The Hustler*, in
the early parts of the *Autobiography of Malcolm X*, and in
the escapades and comments of Langston Hughes' "Mr.
Semple" (that modern Brer' Rabbit), one sees the other side
of the story: the cunning, creative Black individual in his
struggle against the cruel closed society and the wide repertoire of mechanisms and roles played by Black people in their
efforts to "make it," "beat the system," or "put on." The resources and styles differ for various classes of people and in
various situations.

Other students of personality suggest wide variation in
responses among contemporary victims of oppression and
prejudice. Pettigrew points out that there are three kinds of
reactions to oppression—moving toward, against, or away
from the oppressor.[17] Allport views clowning as an intro-
punitive and cunning as an extra-punitive response, but both
as pretensive or elusive measures which allow the victim to
"escape" the system often unnoticed. The reason why the
escape is unnoticed is because such measures "fit" so well the
prejudicial stereotypes entertained about the actor or his
group. Thus while he escapes, he continues to reinforce the
stereotype and fulfill the prophecy. He thus does not fully
escape nor destroy the system.[18]

We think, in fact, that Elkins' analysis falters because he
inadvertently accepts the stereotype of the clown or Sambo
as given. He then proceeds to explain it and use it to chastise
the system, as well as to demand a change. As Allport points
out: "If the master jokes, the slave laughs; if the master storms,
the slave quails; if the master wants flattery, the slave gives it.

[17] Thomas F. Pettigrew, *A Profile of the Negro American* (Princeton,
1964).
[18] Gordon Allport, *The Nature of Prejudice* (New York, 1958). See
also Orlando Patterson, *The Sociology of Slavery* (London, 1967).

And if the master wants to be amused, the slave sometimes obligingly plays the clown." Differentiation between meaning of category and meaning of conduct is manifested in the following statement by Fanon: "It is the white man who creates the Negro. But it is the Negro who creates Negritude."[19] Even though it be positive, Fanon avoids equivocating between Negro and Negritude. Even though it be innocent, Elkins equivocates between *being* and *playing* the clown. Elkins makes the same mistakes as some of the masters he condemns. Others knew better. As a supposedly "unbiased" intellectual he compounds the problems, and his treatise contributes weightedly to the verification of a stereotype which some antebellum white men merely entertained but others exploited for their own ends—a stereotype which is inaccurate about the past and harmful as a ploy for correcting the present.[20] Sadly we find it possible to quote Lerone Bennett's commentary on William Styron with reference to Elkins: "The fascination horror of a bigot may be more compelling than the fascination-anxiety of a white liberal."[21] But then

[19] Franz Fanon, *A Dying Colonialism* (New York, 1967).

[20] Glazer and Moynihan have made rather bold projective assertions about the persistence of Sambo among North American Blacks. Nathan Glazer, Introduction to the 1962 paperback edition of *Slavery*, vii; Daniel Patrick Moynihan, *The Negro Family: The Case for National Action* (Washington, D.C., 1965), 15–16. Some Black scholars have almost fallen into the trap of appearing to implicitly support Elkins' thesis in their efforts to explain Sambo. See James Comer, "Individual Development and Black Rebellion, Some Parallels," *Midway* (1968), 33–45; Grier and Cobbs, *Black Rage*, 60. For rejections of the notion of persistence using Reconstruction, see Amistead Robinson, "The Reconstruction in Memphis: A Test of the Elkins Thesis," unpublished senior essay in history, Yale University, 1969; Willie Lee Rose, *Rehearsal for Reconstruction: The Port Royal Experiment* (New York, 1967); Herbert Gutman, *The Invisible Fact*, forthcoming; and Thomas Holt, "The Emergence of Black Political Leadership during Reconstruction, 1865–1890," proposal for a Ph.D. dissertation, Yale University.

[21] Lerone Bennett, "Nat's Last White Man," in John Henrik Clarke (ed.), *William Styron's Nat Turner: Ten Black Writers Respond* (Boston, 1968).

Styron seemingly derived some of his notions or defense of *his* Nat Turner from Elkins' Sambo.

SLAVES AS MEN

Crucial in the understanding of slavery is the issue of the definition of man by other men, and of course the purposes underlying and the treatments and interactions accompanying such definitions.[22] Elkins' notion of *moral personality* stresses the presumably internalized psychological attributes of the individual, and accordingly presents the defeated slaves as deficient men. Tannenbaum, upon whom Elkins draws heavily, also concedes the lack of *moral personality* on the part of the North American slaves, but he defines personality in terms of the social denial of full-fledged and equal status to the ex-slaves by their former masters. Although there seems to be a controversy developing among historians on the nature of *slave personality*,[23] it is obvious that Elkins does not consider the possibility that slaves—as displaced or bicultural Africans with a past and folklore, and more so as a fairly stabilized status group in a persistently segregated society—would have

[22] Frank Tannenbaum, *Slave and Citizen* (New York, 1963), vii; Eric Williams, "Race Relations in Caribbean Society," in Vera Rubin (ed.), *Caribbean Studies: A Symposium* (Seattle, 1960), 54–59.

[23] Mina Davis Caulfield, "Slavery and the Origins of Black Culture: Elkins Revisited," in Peter Rose (ed.), *Americans from Africa* (New York, 1969), 171–91; M. I. Finley, "Slavery," *International Encyclopedia of the Social Sciences* (New York, 1968); Mary Agnes Lewis, "Slavery and Personality," herein; David McClelland, *The Achieving Society* (Princeton, 1961); Richard Morse, "Comments on Degler's 'Slavery in the United States and Brazil: An Essay in Comparative History,'" unpublished; Rose, *Rehearsal for Reconstruction;* Arnold A. Sio, "Society, Slavery, and the Slave," *Social and Economic Studies,* 16 (1967); Earl E. Thorpe, "Chattel Slavery and Concentration Camps," herein.

retained or developed as part of their *underlife*[24] a notion of manhood distinct from or even complementary to that of their masters. Consequently, Elkins finds himself hard put (1) to demonstrate that the prevalence of Sambo was indeed an *empirical reality* rather than a *conceptual construct,* (2) to logically detach this construct from the naive, if not racist, view traditionally entertained about Black men in white America, and (3) to avoid the ethnocentric myth that man is truly man only to the extent that his personality and career approximate the total embodiment of the "virtues" of the capitalistic-Calvinistic-bureaucratic ethos embraced by *white* North America.[25]

[24] A Black undergraduate student at Yale insisted that rather than "underlife" (*modus operandi*) the term should be "the life" (*modus vivendi*). Notwithstanding the tacit chauvinism, and perhaps a hindsighted version at that, the contention represents a way of viewing and directing empirical inquiry toward discerning the actual behavior, norms, and values of slaves as expressed by themselves. The concern with viewing the slave as an informant and the using of slave narratives as information were recurrent themes of my students at a seminar session in introductory Afro-American Studies at which Mr. Elkins was the guest speaker. See George Rawick, *The American Slave: A Composite Autobiography,* forthcoming, and Norman Yetman, *Life in the Peculiar Institution,* forthcoming. There are a number of Black scholars, John Blassingame, Arna Bontemps, Michael Cooke, and Carrol Nichols among others, who are now re-examining the Black autobiography from this new perspective as well.

[25] Marx, Veblen, and even Weber have raised issues with the *dehumanized* aspects of that model of man. See here the reactions of a contemporary *nonviolent* Black leader and Christian minister of God: ". . . there's nothing to be learned from the white man's idea of manhood. An American man is identified by his weapon, by what he controls. American men are obsessed; they are gratified by making money they can't even spend, which is a kind of emptiness of the soul. Real manhood should be defined by the ability to help and to heal, by an extension of the mind, by knowledge exerting its power over ignorance. Real manhood comes from helping others to be free, by breaking the bonds of slavery." Jessie Jackson, "Candid Conversation," *Playboy,* 18 (November, 1969), 290.

Two figures who are still celebrated as articulate, authentic spokesmen for their people at widely different points of time in history have been known to dramatically refute the notion of the undisputable role of white

Elkins' analysis also accepts as given the "over-socialized concept of man"[26] and the consensual view of society, which denies the individual freedom or variability. It assumes a one-to-one relation between institutional context and human conduct. Accordingly, the individual internalizes his role and the value of his society, as well as the value of being a member of that society. Through internalizations and social controls the individual learns and tends to conform, lest he lose his highly cherished membership in society and be punished as a deviant. This analysis, though, is faulty and restricting, for the slave was located in two completely different and conflicting groups and cultures—a stabilized plural situation. He was exposed to two diametrically different value systems or role expectations—slave and free. Thus, if we accept the conformity-deviation dichotomy which underlies the consensual approach, the slave was at one and the same time deviant and conformist. He could be a conformist to the slave role and thus a deviant from the ideal role of the free human being in the larger group, or he could be deviant from the slave role and conform to the ideal role of the free human being in the larger society. If he were both at the same time he would be neurotic, to say the least, much in the fashion of the Nat Turner depicted by Styron or the Black male depicted by Moynihan.

If, on the other hand, a more voluntaristic and bicultural view of man and a more pluralistic view of society were taken by Elkins, the slave would have been perceived as having more choices of behaving. Thus the prevalence of certain role

---

men as positive models for Blacks. Frederick Douglass called them "robbers" and "deceivers"; Malcolm X called them "white, blue-eyed devils." Apparently this tradition of refutation was overlooked by Elkins.

[26] See Dennis Wrong, "The Over-Socialized Conception of Man in Modern Sociology," *American Sociological Review*, 26 (April, 1961), 185–93.

patterns and choices, rather than personality, would have become the issue to be explained. In our own voluntaristic-pluralistic approach we have accepted the contextual presentation of Elkins, but then have asked for consideration of the kinds of choices there were available to the slaves and to explain the choices they tended to practice most often. From such a viewpoint, in addition to strict conformity to one *or* the other role definition, slaves could play parts of both, at the same or at different times. And they could play whatever they chose to play in "bad faith" or in "ecstasy." Such possibilities are heightened in stabilized *plural* situations such as the slave plantation. The point is that a voluntaristic, variable, creative, narcissistic view of man and a complex, pluralistic view of society would have allowed Elkins to consider (1) the institutional incongruence which mitigated against total closure as represented by the slave plantation and (2) the fact that eventually various levels of escaping totality would have been devised by the slaves despite the controls. The totality of the plantation context was more apparent than real and the conduct of the slaves was less controlled than it seemed. In other words, like other forms of social organization, total institutions *not only control individuals, they also create individuals who learn to escape them by various forms of expression, illusions, and actions.*[27] It is this resilience, resourcefulness, and recalcitrance that Black people call *soul,* and Goffman defines as *self:*

> The individual [is] . . . a stance-taking entity, a something that takes up a position somewhere between identification with an organization and opposition to it, and is ready at the slightest pressure to regain its balance by shifting its in-

[27] See Peter Berger, *Invitation to Sociology* (New York, 1963).

volvement in either direction. It is thus *against something* that the self can emerge.[28]

ELKINS' CONCLUSIONS
AS THESES, NOT FINDINGS

To put it succinctly, our criticisms of Elkins are directed not to his history but rather to his sociology—to its overly deterministic and prematurely comparative features. Despite our criticisms, Elkins' treatment of slavery has profound significance to those social scientists and historians interested in the behavior of captive men—past, present, and future. It represents the most provocative and successful effort yet to reopen the study of slavery, an event of the past, on terms amenable to behavioral analysis. The cries for American scholars to interrelate behavioral and historical approaches in their studies of human affairs have been recurrent. Perhaps the best-known advocate among sociologists has been C. Wright Mills.[29] Among American historians the plea has been even more direct. Hofstadter, for example, called for a behavioral approach to the study of slavery, one which will reflect the standpoint of the slaves.[30]

This request by Hofstadter has not been easy to fulfill. The empirical, particularly the phenomenological, study of

[28] Goffman, *Asylums*, 320.

[29] Mills states it as follows: "The problems of our time . . . cannot be stated adequately without consistent practice of the view that history is the shank of social study, and recognition of the need to develop further a psychology of man that is sociologically grounded and historically relevant. Without use of history and without an historical sense of psychological matters, the social scientist cannot adequately state the kinds of problems that ought now to be the orienting points of his studies." *The Sociological Imagination* (New York, 1959), 143.

[30] Richard Hofstadter, "U. B. Phillips and the Plantation Legend," *Journal of Negro History*, 29 (1944), 109–24.

human behavior requires the *accessible presence* of the *actors* themselves. However at one time most slaves were foreigners, at another time they were illiterate and restricted, and at this time they are dead and of a distant past. Notwithstanding the immense wealth of folklore available, there are few auto-biographies and interviews of slaves whose authenticity and representativeness would allow fullest confidence for gen-eralizing about slavery. At this moment in time the records of masters, witnesses, and historians, like some of the alleged autobiographies of slaves, are being viewed askance by serious scholars. Our concern then must be to get more adequate insights or impressions *as a first step*, rather than spuriously claim accuracy about slavery. Elkins' treatment of slavery brought us closer to such insights by his analogy of the slave plantation to the concentration camp, a like-situated system of captive men.[31] Elkins did not reach the level of *under-standing phenomenologically* the behavior of inmates or slaves but his work took us to the threshold of analyzing the institutions to which such men were confined.

In this paper, we have approached Elkins' statements, especially regarding the *prevalence* of a Sambo personality, as *theses*—logical possibilities rather than empirical claims. After all, his study did not include field work nor primary research. It was largely an effort to reinterpret positions and synthesize the teachings of various relevant fields of study. We have criticized his effort on grounds of its naive deter-ministic exaggerations and we have magnified the extent and number of conclusions that would follow a more humanistic sociological approach. By so doing we have tried to lift the

[31] Lasch and Fredrickson inadvertently extended the analogy even fur-ther as they used both Goffman's asylums and Sykes' maximum security penitentiary to challenge Elkins' conclusion. See Bryce-Laporte, "The Con-ceptualization of the American Slave Plantation," for other proposed an-alogies.

topic of American slavery out of the arena of ideological and historistic polemics. American slavery is not simply an historical or symbolic artifact. It is a period of human experience, the causes, contexts, and consequences of which are yet to be fully understood in behavioral terms. We have tried to present the case that the study of slavery can be carried out by studying like-situated men in like-situated institutions— some of which exist in our midst even today. By the same token a more systematic study of the slave plantation and its inmates as part of the *genre* of total institution should provide much more plausible and verifiable propositions about the relation between behavior of captive men and the institutional-ideological context of their captivity, without limitation to a single period, institution, people, or society. These propositions need not be present-time oriented nor confined to the U.S. Black population.

Other critics have chosen to view Elkins' assertions as stated *findings*. But then some of these critics have proceeded to attempt to disprove these findings or to better explain them. In our opinion many such critics commit the same mistake that they attribute to Elkins of positing as a general, factual truth something that has not been and, perhaps, cannot quite yet be tested empirically.[32] The traditional methodological tools of history and the social sciences are inadequate for testing long-dead, illiterate, subjugated men in sufficient numbers, depth, or variety to either support or disprove such alleged empirical claims. The logic of internal consistency so

---

[32] This criticism is directed less to those who view his statements as predictive, explanatory, or relational *hypotheses*, and are now *testing* them on different levels or by use of various creative empirical methods. See Joseph Boskin, "Black Humor and Black Militancy," forthcoming; Robert Marsh, "The Bearing of Comparative Analysis on Sociological Theory," *Social Forces*, 43, No. 2; or Norman Yetman, "Testing Elkins' 'Sambo' Thesis: Some Preliminary Problems," unpublished manuscript.

useful in winning debates may be necessary, but is not sufficient for verifying empirical relations. For these critics Elkins has served best as a straw man to give them audience on a topic worth airing. Hopefully they will begin to see him also as a scholar who boldly applied academic borrowing and new scholarship to a subject still worth studying: The slaves are dead but their successors and substitutes are living.

Yes (we) Black men are still living! And it is in our self interest, our ancestors' and our offspring's, that we strive to correct the vestiges of any image which can be injurious to our integrity and inaccurate of our being. We must search for another scholarly way to lay bare the cruelties of our conditions without further degrading our identity as men—proud, normal, and equal men. All God's chillun got soul! Moreover, there is need for us to discern the resilience and resourcefulness that we derived from and developed despite such conditions. What is needed then is new scholarly redirection so that such resilience and resourcefulness may be utilized to improve the lives—chances, social conditions, images, and being—of Black men, once captive, somewhat still captive men.

American Slaves and Their History

EUGENE D. GENOVESE

The history of the American lower classes has yet to be written. The ideological impact of the New Left, the intellectual exigencies of the black liberation movement, and the developing academic concern for the cultural aspects of politics and history have all converged to produce the expectation that this history will be written. If even a small percentage of the praise heaped upon E. P. Thompson's *The Making of the English Working Class* could be translated into an effort to extend its achievement, the future would be bright. Good work is finally being done, although little by those who periodically issue manifestoes on the need to rewrite history "from the bottom up."

History written from the bottom up is neither more nor less than history written from the top down: It is not and cannot be good history. Writing the history of a nation without considering the vicissitudes of a majority of its people is not a serious undertaking. Yet it is preposterous to suggest that there could conceivably be anything wrong with writing a book about the ruling class alone, or about one or another elite, or about any segment of society, however small. No subject is too limited to treat.

But a good historian writes well on a limited subject while

taking account (if only implicitly and without a single direct reference) of the whole, whereas an inferior one confuses the need to isolate a small portion of the whole with the license to assume that that portion acted in isolation. One may, for example, write Southern history by focusing on either blacks or whites, slaves or masters, tenant farmers or landlords; but the one cannot be discussed without an understanding of the other.

The fate of master and slave was historically intertwined, and formed part of a single social process; each in his own way struggled for autonomy—struggled to end his dependence upon the other—but neither could ever wholly succeed. The first problem in the writing of social history lies in this organic antagonism: We tend to see the masters in their own terms, without acknowledging their dependence upon the slaves; but we also tend to see the slaves in the masters' terms, without acknowledging the extent to which the slaves freed themselves from domination.

There cannot be, therefore, any such thing as "history from the bottom up," but there can and should be good histories of "the bottom." A good study of plantation architecture, apart from its contribution to aesthetics, would be one that grasped the social link between the culture of the Big House and that of both the slave quarters and small nonslaveholding farm houses, for the Big House, whatever else it did, served to impress men in humble circumstances. Such a study need never mention the slave quarters or the farm houses, but if the essential insight fails or remains undeveloped and abstract, then the entire effort must remain limited. Should it succeed, then the book would be a valuable contribution to the history of Southern society and its constituent races and classes. To consider such a study "elitist" because it concerns itself with upper-class life or eschews moralistic pronouncements is a modern form of absurdity.

There is much to be said for the current notion that blacks will have to write their own history: Black people in the United States have strong claims to separate nationality, and every people must interpret its own history in the light of its own traditions and experience. At the same time, the history of every people must be written from without, if only to provide a necessary perspective; sooner or later the history of every people must flow from the clash of viewpoints and sensibilities.

But for historians of the South there is a more compelling reason for black and white scholars to live with each other: there is simply no way of learning about either blacks or whites without learning about the other. If it is true, as I suspect, that future generations of black scholars will bring a special viewpoint to Southern history, then their success or failure will rest, in part, on their willingness to teach us something new about the masters as well as the slaves.

I should like to consider some debilitating assumptions often brought by social historians to the study of the lower classes and to suggest a way of avoiding the twin elitist notions that these classes are generally either passive or on the brink of insurrection. We have so many books on slavery in the Old South that specialists need to devote full time merely to keeping abreast of the literature. Yet there is not one book and only a few scattered articles on life in the slave quarters: we must rely mainly on such primary and undigested sources as slave narratives and plantation memoirs. A good student might readily be able to answer questions about the economics of the plantation, the life of the planters, the politics of slavery expansionism, or a host of other matters, but he is not likely to know much about the daily life and thoughts of slaves, about the relationship of field to house slaves, or about the relations between slave driver or foreman and other slaves. To make matters worse, he may well think he knows a good deal, for the literature abounds in undocumented assertions and plausible legends.

The fact remains that there has not been a single study of the slave driver—the most important slave on the larger plantations—and only a few sketchy and misleading studies of house slaves. So far as the life of the quarters is concerned, it should be enough to note that the idea persists, in the face of abundant evidence, that slaves had no family life to speak of. Historians and sociologists, both white and black, have been guilty of reasoning deductively from purely legal evidence—slave marriages were not recognized by law in the United States—and have done little actual research.

I do not propose here to discuss the slave family in detail, or house slaves and drivers for that matter, but should like to touch on all three in order to illustrate a larger point. We have made a grave error in the way in which we have viewed slave life, and this error has been perpetuated by both whites and blacks, racists and anti-racists. The traditional proslavery view and that of such later apologists for white supremacy as Ulrich B. Phillips have treated the blacks as objects of white benevolence and fear—as people who needed both protection and control—and devoted attention to the ways in which black slaves adjusted to the demands of the master class. Abolitionist propaganda and the later and now dominant liberal viewpoint have insisted that the slave regime was so brutal and dehumanizing that blacks should be seen primarily as victims. Both these viewpoints treat black people almost wholly as objects, never as creative participants in a social process, never as half of a two-part subject.

True, abolitionist and liberal views have taken account of the ways in which slaves resisted their masters by shirking, breaking their tools, and even rebelling, but the proslavery view generally noted that much, too, even if from a different

interpretation. Neither has ever stopped to consider, for
example, that the evidence might reflect less a deliberate
attempt at sabotage or alleged Negro inferiority than a set
of attitudes toward time, work, and leisure which black
people developed partly in Africa and partly in the slave
quarters and which constituted a special case of a general pattern of behavior associated with preindustrial cultures.

Preindustrial peoples knew all about hard work and discipline, but their standards were neither those of the factory
nor those of the plantation, and were embedded in a radically
different culture. Yet even such sympathetic historians as
Kenneth Stampp who give some attention to the subject
of slaves generally try to show that slaves exercised some
degree of autonomy in their responses to the blows or
cajoling of their masters. We have yet to receive a respectful
treatment—apart from some brief but suggestive passages in
the work of W. E. B. Du Bois, C. L. R. James, and perhaps
one or two others[1]—of their attempts to achieve an autonomous life within the narrow limits of the slave plantation.
Although family letters and plantation diaries of the whites,
slave narratives, and black folklore are full of the hints and
data needed for such a history, we have yet to have a syn-
thetic record of their incessant struggle to escape from the
culture as well as from the psychological domination of the
master class.

In commenting briefly on certain features of family life,
house slaves, and drivers, I should like to suggest some of
the possibilities in an approach that goes beyond the question,
What was done to the slaves? Namely: What did the slaves

[1] See, e.g., C. L. R. James, "The Atlantic Slave Trade and Slavery: Some
Interpretations of Their Significance in the Development of the United
States and the Western World," *Amistad*, #1 (Vintage Books, 1970).
Du Bois's writings are full of important ideas and hypotheses. See especially
Black Reconstruction in America and *Souls of Black Folk*.

do for themselves and how did they do it? In a more extensive presentation it would be possible, indeed necessary, to discuss slave religion, entertainment, songs and dances, and many other things. But perhaps we may settle for a moment on one observation about slave religion.

We are told a great deal about the religious instruction of the slaves, by which is meant the attempt to inculcate a version of Protestant Christianity. Sometimes this instruction is interpreted as a good thing in itself and sometimes as a kind of brainwashing, but we may leave this question aside. Recently, Vincent Harding, following Du Bois's suggestive probing, has offered a different perspective and suggested that the slaves had their own way of taking up Christianity and forging it into a weapon of active resistance.[2] Certainly we must be struck by the appearance of one or another kind of messianic preacher in almost every slave revolt on record. Professor Harding therefore asks that we look at the slaves as active participants in their own religious experience and not merely as objects being worked on by slaveholding ideologues.

This argument may be carried further to suggest that a distinctly black religion, at least in embryo, appeared in the slave quarters and played a role in shaping the daily lives of the slaves. In other words, quite apart from the problem of religion as a factor in overt resistance to slavery, we need to know how the slaves developed a religious life that enabled them to survive as autonomous human beings with a culture of their own within the white master's world.

One of the reasons we know so little about this side of slavery—and about all lower-class life—is that it is undramatic. Historians, white and black, conservative, liberal, and radical,

---

[2] Vincent Harding, "Religion and Resistance among Antebellum Negroes, 1800–1860," August Meier and Elliott Rudwick, eds., *The Making of Black America* (New York, 1969), I, 179–97.

tend to look for the heroic moments, either to praise or to excoriate them. Yet, if a slave helped to keep himself psychologically intact by breaking his master's hoe, he might also have achieved the same result by a special effort to come to terms with his God, or by loving a woman who shared his burdens, or even by aspiring to be the best worker on the plantation.

We tend to think of someone who aspires to be a good slave as an Uncle Tom, and maybe we should. But human beings are not so simple. If a slave aspires to a certain excellence within the system, and if his implicit trust in the generous response of the master is betrayed, as often it must be in such a system, then he is likely to be transformed into a rebel. If so, he is likely to become the most dangerous kind of rebel, first because of his smashed illusions and second because of the skills and self-control he taught himself while he was an Uncle Tom. The historical record is full of people who were model slaves right up until the moment they killed their overseer, ran away, burned down the Big House, or joined an insurrection.

So what can be said about the decidedly non-Christian element in the religion of the slave quarters? The planters tell us repeatedly in their memoirs and letters that every plantation had its conjurer, its voodoo man, its witch doctor. To the planters this meant a residue of African superstition, and it is of course possible that by the 1830s all that remained in the slave quarters were local superstitions rather than continuing elements of the highly sophisticated religions originally brought from Africa. But the evidence suggests the emergence of an indigenous and unique combination of African and European religious ideas, adapted to the specific conditions of slave life by talented and imaginative individuals, and representing an attempt to establish a spiritual life adequate to the task of linking the slaves with the powerful culture of the masters while providing for a high degree of separation and cultural autonomy.

When we know enough of this story we shall know a good deal about the way in which the culture of an oppressed people develops. We often hear the expression "defenseless slaves," but, although any individual at any given moment may be defenseless, a whole people rarely if ever is. A people may be on the defensive and dangerously exposed, but it often finds its own ways to survive and fight back. The trouble is that we keep looking for overt rebellious actions—a strike, a revolt, a murder, arson, tool-breaking—and often fail to realize that in given conditions and at particular times the wisdom of a people and their experience in struggle may dictate a different course, one of keeping together. From this point of view, the most ignorant of the field slaves who followed the conjurer on the plantation was saying no to the boss and seeking a form of cultural autonomy. That the conjurer may in any one case have been a fraud and even a kind of extortionist, and in another case a genuine popular religious leader, is, from this point of view, of little importance.

Let us take the family as an illustration. Slave law refused to recognize slave marriages and family ties. In this respect United States slavery was far worse than Spanish American or Luso-Brazilian slavery. In those Catholic cultures the Church demanded and tried to guarantee that slaves be permitted to marry and that the sanctity of the slave family be upheld. As a result, generations of American historians have concluded that American slaves had no family life and that Cuban and Brazilian slaves did.

This judgment will not bear examination. The slave trade to the United States was closed early: no later than 1808—except for some cases of smuggling which are statistically insignificant—and in fact decades earlier for most states. The rise of the Cotton Kingdom and the great period of slavery expansion followed the closing of the slave trade. Slavery, in the numbers we are accustomed to thinking of, was a product of the period following the end of African importations. The slave force that was liberated during and after the War for Southern Independence was overwhelmingly a slave force born and raised in this country.

We have good statistics on the rate of increase of that slave population and there can be no doubt that it compared roughly to that of the whites—apart from the factor of immigration—and that, furthermore, it was unique among New World plantation slave classes. An early end to the slave trade, followed by a boom in cotton and plantation slavery, dictated a policy of encouraging slave births. In contrast, the slave trade remained open to Cuba and to Brazil until the second half of the nineteenth century; as a result, there was little economic pressure to encourage family life and slave-raising. In Brazil and Cuba far more men than women were imported from Africa until late in the history of the respective slave regimes; in the Old South a rough sexual parity was established fairly early. If, therefore, religion and law militated in favor of slave families in Cuba and Brazil and against them in the Old South, economic pressure worked in reverse. The result was a self-reproducing slave force in the United States and nowhere else, so far as the statistics reveal.

It may be objected that the outcome could have reflected selective breeding rather than family stability. But selective breeding was tried in the Caribbean and elsewhere and never worked; there is no evidence that it was ever tried on a large scale in the South. Abolitionists charged that Virginia and Maryland deliberately raised slaves—not merely encouraged but actually fostered slave breeding. There is, however, no evidence for slave breeding on a significant scale. If slave-raising farms existed and if the planters were not complete fools, they would have concentrated on recruiting women of childbearing age and used a relatively small number of studs. Sample studies of major slave-exporting counties in Virginia and Maryland show no significant deviations from the patterns in Mississippi or other slave-buying regions.

It is clear that Virginia and Maryland—and other states as well—exported their natural increase for some decades before the war. But this was a process, not a policy. It reflected the economic pressures to supplement a waning income from agriculture by occasional slave sales; it was not incompatible with the encouragement of slave families and in fact reinforced it. Similarly, planters in the cotton states could not work their slaves to death and then buy fresh ones, for prices were too high. They had been too high from the very moment the Cotton Kingdom began its westward march and, therefore, a tradition of slave-killing never did take root. As time went on, the pressures mounted to provide slaves with enough material and even psychological satisfaction to guarantee the minimum morale needed for reproduction.

These standards of treatment—food, living space, time off, etc.—became part of the prevailing standard of decency, not easily violated by greedy slaveholders. In some respects the American slave system may have been the worst in the world, as Elkins and others insist. But in purely material terms, it was probably the best, for the evidence left by participants, travelers, and official reports shows that American slaves were generally better fed, clothed, housed, and worked than those of Cuba, Jamaica, Brazil, or elsewhere.

But the important thing here is that the prevailing standard of decency was not easily violated because the slaves had come to understand their own position. If a master wished to keep his plantation going, he had to learn the limits of his slaves' endurance. If, for example, he decided to ignore the prevailing custom of giving Sundays off or of giving an extended Christmas holiday, his slaves would feel sorely tried and would certainly pay him back with one or another form of destruction. The slaves remained in a weak position, but they were rarely completely helpless, and by guile, brute courage, and a variety of other devices they taught every master just where the line was he dared not cross if he wanted a crop. In precisely this way, slaves took up the masters' interest in their family life and turned it to account. The typical plantation in the Upper South and the Lower was organized by family units. Man and wife lived together with children, and to a considerable degree the man was in fact the man in the house.

Whites violated black family life in several ways. Many families were disrupted by slave sales, especially in the Upper South where economic pressures were strong; white men on the plantations could and often did violate black women: nothing can minimize these injustices. The frequency of sales is extremely hard to measure. Many slaves were troublesome and sold many times over; this inflated the total number of sales but obscured the incidence of individual transfers.

The crimes against black people are a matter of record, and no qualifications can soften their impact. But it is not at all certain that most slaves did not live stable married lives in the quarters despite the pressures of the market. I do not wish to take up the vexing question of the violation of black women here, but certainly there was enough of it to justify the anger of those who condemned the regime on this ground alone. The evidence, however, does not warrant an assumption that a large percentage of black plantation women were so violated. In other words, for a judgment on the moral quality of the regime, the problem was extremely important; for an assessment of the normal life of the slaves it was much less so.

What the sources show—both the plantation diaries and record books and letters of the masters and also the reports of runaway slaves and ex-slaves—is that the average plantation slave lived in a family setting, developed strong family ties, and held the nuclear family as the proper social norm. It is true that planters who often had to excuse others, or even themselves, for breaking up families by sale, would sometimes argue that blacks did not really form deep and lasting attachments, that they lacked a strong family sense, that they were naturally promiscuous, and so forth. Abolitionists and former slaves would reinforce the prevalent notion by saying that slavery was so horrible no real family tie could be maintained. Since planters, abolitionists, and former slaves all said the same thing, it has usually been taken as the truth. Only it was not.

In the first place, these various sources also say the opposite, which we rarely notice. Planters agonized over the breakup of families and repeatedly expressed regrets and dismay. Often, they went to great lengths to keep families together at considerable expense, for they knew how painful it was to enforce separations. Whether they were motivated by such material considerations as maintaining plantation morale or by more lofty sentiments is beside the point. They often demonstrated that they knew very well how strong the family ties were in the quarters. Planters encouraged the slaves to live together in stable units, for they recognized that a man was easier to control if he had a wife and children to worry about.

The slaves, on their side, behaved, of course, in various ways. Some were indeed promiscuous, although much of the charge of promiscuity stemmed not so much from actual promiscuity as from sequential polygamy. They did change partners more often than Victorian whites said they could stomach. (In this respect, they might be considered among the forerunners of the white middle-class sexual morality of the 1960s.) I stress these matters, the interest of the master in slave family stability and the effort of the slave to protect his stake in a home, however impoverished, because it is now fashionable to believe that black people came out of slavery with little or no sense of family life. But if so, then we need to know why so many thousands wandered over the South during early Reconstruction looking for their spouses or children.

We do not know just how many slaves lived as a family or were willing and able to maintain a stable family life during slavery. But the number was certainly great, whatever the percentage, and as a result, the social norm that black people carried from slavery to freedom was that of the nuclear family. If it is true that the black family has disintegrated in the ghettos—and we have yet to see conclusive evidence of this—then the source will have to be found in the conditions of economic and social oppression imposed upon blacks during recent decades. The experience of slaves, for all its tragic disruptions, pointed toward a stable postslavery family life, and recent scholarship demonstrates conclusively that the reconstruction and postreconstruction black experience carried forward the acceptance of the nuclear-family norm.[3]

---

[3] Herbert Gutman has presented several papers to scholarly meetings and is close to completing a major book on the historical development of the black family from slavery to World War I. I am indebted to him for allowing me to see the manuscript in progress and for discussing the data with me.

Let us consider the role of the male and the legend of a slave matriarchy. Almost all writers on slavery describe the slave man as a guest in the house, who could have no role beyond a purely sexual one. The slave narratives and the diaries and letters of white plantation owners tell us something else. The position of the male slave was undeniably precarious and frustrating. If his wife was to be whipped, he had to stand by and watch; he could not fully control his own children; he was not a breadwinner in the usual sense. There were severe restrictions imposed upon the manifestations of what we somewhat erroneously call manliness. But both masters and former slaves tell us about some plantations on which certain women were not easily or often punished because it was readily understood that to punish the woman it would be necessary to kill her man first.

These cases were the exception, but they tell us that the man felt a duty to protect his woman. If circumstances conspired to prevent his fulfilling that duty, those circumstances often included the fact that his woman did not expect him to do so and indeed consoled him by acknowledging the futility of such a gesture. We cannot know what was said between a man and a woman when they lay down together at night after having experienced such outrages, but there are enough hints in the slave narratives to suggest that both knew what a man could do, as well as what he "should" do, especially when there were children to consider. Many scholars suggest that black women treated their men with contempt for not doing what circumstances made impossible. This is a deduction from tenuous assumptions; it is not a demonstrated fact.

Beyond that, the man of the house did do various things. He trapped and hunted animals to supplement the diet in the quarters, and in this small but important and symbolic way he was a breadwinner. He organized the garden plot and presided over the division of labor with his wife. He disciplined his children—or divided that function with his wife as people in other circumstances do—and generally was the source of authority in the cabin. This relationship within the family was not alway idyllic. In many instances, he imposed his authority over both wife and children by force. Masters forbade men to hit their wives and children and whipped them for it; but they did it anyway and often. And there is not much evidence that women readily ran to the masters to ask that their husbands be whipped for striking them.

The evidence on these matters, even from the slave narratives, is fragmentary, but what it suggests is that the men asserted their authority as best they could; that the women expected to have to defer to their husbands in certain matters; and that both tried hard to keep the master out of their lives. The conditions were unfavorable, and perhaps many men did succumb and in one way or another became emasculated. But we might also reflect on the ways in which black men and women conspired to maintain their own sense of dignity and their own autonomy by settling things among themselves and thereby asserting their own personalities.

Black women have often been praised—and justly so—for their strength and determination in holding their families together during slavery, when the man was supposedly put aside or rendered irrelevant. It is time, I think, to praise them for another thing which large numbers of them seem to have been able to do: to support a man they loved in ways deep enough and varied enough to help him to resist the mighty forces for dehumanization and emasculation. Without the support of their women, not many black men could have survived; but with it—and there is plenty of testimony that they often had it—many could and did.

If our failure to see the plantation from the vantage point of the slave quarters has led us to substitute abstractions for research on the slave family, so has it saddled us with unsubstantiated and erroneous ideas on house slaves. According to the legend, house slaves were the Uncle Toms of the system—a privileged caste apart, contemptuous of the field hands, jealous of their place in the affection or at least attention of the white master and mistress, and generally sellouts, "white man's niggers." Like most stereotypes this one has its kernel of truth; there were indeed many house slaves who fit the description. But in 1860 roughly half the slaves in the South lived on farms of twenty or fewer slaves; another 25 percent lived on plantations of between twenty and fifty slaves. Only 25 percent, in other words, lived on plantations of fifty or more, and of these, the majority lived on units of fewer than 100—that is, on units of fewer than twenty slave families. In short, the typical house slave worked either on a small farm or, at best, on a moderate-sized plantation. Only a few lived and worked on plantations large enough to permit the formation of a separate group of house slaves—of enough house slaves to form a caste unto themselves.

The idea of the fancy-dressed, uppity, self-inflated house slave who despised the field blacks and identified with the whites derives from those who lived in the towns and cities like Charleston, New Orleans, Natchez, and Richmond. These town house slaves and a small group of privileged house slaves on huge plantations could and sometimes did form a separate caste having the qualities attributed to them in the literature. Certainly the big planters and their families, who left most of the white family records that have been the major source, would likely have remembered precisely these slaves. Even these blacks deserve a more careful look than they have received, for they were much more complicated people than we have been led to believe. The important point, however, is that the typical house slave was far removed from this condition. He, or more likely she, worked with perhaps one to three or four others on an estate too small to permit any such caste formation.

If the typical house slave was an Uncle Tom and a spoiled child of the whites, then we need to be told just why so many of them turn up in the records of runaways. There is abundant evidence from the war years. We hear much about the faithful retainers who held the Yankees off from the Big House, or protected young missus, or hid the family silver. Such types were not at all rare. But they do not appear to have been nearly so numerous as those house slaves who joined the field slaves in fleeing to the Yankee lines when the opportunity arose.

The best sources on this point are the letters and diaries of the planters themselves who were shocked at the defection of their favorite slaves. From a vast body of published and unpublished writing by Southern whites on their war experience we learn that they could readily understand the defection of the field hands, whom they considered stupid and easily led, but were unable to account for the flight—with expressions sometimes of regret and sometimes of anger and hatred—of their house slaves. They had always thought that they knew these blacks, loved them, were loved by them; and they considered them part of the family. One day they learned that they had been deceiving themselves, that they had been living intimately with people they did not know at all. The house slaves, when the opportunity presented itself, responded with the same range of behavior as did the field slaves: they proved themselves to be just as often rebellious and independent as docile and loyal.

This display of independence really was nothing new.

If it is true that house slaves were often regarded as traitors to the black cause during slave rebellions, it is also true that their appearance in those rebellions was not so rare as we are led to believe. Consider the evidence from the abortive slave rebellion led by Denmark Vesey in Charleston in 1822. One slave leader, in an often-quoted remark, said not to trust the house slaves because they were too closely tied to the whites, and, indeed, several house slaves did turn informers. But we ought also to note that some of the toughest and most devoted leaders of Vesey's rebellion were themselves house slaves. Indeed, the greatest scandal was the role played by the most trusted slaves of the governor of South Carolina.

Certainly, the role of the house slave was always ambiguous and often treacherous. But if many house slaves betrayed their fellows, many others collected information in the Big House and passed it on to the quarters. We know how well informed the field slaves were about movements of Yankee troops during the war; we know that these field slaves fled to the Yankee lines with uncanny accuracy in timing and direction. Probably no group was more influential in providing the necessary information than those same house slaves who are so often denigrated.

The decision of slaves, whether house slaves or not, to protect whites during slave insurrections or other catastrophes, hardly proves them to have been Toms. The master-slave relationship, especially when it occurred in the intimacies of the Big House, was always profoundly ambivalent. Many of the same slaves who protected their masters and mistresses from harm and thereby asserted their own humanity were anything but docile creatures of the whites.

Since most house slaves worked on estates too small for a separate existence, their social life was normally down in the slave quarters and not apart or with the whites. Women usually predominated in the house, and even when they did not, the group was too small for natural pairing off. A large number of house slaves married field hands, or more likely the more skilled artisans or workers. Under such circumstances, the line between house slaves and field hands was not sharp for most slaves. Except on the really large plantations, house slaves were expected to help out in the fields during picking season and during emergencies. The average house slave got a periodic taste of field work and had little opportunity to cultivate airs.

There are two general features to the question of house slaves that deserve comment: first, there is the ambiguity of their situation and its resultant ambivalence toward whites; the other is the significance of the house slave in the formation of a distinctly Afro-American culture. The one point I should insist upon in any analysis of the house slave is ambivalence. It is impossible to think of people, black and white, slave and master, thrown together in the intimacy of the Big House without realizing that they had to emerge loving and hating each other.

Life together meant sharing pains and problems, confiding secrets, having company when no one else would do, being forced to help one another in a multitude of ways. It also meant experiencing in common, but in tragically opposite ways, the full force of lordship and bondage: that is, the full force of petty tyranny imposed by one woman on another; of expecting someone to be at one's beck and call regardless of her own feelings and wishes; of being able to take out one's frustrations and disappointments on an innocent bystander, who would no doubt be guilty enough of something since servants are always falling short of expectations.

To illustrate the complexity of black slave behavior in the Big House, let us take a single illustration. It is typical in that it catches the ambiguity of those enmeshed and yet hostile lives. Beyond that it is of course unique, as is all individual experience. Eliza L. Magruder was the niece of a deceased planter and politician from the Natchez, Mississippi, region and went to live with her aunt Olivia, who managed the old plantation herself. Eliza kept a diary for the years 1846 and 1847 and then again for 1854 to 1857.[4] She may have kept a diary for the intermittent years, but none has been found. In any case, she has a number of references to a slave woman, Annica, and a few to another, Lavinia. We have here four women, two white and two black, two mistresses and two servants, thrown together in a single house and forced on one another's company all year long, year after year.

On August 17, 1846, Eliza wrote in her diary more or less in passing, "Aunt Olivia whipped Annica for obstinacy." This chastisement had followed incidents in which Annica had been "impudent." About a month later, on September 11, Annica took another whipping—for "obstinacy." Eliza appears to have been a bit squeamish, for her tone, if we read it correctly, suggests that she was not accustomed to witnessing such unpleasantness. On January 24, 1847, she confided to her diary, "I feel badly. Got very angry and whipped Lavinia. O! for government over my temper." But as the world progresses, so did Eliza's fortitude in the face of others' adversity. When her diary resumed in 1854, she had changed slightly: the squeamishness had diminished. Annica had not changed: she remained her old, saucy self. October 26, 1854: "Boxed Annica's ears for impertinence."

Punctuated by this war of wills, daily life went on. Annica's mother lived in Jackson, Mississippi, and mother

---

[4] Ms. diary in Louisiana State University library, Baton Rouge, La.

and daughter kept in touch. Since Annica could neither read nor write, Eliza served as her helpmate and confidante. December 5, 1854: "I wrote for Annica to her mother." Annica's mother wrote back in due time, no doubt to Annica's satisfaction, but also to her discomfiture. As Eliza observed on January 25, 1855, "Annica got a letter from her mammy which detected her in a lie. O! that negroes generally were more truthful." So we ought not to be surprised that Eliza could write without a trace of the old squeamishness on July 11, 1855, "I whipt Annica."

The impertinent Annica remained undaunted. November 29, 1855: "Aunt Olivia gave Annica a good scolding and made her ask my pardon and will punish her otherwise." Perhaps we should conclude that Annica's behavior had earned the undying enmity of the austere white ladies, but some doubts may be permitted. On July 24, 1856, several of their neighbors set out on a trip to Jackson, Mississippi, where, it will be recalled, Annica's mother lived. Aunt Olivia, with Eliza's concurrence, sent Annica along for a two-week holiday and provided ten dollars for her expenses. On August 3, Annica returned home in time for breakfast.

On September 4, 1856, "Annica was very impertinent, and I boxed her ears." Three days later, wrote Eliza, "I kept Annica in in the afternoon for impudence." The next day (September 8) Eliza told Aunt Olivia about Annica's misconduct. "She reproved her for it and will I suppose punish her in some way." Again in November, on the tenth day of the month, "Aunt Olivia whipt Annica for impertinence."

At this point, after a decade of impudence, impertinence, obstinacy, whipping, and ear-boxing, one might expect that Annica would have been dispatched to the cotton fields. But she remained in the Big House. And what shall we make of such an incident as occurred on the night of December 29,

1856, when poor Annica was ill and in great pain? It is not so much that Eliza sat up with her, doing what she could; it is rather that she seemed both concerned and conscious of performing a simple duty. On the assumption that the illness left Annica weak for a while, Eliza of course still had Lavinia. January 30, 1857: "I boxed Lavinia's ears for coming up late when I told her not."

On April 23, 1857, Annica greatly pleased Eliza by making her a white bonnet. But by April 26, Annica was once again making trouble: "Aunt Olivia punished Annica by keeping her in her room all afternoon." And the next day: "Aunt Olivia had Annica locked up in the garret all day. I pray it may humble her and make further punishment unnecessary."

On August 18, 1857, "Aunt Olivia held a court of enquiry, but didn't find out who ripped my pattern." There is no proof that Annica did it; still, one wonders. Two weeks later in Miss Eliza's Sunday school, "Annica was strongly tempted to misbehave. I brought her in however." The entries end here.

Let us suppose that the ladies had carried their household into the war years: What then? It would take little imagination to see Annica's face and to hear her tone as she marched into the kitchen to announce her departure for the federal lines. It would not even take much imagination to see her burning the house down. Yet she seems never to have been violent, and we should not be too quick to assume that she would easily have left the only home that she had known as an adult and the women who wrote letters to her mother, exchanged confidences with her, and stayed up with her on feverish nights. The only thing we can be sure of is that she remained impudent to the day she died.

What I think this anecdote demonstrates above all is the ambivalence of relations in the Big House and the stubborn struggle for individuality that house slaves, with or without the whip, were capable of. Yet it may also hint at another side of their experience and thereby help to explain why so many black militants, like so many historians before them, are quick to condemn the whole house-slave legacy as one to be exorcized. The house slaves were indeed close to the whites, and of all the black groups they exhibit the most direct adherence to certain white cultural standards. In their religious practices, their dress, their manners, their prejudices, they were undoubtedly the black group most influenced by Euro-American culture. But this kind of cultural accommodationism was by no means the same thing as docility or Uncle Tomism. Even a relatively assimilated house slave could and normally did strike back, assert independence, and resist arbitrariness and oppression.

We are today accustomed to thinking of black nationalists as "militants" and civil rights integrationists as "moderates," "conservatives," or something worse. Yet Dr. Martin Luther King and his followers were and are militant integrationists, prepared to give up their lives for their people; on the other hand, there are plenty of black nationalists who are anything but militant. The tension between integration and separatism has always rent the black community, but now it has led us to confuse questions of militancy with those of nationalism. In fact, the combinations vary; there is no convincing way to categorize integrationists or separationists as either militant or accommodating. Field hands or house slaves could be either docile, "accommodating," or rebellious, and it is likely that most were all at once.

If today the house slaves have a bad press, it is largely because of their cultural assimilationism, from which it is erroneously deduced that they were docile. The first point may be well taken; the second is not. LeRoi Jones, for example, in his brilliant book *Blues People*, argues convincingly that field slaves had forged the rudiments of a distinct Afro-American culture, whereas the house slaves largely took over the culture of the whites. He writes primarily about black music, but he might easily extend his analysis to language and other fields. There are clearly two ways of looking at this side of the house-slave experience. On the one hand, the house slaves reinforced white culture in the slave quarters; they were one of the Americanizing elements in the black community; on the other hand, they wittingly or unwittingly served as agents of white repression of an indigenous Afro-American national culture.

Of course, both these statements are really the same; it is merely that they differ in their implicit judgments. But we ought to remember that this role did not reduce the house slaves who were in their own way often rebellious and independent in their behavior. Therefore, even these slaves, notwithstanding their assimilationist outlook and action, also contributed in no small degree to the tradition of survival and resistance to oppression that today inspires the black liberation movement.

If today we are inclined to accept uncritically the contemptuous attitude that some critics have toward the house slave, we might ponder the reflections of the great black pianist Cecil Taylor. Taylor was speaking in the mid-1960s—a century after slavery—but he was speaking of his father in a way that I think applies to what might be said of house slaves. Taylor was talking to A. B. Spellman, as reported in Spellman's book, *Four Lives in the Bebop Business:*

> Music to me was in a way holding on to Negro culture, because there wasn't much of it around. My father has a great store of knowledge about black folklore. He could

talk about how it was with the slaves in the 1860's, about the field shouts and hollers, about myths of black people. . . . He worked out in Long Island for a State Senator. He was a house servant and a chef at the Senator's sanatorium for wealthy mental wrecks. And actually it was my father more than the Senator himself who raised the Senator's children. . . .

And I really used to get dragged at my father for taking such shit off these people. I didn't dig his being a house servant. I really didn't understand my old man; well, you're my generation and you know the difference between us and our fathers. Like, they had to be strong men to take what they took. But of course we didn't see it that way. So that I feel now that I really didn't understand my father, who was a really lovely cat. He used to tell me to stay cool, not to get excited. He had a way of letting other people display their emotions while keeping control of his own. People used to say to me, "Cecil, you'll never be the gentleman your father was." That's true. My father was quite a gentleman. . . . I wish that I had taken down more about all that he knew about black folklore, because that's lost too; he died in 1961.

Finally, we must consider another misunderstood group of slaves—the drivers. These black slave foremen were chosen by the master to work under his direction or that of an overseer and to keep the hands moving. They would rouse the field slaves in the morning and check their cabins at night; would take responsibility for their performance; and often would be the ones to lay the whip across their backs. In the existing literature the drivers appear as ogres, monsters, betrayers, and sadists. Sometimes they were. Yet Mrs. Willie Lee Rose, in her book *Rehearsal for Reconstruction*, notes that it was the drivers in the Sea Islands who kept the plantations together after the masters had fled the approach of the

Yankees, who kept up discipline, and who led the blacks during those difficult days.

Now, it is obvious that if the drivers were as they are reported to have been, they would have had their throats cut as soon as their white protectors had left. In my own researches for the war years I have found repeatedly, almost monotonously, that when the slaves fled the plantations or else took over plantations deserted by the whites, the drivers emerged as the leaders. Moreover, the runaway records from the North and from Canada reveal that a number of drivers were among those who successfully escaped the South.

One clue to the actual state of affairs may be found in the agricultural journals for which many planters and overseers wrote about plantation matters. Overseers often complained bitterly that masters trusted their drivers more than they trusted them. They charged that often overseers would be fired at the drivers' instigation and that, in general, masters were too close to their drivers and too hostile and suspicious toward their white overseers. The planters did not deny the charges; rather, they admitted them and defended themselves by arguing that the drivers were slaves who had earned their trust and that they had to have some kind of check on their overseers. Overseers were changed every two or three years on most plantations whereas drivers remained in their jobs endlessly. Usually any given driver remained in his position while a parade of overseers came and went.

It had to be so. The slaves had to be controlled if production was to be on schedule, but only romantics would think that a whip alone could effect the result. The actual amount of work done and the quality of life on the plantation were a consequence of a compromise between masters and slaves. It was a grossly unfair and one-sided compromise, with the master holding a big edge. But the slaves did not simply lie down and take whatever came. They had their own ways of foot-dragging, dissembling, delaying, and sabotaging.

The role of the driver was to minimize the friction by mediating between the Big House and the quarters. On the one hand he was the master's man: he obeyed orders, inflicted punishments, and stood for authority and discipline. On the other hand, he could and did tell the master that the overseer was too harsh, too irregular; that he was incapable of holding the respect of the hands; that he was a bungler. The slaves generally knew just how much they had to put up with under a barbarous labor system but they also knew what even that system regarded as going too far. The driver was their voice in the Big House as he was the master's voice in the quarters.

Former slaves tell us of drivers who were sadistic monsters, but they also tell us of drivers who did everything possible to soften punishments and to protect the slaves as best they could. It was an impossible situation, but there is little evidence that drivers were generally hated by the field hands.

The selection of a driver was a difficult matter for a master. First, the driver had to be a strong man, capable of bullying rather than of being bullied. Second, he had to be uncommonly intelligent and capable of understanding a good deal about plantation management. A driver had to command respect in the quarters. It would be possible to get along for a while with a brutal driver who could rule by fear, but, generally, planters understood that respect and acquiescence were as important as fear and that a driver had to do more than make others afraid of him. It was then necessary to pick a man who had leadership qualities in the eyes of the slaves.

The drivers commanded respect in various ways. Sometimes they became preachers among the slaves and got added prestige that way. Sometimes, possibly quite often, they acted as judge and jury in the quarters. Disputes among slaves arose often, generally about women and family matters. If there were fights or bitter quarrels and if they were called to the attention of the overseer or the master, the end would be a whipping for one or more participants. Under such circumstances, the driver was the natural choice of the slaves themselves to arbitrate knotty problems. With such roles in and out of the quarters, it is no wonder that so many drivers remained leaders during and after the war, when the blacks had the choice of discarding them and following others.

Every kind of plantation had two kinds of so-called "bad niggers." The first kind were those so designated by the masters because they were recalcitrant. The second kind were those so designated by the slaves themselves. These were slaves who may or may not have troubled the master directly but were a problem to their fellow slaves because they stole, or bullied, or abused other men's women. The driver was in a position to know what was happening in the quarters and to intervene to protect weaker or more timid slaves against these bullies. In short, the driver's position was highly ambiguous and on balance was probably more often than not positive from the slaves' point of view. Whatever the intentions of the master, even in the selection of his own foremen—his own men, as it were—the slaves generally were not passive, not objects, but active agents who helped to shape events, even if within narrow limits and with great difficulty.

We know that there were not many slave revolts in the South and that those that did occur were small and local. There were good reasons for the low incidence of rebellion: In general, the balance of forces was such that revolt meant suicide. Under such conditions, black slaves struggled to live as much as possible on their own terms. If their actions were less bombastic and heroic than romantic historians would like us to believe, they were nonetheless impressive in their assertion of their resourcefulness and dignity, and a strong sense of self and community. Had they not been, the fate of black America after emancipation would have been even grimmer than it was. For the most part the best that the slaves could do was to live, not merely physically but with as much inner autonomy as was humanly possible.

Every man has his own judgment of heroism, but the kind of heroism alluded to by Cecil Taylor in his moving tribute to his father is worth recalling. There are moments in the history of every people—and sometimes these historical moments are centuries—in which they cannot do more than succeed in keeping themselves together and maintaining a sense of individual dignity and collective identity. Slavery was such a moment for black people in America, and their performance during it bequeathed a legacy that combined negative elements to be exorcized[5] with the decisive elements of community and self-discipline. If one were to tax even the privileged house slaves or drivers with the question, "Where were you when your people were groaning under the lash," they could, if they chose, answer with a paraphrase of the Abbé Sieyès, but proudly and without his cynicism, "We were with our people, and together we survived."

[5] I have discussed some of these negative features in "The Legacy of Slavery and the Roots of Black Nationalism," *Studies on the Left*, VI (Nov.–Dec., 1966), 3–26. I stand by much of what I wrote there, but the essay is doubtless greatly weakened by a failure to appreciate black slave culture and its political implications. As a result, the political story I tried to tell is dangerously distorted. Still, that legacy of slavishness remains an important part of the story, and I think I identified some of its features correctly. I am indebted to many colleagues and friends for their criticism, without which I could not have arrived at the reconsiderations on which the present essay is based; in particular, the criticism of George Rawick has been indispensable.

PART FOUR

REAPPRAISAL

Slavery and Ideology

STANLEY M. ELKINS

When I first became interested in the subject of slavery more than fifteen years ago, I was greatly struck by what seemed to me the "closed" character of the argument as it had been carried on by publicists and scholars over several prior generations. "To the present day," I said in the opening pages of my book, "the rhythm of 'right' and 'wrong' which characterized antebellum discourse on the subject of slavery has retained much of its original simplicity and vigor." It seemed then that some effort needed to be made to break the grip of the old argument, and to interrupt this persistent "rhythm of 'right' and 'wrong.' " That is, I did not believe that further insights were to be gained by continuing the discourse as though the brutality and inhumanity of American Negro slavery were still a matter of question. On those terms, I felt, the debate had been settled. I urged that the terms now be changed, and that the debate be continued on newer and less familiar ground. Specifically, I believed that by examining the implications of cross-cultural comparisons, and by raising the issue of institutions and their impact upon individuals, one might thereby loosen the coercions of the old debate and open up new lines of exploration. Since that time, such explorations have in fact occurred, and a new debate has replaced the old.

The present occasion, to which I have been invited to contribute, bears impressive testimonial of this.

And yet this same occasion, dealing as it does with my own
work, confronts me with certain ironic embarrassments. I
began that work in an effort to break out of a closed cycle,
but hardly foresaw that the time might come when I would be
locked in another, this time partly of my own making. The
terms of today's debate are very different from what they
were then. But the debate itself, and the rhythm of it, have
now taken on qualities uncomfortably similar to those I
found so coercive when I first began. That I myself should
be largely responsible for a state of things comparable to the
one I originally resisted hardly makes the embarrassment less
acute. Consequently, I have come to think that it would be
not at all a bad thing if the terms were once again changed.

How all this came about, and how the outlines of the
present debate emerged, may be seen from the critical writings to which my work has given rise. This criticism falls
into three broad categories. How significant, it asks, were the
differences between North American and Latin American
slavery? How adequate is such an analogy as the Nazi concentration camp, with its implications for human personality,
when applied to the complex reality of American Negro
slavery? What real bearing does the idea of anti-institutionalism in American life have on the problem of American abolitionism? These three questions, of course, encompass a good
many others, as a close reading of the critical essays will
reveal. The criticism has been formidable, salutary, and
enormously instructive. At the same time it does form a certain pattern, and has created a new rhythm of its own.

I am thus faced with certain choices regarding what the
present occasion requires of me. One choice would be simply
to take up the principal commentaries, point by point, and

"answer" them seriatim. From the standpoint of their quality, justice would certainly seem to call for some such effort. But here I would be confronted with endless difficulties. For one thing, certain of the criticisms, being correct, are by the same token unanswerable. But as for the rest, were I to approach them on their merits, I would be forced to undertake a range of supplementary investigation and scholarship that would be well beyond my competence. Faced with that, I should be powerfully tempted to beg off, concede the field, and go about other business. And yet I do retain certain convictions about my own work, and the number of concessions I am willing to make does have its limits.

Another choice would be to proceed as though all the criticism were helpful, at least in its effect, and to try to project what my book might have been like if I had had the benefit of it beforehand—or if, instead of having written it then, I were writing it now. But it took little reflection to make the artificiality of such a course apparent. In subsequent editions of their work, few authors have been known to change a single word of what they originally wrote, and I think I can now understand why. The very criticism they have received, the subsequent knowledge they have acquired, the afterthoughts they have entertained, all make it literally impossible to imagine what it would be like to start over. At the same time, why should it be assumed that the conceptual framework which I found meaningful ten years ago, and within which the question is still being debated, is necessarily the most serviceable one for future debates? Conceivably it is not; others are surely possible.

All of which leads to a third alternative, one that to me seems much more constructive than either of the others. What my critics have written is important, and must be taken account of. But I wish to do this with other purposes in mind than simply "vindicating" *Slavery*. I should like to make certain predictions about the future course of the argument. I am assuming that the present one has taken on a certain repetitiveness and acquired certain locked-in features, that this could in time become dangerously stultifying, and that the cycle once more can and should be broken. A new object of interest—the phenomenon of ideology—has arisen in other areas of historical study within the past five years. Ideology is a subject that has to be thought about and written about with standards we are only beginning to get used to. It is this phenomenon and this interest, I should guess, that may create new or altered perspectives in the study of slavery.

II

In the years since I made my proposal, following the lead of Frank Tannenbaum's *Slave and Citizen*, that many important insights were to be derived from comparisons of North American and Latin American slavery, there has been considerable dispute over what such comparisons, if systematically carried out, might be expected to yield. Underlying this debate, if I may simplify it momentarily, is a philosophical question having to do with method. It is a question not simply of models of explanation, but of why one constructs such "models" in the first place, and of what it is one wants to explain with them. In this instance, concerning the slave systems in Anglo-American and Latin American cultures, there are a number of writers—most prominently David Brion Davis, and to a qualified degree Eugene Genovese—who believe that the broad similarities between these systems are more significant than the differences. I, on the other hand, was far more impressed by the contrasts, and laid out my discussion accordingly.

I was struck by the way in which the arrangements of law, custom, and institutions—including those of religion—in the American South evolved along lines so precisely parallel with, and supportive of, the full development of slavery and plantation capitalism. It was apparent that no official contrary standards could emerge in Southern society which might interfere with such a system or complicate its workings. The logic of all this was embodied in a racism the massive consistency of which kept that society united behind slavery while it existed, and continued to operate as a barrier to full freedom long after slavery was dead. In the way in which law, custom, and institutions impinged on slavery in Latin American society, on the other hand, I could perceive no such parallelism, no such logic, no such consistency. The complexities of the slave system there, and the subtle gradations in racial attitudes which accompanied it, are baffling to any American who tries to penetrate them, conditioned as he is to the comparative simplicities of his own society's experience with slavery. To the outside observer, then as now, the Latin American slave population somehow did not seem as totally "enslaved" as it logically ought to have been, since men and women kept leaving it by a variety of exits; nor did color, as a barrier to advancement in free society, operate with anything like the inexorability that his own historical experience would lead him to expect. But why? Why this difference? The question was deeply interesting to me, as it was to Tannenbaum.

In order to deal with it, I lumped the entire Hispanic American and Luso-Brazilian experience together, as Tannenbaum had done, for the purpose of the comparison with the

STANLEY M. ELKINS

STANLEY M. ELKINS

American South. I reasoned that there must have been countervailing institutional forces in both these Latin cultures, generating standards not always consonant with those of chattel slavery, that served both to blunt the full force of slavery itself and to blur the line between slavery and freedom. In attempting to locate such forces I found, or thought I had found, what I was looking for in the form of a royal officialdom which saw to the enforcement of a body of law governing the treatment of slaves and protecting their rights, as well as of a Church whose interest it was to see that all men—slaves included—should be gathered together in the Faith. This rather abstract framework—overly abstract, perhaps—does seem to have been borne out fairly well by studies since made by others of parts of the Spanish Empire.[1] But the same framework, as critics have pointed out to me, cannot be applied to Brazil in anything like the same way. The Portuguese Crown never had the effectiveness in Brazil that the Spanish Crown at the height of its power could claim over its own New World colonies. Repeated royal edicts from Lisbon against the mistreatment of slaves, for example, had minimal results, and expectations of legal redress for abuses were chronically precarious. In the boom plantation areas—the coffee regions of Brazil and even the sugar estates of nineteenth-century Cuba—slavery was full of horrors. Nor did the Church in Brazil, in its official, institutional capacity, have quite the direct impact upon slave life that my schematic treatment seemed to suggest, at least not on the plantations. Nearly all planters maintained private chapels, but despite the heavy Catholic symbolism that characterized daily life

---

[1] E.g., Herbert S. Klein, *Slavery in the Americas: A Comparative Study of Cuba and Virginia* (Chicago, 1967); Norman Meiklejohn, "The Observance of Negro Slave Legislation in Colonial Nueva Granada" (Unpub. Ph.D. diss., Columbia University, 1968).

and personal relations among masters and slaves, priests were found only on the larger estates, while on most others clerical visits were very irregular. And although the Church's official position was one of racial equality, it was much breached in practice, and the Church's zeal for mitigating the rigors of Negro slavery was hardly on a level with its opposition to Amerindian slavery.[2]

A purely institutional scheme, therefore, if it were to embrace satisfactorily the conditions and impact of slavery in both Brazil and the Spanish colonies, would need to be arranged in a form both more enlarged and more refined than the one proposed in my own brief discussion. I remain—not perversely, I think—more convinced than ever that this is entirely possible. But since for my particular purposes the social end-products of both systems were functionally interchangeable, I was not moved as much as I should have been to pursue such refinements at the time. Had I done so, I would not have required the law and official authority in Brazil to bear quite so many of the burdens, and would have supplemented this with a far heavier emphasis than I gave to the authority of tradition and custom, about which there is a variety of evidence. As for the Brazilian Church, picturing it as a single institution speaking with a single voice is misleading, certainly with regard to the many points at which it touched slavery. A proper picture of the Church's true authority in this realm would require proportionally greater

[2] These points are stressed in Eugene D. Genovese, "Rebelliousness and Docility in the Negro Slave," herein; David Brion Davis, *The Problem of Slavery in Western Culture* (Ithaca, 1966), 223–90, an excerpt from which is included here; Marvin Harris, *Patterns of Race in the Americas* (New York, 1964), also included in this volume; Stanley J. Stein, *Vassouras: A Brazilian Coffee County, 1850–1900* (Cambridge, 1957), 132–95; and C. R. Boxer, *Race Relations in the Portugese Colonial Empire, 1415–1825* (Oxford, 1963).

emphasis on the subsidiary institutions which it fostered and protected—most prominently the Negro lay brotherhoods—as well as on the variety of ways in which personal relations were affected by Catholic practice. For forcing me to think such modifications through (I shall say more about them shortly), I have particularly to thank Genovese and Davis, whatever the discomfiture they may have caused me.

The very surge, however, that has gone into their line of criticism, salutary as it is, has generated certain side effects that discomfit me for quite other reasons, and that are not so salutary. What they should have taxed me for was making insufficient discriminations within Latin American society—and in a very limited sense, they have. But more fundamentally their effort is to break down my entire scheme of contrasts with North America through the technique of citing exceptions, the cumulative effect of which is to blur *all* discriminations—discriminations so strikingly gross as to have been perfectly obvious to every outsider who observed and wrote about slavery in nineteenth-century Brazil.

Let me revert for a moment to the philosophical question I mentioned earlier regarding assumptions about method: the question of what it is that one expects to accomplish with the comparative approach to historical problems. My conviction on this is that the usefulness of comparison as an analytical device, great as it is, cannot be made to extend beyond fairly restricted purposes. For instance, a case can certainly be made for analogies, if one uses them metaphorically and does not claim too much for them. Or, a comparative survey whose aim is to exhibit a series of sharp contrasts, say between two or more sets of cultural phenomena, seems equally defensible. The critical test they have to meet is simply that of effectiveness: what such devices do for heightening perception. On the other hand, a comparative effort whose primary attention is upon the broad parallels and similarities between cultures will always end, it seems to me, not by heightening perception at all, but by dulling it. To the extent that Davis and Genovese have emphasized the features that slave systems everywhere have had in common—placing the United States, whose system was the most socially damaging of modern times, side by side with Brazil, where the social consequences of slavery were dramatically different—to that extent do they reduce and homogenize the slave experience of the entire Western Hemisphere. I cannot see the gain in this, and I would urge with all due respect that such a drift be resisted. It would be regrettable if, after all our discourse, we should find ourselves back where we started.[3]

One must, at any rate, protect the clarity of one's gross perceptions. Among the very grossest of these, when it is a question of comparing the slave society of Brazil with that of North America, is that concerning the rate and frequency of manumissions. Of the total Negro population of the American slave states in 1860, more than 90 per cent were still in slavery; in Brazil at the same time, more than half were already free, and the proportion of free to slave, which had been steadily rising since the eighteenth century, would continue to do so over the ensuing 28 years.[4] This is the key fact

[3] In justice to Genovese I should note that when in his opinion "homogenization" has gone too far, he too feels impelled to move against it. I refer to his sharp critique of Carl Degler's paper, "Slavery in the United States and Brazil: An Essay in Comparative History," read at the annual meeting of the Organization of American Historians at Philadelphia, April 19, 1969, and published in *American Historical Review*, LXXV (Apr. 1970), 1004–28.

[4] In comparison to the steady rise in the numbers of free colored in relation to slaves in Brazil throughout this period, the free-slave ratio among the total colored in the United States (for the entire country) remained strikingly stable. Indeed, by 1860 it had actually declined to 11.0% from the 11.9% of 1850 and 13.4% of 1840. On the other hand, an examination of early manuscript census materials in Brazil has led Herbert Klein

one has to work with; everything of consequence regarding the entire problem is directly related to it. The very high rate of manumission in Brazil throughout the period of slavery, and, conversely, the large and ever increasing numbers of former slaves functioning in free society there, affected the position not only of freedmen but of persons still in slavery. It affected, in short, the whole character of the slave system; it was a social fact, moreover, that simply did not exist in the United States. And fundamentally it was upon this basis, rather than on grounds of physical treatment, that observers invariably referred to the Brazilian slave system as the "mildest" in the Western Hemisphere.

How are we to account for this, and what are we to make of it? As for the law and its enforcement in Brazil, no modern study has as yet been made, and until one is, generalizations can hardly be made with much precision. We do know from the recent studies of colonial Bahia by A. J. R. Russell-Wood that aggrieved slaves found direct access to the sovereign remarkably simple. But though Spix and Martius, Walsh, Koster, and Mansfeldt insisted that masters were liable to punishment for abusing their slaves,[5] instances of cruelty,

---

to estimate that in the closing years of the eighteenth century the proportion of free men within the total colored population already ran as high as 50% in the peripheral regions and between 20% and 30% in the major slave-plantation areas. *Negro Population in the United States, 1790–1915* (New York, 1968), 53–57; Herbert S. Klein, "The Colored Freedmen in Brazilian Slave Society," *Journal of Social History*, III (Fall, 1969), 30–52.

[5] A. J. R. Russell-Wood, *Fidalgos and Philanthropists: The Santa Casa da Misericórdia of Bahia, 1550–1755* (Berkeley, 1968), 139, 257; and "Class, Creed and Colour in Colonial Bahia: A Study in Prejudice," *Race*, IX (Oct. 1967), 133–57. "One curious aspect of the relationship between slave and sovereign was the facility with which any slave and coloured person could appeal directly to the king." *Ibid.*, 151. J. B. von Spix and C. F. P. von Martius, *Travels in Brazil in the Years 1817–1820* (London, 1824), I, 179: R. Walsh, *Notices of Brazil in 1828 and 1829* (Boston, 1831), II, 189; Henry

some bordering on the bizarre, were frequent. Or, in view of the frequency of self-purchase, even most Brazilians seem to have been under the impression that a master was legally obliged to free a slave who could present his purchase price. Apparently no such law existed.[6] But here it was custom and public opinion, applauding *all* forms of manumission, that had the virtual force of law. (Newspaper notices of manumissions were carried under the heading of "Acts Worthy of Praise.")[7] One must, moreover, take account not only of what the law did, but of what it did not do. In the American South there were actual prohibitions in law, as well as sanctions of public opinion, against manumission, against the holding of property, and against the educating of slaves. Such prohibitions were unknown in Brazil.

The very conditions of city life, with enormous numbers of both slave and free colored concentrated in urban centers, represented another fragmenting influence upon Brazilian

---

Koster, *Travels in Brazil* (London, 1817), II, 237; Julius Mansfeldt, *Meine Reise nach Brasilien im Jahre 1821* (Magdeburg, 1828), 92.

The only study ever done on Brazilian slave law, originally published in 1866 and recently reprinted, is Agostinho Marques Perdigão, *A escravidão no Brasil: ensaio historico-juridico-social* (São Paulo, 1944), 2v. It is a study of the jurisprudence of the subject and a commentary on the codes, and is therefore of value for what it reveals of the society's systems of belief (see below), but it contains no systematic information on enforcement. It is comparable to John Codman Hurd's *Law of Freedom and Bondage* and Thomas R. R. Cobb's *Inquiry into the Law of Negro Slavery* for the United States.

[6] Mary W. Williams, "The Treatment of Negro Slaves in the Brazilian Empire: A Comparison with the United States of America," *Journal of Negro History*, XV (July 1930), 332–33; W. D. Christie, *Notes on Brazilian Questions* (London, 1865), 78.

[7] Sir Richard F. Burton, *Explorations of the Highlands of the Brazil* (London, 1869), I, 271–72; Walter Colton, *Deck and Port; or, Incidents of a Cruise in the United States Frigate Congress . . .* (New York, 1860), 112; Pierre Verger, *Flux et reflux de la traite des nègres entre le Golfe de Bénin et Bahia de Todos os Santos du dix-septième au dix-neuvième siècle* (Paris, 1968), 516–18.

slavery. The employment—and self-employment—of slaves as stevedores, boatmen, peddlers, artisans, skilled craftsmen, and small tradesmen had a variety of consequences both inside and outside the system. With the right to retain a portion of their earnings, these individuals regularly bought their way out of slavery, which meant a systematic leakage of ambitious, economically productive non-whites into free society. Moreover, the diversity of roles which these persons could play while still in slavery meant an ongoing rehearsal, as it were, for freedom, and this in turn meant that the shock of transition, either on the individual or on the environing society, was bound to be minimal. The apprenticing of slave craftsmen side by side with free colored apprentices, their subsequent practice of their trade in company with freedmen, and their eventual entry as free men themselves into a world in which all the skilled crafts were dominated by men of color, constitutes the representative example of how the process worked.[8] And the cities themselves were the very places where sentiments least friendly to slavery were fostered. For example, the officer class, largely recruited from the cities, came more and more to resent the use of the army to capture runaway slaves, and the military schools were centers of abolitionism for many years before emancipation. Nor should this be surprising, with a large part of the army's rank and

---

[8] "I have now seen slaves working as carpenters, masons, pavers, printers, sign and ornamental painters, carriage and cabinet makers, fabricators of military ornaments, lamp-makers, silversmiths, jewelers, and lithographers. It is also a fact that sculptures in stone and saintly images in wood are often done admirably by slaves and free blacks. . . . *All* kinds of trades are carried on by black journeymen and boys." Thomas Ewbank, *Life in Brazil; or, A Journal of a Visit to the Land of the Cocoa and the Palm* (New York, 1856), 195. See also Koster, *Travels*, II, 219–20, 260–61; Spix and Martius, *Travels*, I, 197–98; John Luccock, *Notes on Rio de Janeiro and the Southern Parts of Brazil . . . from 1808 to 1818* (London, 1820), 201.

file, and even a proportion of the officers, being made up of Negroes and mulattoes. In the cities of the American South, on the other hand, the conditions of life for slaves were by mid-century being consciously made more and more restricted.[9]

And yet it was the Catholic Church, however diffusely its power may have been exerted, that accounted for the major contrasts in character between the slave system of Brazil and that of the United States. The coercive power of the Church in the Spanish dominions was certainly more direct than in Brazil, and the numbers and quality of the priesthood were higher. But it may be doubted whether the influence of Catholic values and Catholic practice was for that reason any the less pervasive. One of the laws that seems not to have been evaded in Brazil was that requiring Catholic instruction and baptism within a year of the newly imported slave's arrival. Family prayers on the estates, morning and night (priest or no priest), the frequent feast days, and the custom of asking and receiving blessings all seem to have created a special set of personal relationships between masters and slaves, unfailingly commented upon by observer after observer. The many religious holidays, during which it was universally understood that slaves, urban or rural, were free to work for themselves, represented a custom that was not lightly breached. The all-embracing quality of the Faith was noted with wonder by the Protestant John Turnbull, visiting Bahia in 1800: "We found . . . that there was one country in the

[9] Richard Graham, "Causes for the Abolition of Negro Slavery in Brazil: An Interpretive Essay," *Hispanic American Historical Review*, XLVI (May 1966), 127, 134; Koster, *Travels*, I, 59–60; Klein, "Colored Freedmen," 31–33; C. S. Stewart, *Brazil and La Plata: The Personal Record of a Cruise* (New York, 1856), 296; Richard C. Wade, *Slavery in the Cities: The South, 1820–1860* (New York, 1964), 243–46.

338   STANLEY M. ELKINS

world in which religion was fashionable, the churches being crowded with all ranks of people, from the meanest slave to his excellency the governor himself."[10]

It was, moreover, unquestionably the Church that created the moral climate for frequent manumissions. The testimony is overwhelming: manumission was a pious deed, a Catholic duty, an "Act Worthy of Praise." It was done on a variety of occasions: a marriage, a birthday, a church festival, the making of a will. The freeing of a slave infant at baptism—whether through the custom of godparenthood or the practice of free fathers liberating their offspring by slave mothers—was very common. It is no mere coincidence that the great majority of such occasions took place under the direct auspices and encouragement of the Church.[11]

Whereas in locating the sources of the Church's institutional power in Spanish America one looks first to the official hierarchy, in Brazil the counterpart is not so obvious. And yet the power was there, and it may well have been organized in such a way that for day-to-day purposes its impact on the slave system itself was even more effective. A major bulwark, social and financial, to Catholicism and the Catholic establish-

[10] Klein, "Colored Freedmen," 40; Williams, "Treatment of Negro Slaves," 330–31; John Turnbull, *A Voyage Round the World in the Years 1800, 1801, 1802, 1803, and 1804* . . . (London, 1805), I, 23; Koster, *Travels*, II, 239; Thomas Lindley, *Narrative of a Voyage to Brazil* . . . (London, 1805), 176; J. B. Debret, *Voyage pittoresque et historique au Brésil . . . depuis 1816 jusqu'en 1831* . . . (Paris, 1834–39), II, 100, 104; III, 129; Maria Graham, *Journal of a Voyage to Brazil, and Residence There, during . . . 1821, 1822, 1823* (London, 1824), 196. "The people of Brazil, brought more in contact with their slaves, from the mildness of their disposition, and from the effects of their religion which unites them together, mix more with them than in other countries. . . ." Alexander Caldcleugh, *Travels in South America during the Years 1819-20-21* (London, 1825), I, 89.

[11] Herbert S. Klein, "The Integration of the Negro into Latin American Society," paper read at Wayne State University, May 5, 1969, Ms.; Koster, *Travels*, II, 234–36; Barbara Rose Trosko, "The Liberto in Bahia before Abolition" (Unpub. M.A. thesis, Columbia University, 1967), 42–43.

ment in Brazil was the large number of lay brotherhoods that flourished under the aegis and protection of the Church. These brotherhoods served the widest variety of social, benevolent, and charitable functions, extending to the actual building and furnishing of churches, and each played a prominent part in municipal religious life, which included the great public festivals and processions. A number of the brotherhoods were open to slaves, free Negroes, and mulattoes, and these probably did more to mold a self-conscious community of the slaves than did any other social mechanism. "The urban counterpart of the *quilombo*," one writer asserts, "was the brotherhood." The Negro brotherhoods gave their members a set of close fraternal ties with a wide company of fellow Catholics, saw to it that masses and a decent burial were provided for those who died, and maintained a regular fund for purchasing the freedom of those who were in slavery. They spoke in a variety of ways for the interests of their membership, and their influence was frequently exerted with the authorities in cases of injustice. The most powerful Negro brotherhood in Bahia, Our Lady of the Rosary, became, according to Russell-Wood, "the mouthpiece for Negro rights."[12]

---

[12] Roger Bastide, *Les religions africaines au Brésil: vers une sociologie des interpénétrations de civilisations* (Paris, 1960), 73, 158–74; Gilberto Freyre, "Some Aspects of the Social Development of Portuguese America," in Charles C. Griffin, ed., *Concerning Latin American Culture* (New York, 1940), 92–93; Manoel S. Cardozo, "The Lay Brotherhoods of Colonial Bahia," *Catholic Historical Review*, XXXIII (Apr. 1947), 12–30; Verger, *Flux et reflux*, 518–21, 527–28. "For ostensibly religious purposes the Church supported these Negro brotherhoods. Behind this support, however, was its decision to allow the Negroes to protect and defend themselves by forming guilds for their collective efforts towards personal liberty." Trosko, "Liberto in Bahia," 43–44. The quotations are from Russell-Wood, *Fidalgos and Philanthropists*, 142, and "Class, Creed and Colour," 153. The *quilombos* were fortified villages of escaped slaves, the term being used here in the sense of a sanctuary.

The power of the Portuguese Crown to impose its own terms upon the slave system of colonial Brazil could not rival that of the Spanish Crown in Spanish America. Nor could the Brazilian Empire, after 1822, achieve much in the way of centralized authority without the support of the planter class. Yet the fact remains that the interests of the Imperial government with regard to slavery were not those of the *fazendeiros*. For one thing, Brazil's very claims to national sovereignty remained perennially insecure throughout the middle decades of the nineteenth century in the face of constant pressure from the British over the slave trade, the enforcement of slave-trade treaties, and the issue of slavery itself. To such pressures, exerted as they were not only through diplomacy but with the actual use of the Royal Navy, the Brazilian Crown, planters or no planters, found it both expedient and necessary to adjust. Moreover, Dom Pedro II himself, throughout much of his enlightened reign of nearly fifty years, was an ardent abolitionist and made little secret of it. Frequent cues from the Throne did much to establish the emancipationist climate of that reign: the Emperor's freeing of his inherited slaves upon his accession, his personal visit of congratulation to the Benedictines of Rio when they emancipated theirs, his insistence upon freedom for those who served in the Paraguayan War, and his pressure upon the ministry, from the 1860s on, to prepare plans for full emancipation. The 1867 Speech from the Throne was a clear indication to the nation at large that slavery was on its way out. In the end, Pedro II's leadership in this realm may have done much to bring down the monarchy itself, but it also had a great deal to do with bringing down slavery.[13]

[13] Richard Graham, "Causes for Abolition," 129–32; Mary W. Williams, *Dom Pedro the Magnanimous: Second Emperor of Brazil* (Chapel Hill, 1937), 264–87.

In any event, one might have toured the Southern United States from end to end, any time after the mid-1830s, searching in vain for a state governor—or any other prominent public official—willing to take a single step, or to say a single public word, hostile to slavery.

A further test of the Brazilian slave system is surely to be found in the state of race relations in Brazilian society both during and after slavery. The amazement of visitors, especially Americans, at finding "no distinction between white and black, or any of the intermediate colors, which can act as a bar to social intercourse or political advancement," is a repeated and well-known feature of all the travel accounts. There was no segregation in omnibuses, trains, restaurants, or places of entertainment. In the coffee room at the opera house in Rio, wrote Ruschenberger in the 1830s, "Blacks and Whites were gay and noisy, eating and drinking together, apparently on the most intimate terms of equality." Agassiz reported that the students at the elite Colégio Dom Pedro II "were of all colors, from black through intermediate shades to white, and even one of the teachers . . . of a higher class in Latin was a negro." The fastest growing element in nineteenth-century Brazilian society was the free colored—not through natural increase but through miscegenation and manumission—and before the end of slavery the colored were well represented in every major occupation and profession. The process had already been in motion more than two centuries before, when Henrique Dias and several of his Negro captains were awarded titles of nobility and admitted into Iberian military orders for their exploits in the wars against the Dutch. "African blood," wrote John Codman after a visit in 1866, "runs freely through marble halls, as well as in the lowest gutters." To a Brazilian slave looking toward freedom, there existed a variety of models of aspiration everywhere around him. To the American slave, viewing the degraded free Negro in his own society, such models were dismally few. And so they would remain for many years after Emancipation—certainly in contrast to the freely mixed society of post-Imperial Brazil.[14]

I am well aware that the innumerable accounts of humane race relations in Brazil, from slavery times down to the present day—from the writings of Henry Koster and Thomas Ewbank in the nineteenth century to those of Gilberto Freyre, Donald Pierson, Frank Tannenbaum, and Charles Wagley in our own time—have at length induced in a number of scholars a certain fretfulness. Race, they point out, *has* been a factor, and still is; prejudice and discrimination *have* played their part in the ordering of Brazilian social arrangements.[15] It is

[14] John Codman, *Ten Months in Brazil: With Incidents of Voyages and Travels* . . . (Boston, 1867), 153; [William S. W. Ruschenberger], *Three Years in the Pacific: Including Notices of Brazil, Chile, Bolivia, and Peru* (Philadelphia, 1834), 43; Louis and Elizabeth Agassiz, *A Journey in Brazil* (Boston, 1869), 124; Klein, "Colored Freedmen," 31. "Thus, if a man have freedom, money, and merit, no matter how black may be his skin, no place in society is refused him." D. P. Kidder and J. C. Fletcher, *Brazil and the Brazilians, Portrayed in Historical and Descriptive Sketches* (Philadelphia, 1857), 133. "A Southern lady (the wife of the very popular United States Consul at Rio during the administration of President Pierce) used to say that 'the very paradise of the negroes was Brazil;' for there they possess a warm climate, and, if they choose, may make their way up in the world, in a manner which can never be the case in the United States." *Ibid.*, 133n. According to Stewart, "color does not fix the social position here, as with us at home. . . . A slave is a menial, not because he is black, but because he is a slave." *Brazil and La Plata*, 296. W. D. Christie, whose position as British minister required him to be officially jaundiced against Brazilian slavery, conceded that "colour is no obstacle to advancement." *Notes*, 78.

[15] In this connection special mention should be made of the "São Paulo school" of sociology in contemporary Brazil. The "Paulistas" came into being as a self-conscious group largely as a result of a series of studies in race relations in various regions of Brazil financed by UNESCO in the 1950s. In some of these studies the findings reveal a pattern of mild and humane relations generally consistent with that described earlier by Donald Pierson. This category includes the work of Thales de Azevedo (Bahia), Luiz de Aguiar Costa Pinto (Rio de Janeiro), and Charles Wagley (north-

very true that they have. But in what context, and compared to what? Not in any context of comparison that includes the United States. To stress "prejudice" in Brazil, and to equate this with prejudice everywhere, including the American South, seems downright perverse. I am quite certain that insights as to the workings of these two cultures—insofar as they are to be reached by any comparative techniques—will not come through this kind of emphasis. Whatever we do, in short, we ought not to homogenize: not in the realm of slavery and race relations, where they concern Brazil on the one side and the United States on the other, not if we want to learn anything really important about either.

But having said all this, I am brought back to a conviction I expressed at the beginning: it is time the argument were moved to another plane entirely. I would guess, from indications already in the air, that when this occurs it will take the form of broad-scale and intensive researches in the realm of ideology. Ideology is of course related to, and has greatly encroached upon, much of what we have done up to now. But we have barely scratched the surface.

Ideology in its most inclusive sense is a massive end-product —a configuration, a total *gestalt*—of a society's historical ex-

---

east interior). The study done in the south by Roger Bastide and Florestan Fernandes of the University of São Paulo, however, placed much more stress on discrimination, both in historical experience and in contemporary life. Their students, Octavio Ianni and Fernando Henrique Cardoso, have subsequently published work similar in spirit. Summary statements in English which embody the Paulista viewpoint are: O. Ianni, "Race and Class in Brazil," *Présence Africaine*, XXV, No. 53 (1st qu. 1965), 105-19; F. H. Cardoso, "Colour Prejudice in Brazil," *ibid.*, 120-28; and F. Fernandes, "The Weight of the Past," *Daedalus*, XCVI (Spring 1967), 560-79. Fernandes' book *A integrecão do negro na sociedade de classes*, originally published in 1965, has recently been condensed and translated into English as *The Negro in Brazilian Society* (New York, 1969).

perience, its norms, its values, its fears and prejudices, its material interests, and its habits of mind. The world-views of societies, or of groups within societies, are inferrable not only from their formal writings but from their bodies of law, political arrangements, social customs, ceremonial behavior, imaginative literature, and responses to real or imagined crisis. We do know something—though we could stand to know a great deal more—about the ideological dynamics that have moved our own society from time to time. But how much do we know, in this respect, of Latin American society? What do we have in systematic and comprehensive form that seeks to place in ideological context the emotional, moral, and intellectual responses of these societies, say, to problems of slavery and race? There is at present little that I know of.[16] A projection or two, however, might be ventured as to the categories and components that will make up such inquiries when they do appear, as they surely will.

A major one would be class, with all the vestigial pre-capitalist attitudes that went with it. Taking into account, as one must, that color has been an item of strong prejudice in all Western societies including those of Latin America, one might well ask how such an element as race tended to be contained, modified, and even transformed over time by assumptions about rank, hierarchy, and class. What were those assumptions, what was their historic background in the experience of Spain and Portugal, and how were they expressed?[17] In the case, say, of Brazil, what sort of psychological

[16] The work of Gilberto Freyre on Brazil might be regarded as an exception, though it could be objected (I think properly) that its principal value lies not so much in systematic analysis but rather in whatever inferences are to be drawn (in this case, with regard to social ideology) from the author's suggestive and wide-ranging impressionism.

[17] Some suggestions in this realm are contained in Richard M. Morse, "Toward a Theory of Spanish American Government," *Journal of the History of Ideas*, XV (Jan. 1954), 71-93. Another such effort is Alexandre

protection did a complex class system provide for the society at large against the spectacle of a steady infusion of free blacks and mulattoes into its social and economic life? They must have been considerable, in view of that society's very limited inclination to hold the line at any given point on such matters as freedom of movement, holding of property, commercial activity, education, miscegenation, and manumission.

Another ideological category most certainly would concern the Church and Catholic culture. The "climate of moral opinion," "the ability of the Catholic Church to help shape the ethos of slave society" (to use Genovese's words), is a great subject for study in itself. The Church made its terms with slavery. But what was the tone and style with which it did so? What was the quality of the Iberian experience that accounts for the Church's extraordinary impulse to *absorb?* Many things would come under some such heading: the acculturation of Moors, Jews, and Negroes; the extension of the sacraments to all men; the syncretization of African cults under the Church's aegis; the encouragement of slave and free colored religious brotherhoods. What sort of attitudes grew out of all this, and how were they expressed? What was the form taken by those convictions about paternity that moved so many free fathers to liberate their slave children at baptism, or that protected a slave's free time, or that placed such approval on manumission? What was it that made the Church and the relationships associated with it the "primary factors," as one student finds, "in the assimilated liberto's life"?[18] And finally, we need to know more than we do about

---

Lobato, "Permanence and Change in Overseas Portuguese Thought," in Raymond S. Sayers, ed., *Portugal and Brazil in Transition* (Minneapolis, 1968), 93–107.

[18] "Undeniably, the outstanding aspect of the last wills and testaments [of freed slaves] was the religious proclamation of their Catholic faith. For

the ways in which Catholic norms left their impress upon the
slave codes themselves. The degree to which the codes were
enforced in different times and places, under the stress of
varying local conditions, constitutes one kind of historical
problem. But another concerns the things such codes can tell
us, whatever those conditions, about what a society *believed*.[19]

Then there is the fascinating question—particularly in the
case of Brazil—of a society's racial picture of itself, and of
what effect this may have on its attitudes about "race" in
general. Earlier notions about racial purity in Brazil, as we
know, tended to break down over time. There has been much
speculation as to the causes. The heritage of experience with
the Moors, widespread habits of miscegenation owing to the
scarcity of white women in the early days, the tolerance of
enveloping Catholic values, and so on—there is no certain
formula as to how to strike the balance.[20] But we do know
something about the results, and in a general way how the
society feels about them now.

Even while slavery still existed in Brazil, according to

---

example, the African Felizberta Maria de Jesus declared she was a member
of the Irmandades of São Benedicto, Santa Efiginia, of Jesus, Maria e José,
of the Carmo, of the Rosário de João Pereira and the Rosário e Baixa de
Sapateiros!" Trosko, "Liberto in Bahia," 65.

[19] See again Morse, "Theory," 72–73. Professor Morse, a strong opponent
of "homogenization," questions the tendency of some American historians
to assimilate the experience of slavery in Brazil and that in the United
States to anything resembling a common or comparable cultural context.
In a critique of the paper by Carl Degler mentioned above (see footnote 3),
he says: "[W]e must recognize that generalizations about slavery, race relations, forms of prejudice and discrimination, rebellions and protest movements will be random and incoherent unless they can be related to [the]
central premises of belief systems which prevailed in the respective societies."

[20] Attempts to strike such a balance include H. Hoetink, *The Two
Variants in Caribbean Race Relations: A Contribution to the Sociology of
Segmented Societies* (London, 1967); and Pierre L. van den Berghe, *Race
and Racism: A Comparative Perspective* (New York, 1967).

Thomas Skidmore, virtually no one believed in the actual biological inferiority of the colored peoples. Race, accordingly, had little to do with that, but it did have something to do with social inferiority. It was therefore desirable to "whiten" the dark-skinned people—an ideal, indeed, which for generations had had its practical application. It was done either through talent and money, which simply redefined a man as "white" when he was really dark, or it was done through miscegenation. Miscegenation was thus a good thing because it "whitened" (whereas in the United States it was a bad thing because it darkened). It was such a way of looking at their own society, for example, that permitted Brazilian intellectuals, despite their feelings of cultural inferiority, to resist the coercions of European racist thought in the years prior to World War I. Patriotism and national pride had no choice but to defend the mixed Brazilian type, who by then was clearly beyond all hope of racial "purity."[21]

With this entire ideological *gestalt*—historical and contemporary—reconstructed, one may be in a position to understand both why ordinary Brazilians find discussions of the "race problem" in the United States incomprehensible, and why a modern Brazilian intellectual should find it so natural to conclude one of his books by serenely referring to his country as "more and more a racial democracy."[22] And going back to slavery times, one can better assess the chances, say, of the *fazendeiro* class's imposing a contrary set of standards on the rest of Brazilian society, beyond a pale and apologetic version

[21] Thomas E. Skidmore, "Brazilian Intellectuals and the Problem of Race, 1870–1930," Graduate Center for Latin American Studies, Vanderbilt University, Occasional Paper No. 6, 1969.

[22] Donald Pierson, *Negroes in Brazil: A Study of Race Contact at Bahia*, 2nd ed. (Carbondale, 1967), xxix–xxx; Gilberto Freyre, *The Mansions and the Shanties: The Making of Modern Brazil* (New York, 1963), 431. "Brazilians," according to Charles Wagley, "can still call their society a racial democracy." *Race and Class in Rural Brazil*, 2nd ed. (New York, 1963), 2.

of the "necessary evil" argument. Thus with ideology as the governing concept, it becomes easier to see that whereas fragmenting such a *gestalt* by concentration upon counter examples may be useful for some purposes, for others it is gravely misleading. For it *is* a kind of totality, the whole being more significant than the parts, and serves to exhibit in relief those very distinctions between cultures that are most worth grasping.

Moreover, one may, if one wishes, view ideologies comparatively. One may examine with fresh appreciation the slave ideology of the antebellum American South, supported as it was not only by the South's leading "theorists"—Calhoun, Fitzhugh, Simms, Hammond, and all the rest—as well as by every argument on racial inferiority then known, but also by every social, political, legal, and religious institution which that society contained.

III

No section of my book has been the subject of so much discussion and criticism as the one entitled "Slavery and Personality." In it, I proposed an analogy between North American slavery in the nineteenth century and the Nazi concentration camps of the twentieth, using the analogy both to draw implications for human personality in an extreme relationship of power and dependency, and to explore the psychological setting in which a childish "Sambo" type might have been fostered among large numbers of American slaves. There have been numerous objections to this. Some have resisted the implication that the slave system could have been as psychologically coercive as the concentration camp image, with all its emotional impact, suggests. There have been many difficulties over Sambo. How prevalent was Sambo as a type—or, for that matter, was he even real? To what extent were Sambo-like characteristics truly internalized, and to what extent were such characteristics, when they appeared, simply a deliberate response to the expectations of white men?

Discussion on all this was originally very heated, and enough of it occurred while the book was still in manuscript that I was able to comment on the main outlines of it in an appendix to the first edition. Since that time, however—though the basic objections continue to be those made from the beginning—the discussion has become much more subtle and sophisticated. It has been conceded that the use of analogy in itself, as an analytical device, is legitimate. The critical question has shifted to that of whether the particular analogy I used is necessarily the most effective one for the purpose. Certain refinements on my theoretical apparatus have been proposed using institutions less extreme than the concentration camp, the better to account for the variety of behavior and personality patterns to be observed within the institution of slavery. Here I have found the essays by George Fredrickson and Christopher Lasch, and by Roy Bryce-Laporte (both included in this volume), very illuminating.

But before proceeding to their work, I shall have to say something about that of Genovese.[23] Genovese's critique of this section falls somewhat outside the pattern just referred to, inasmuch as it forms an integral part of his discussion of the previous section and is consistent with his argument that slavery in all times and places has produced similar effects. Unlike many of the critics, Genovese is willing to concede the reality of Sambo—he calls it the "slavish personality"—

[23] "Rebelliousness and Docility," cited above. Bryce-Laporte's essay is drawn from his dissertation, "The Conceptualization of the American Slave Plantation as a Total Institution" (UCLA, 1968).

but insists that such a type was not unique to American slavery. Citing evidence from various cultures, including Brazilian and even Arabic, he asserts that Sambo existed wherever slavery existed.

Genovese further argues that my notion of absolute power, in relation to the complex realm of alternatives and probabilities that constituted the historical reality of slavery, was not sufficiently discriminating to deal either with the many spaces in the system or with a range of deviant behavior, including rebelliousness, among the slaves themselves. My "greatest weakness," he says, is my "inability to accept the principle of contradiction, to realize that all historical phenomena must be regarded as constituting a process of becoming, and that, therefore, the other-sidedness of the most totalitarian conditions may in fact represent the unfolding of their negation." The contradictions within Sambo, for instance, might very well reach the point of transforming him, under certain conditions, into a Nat Turner.

I gather that Genovese would actually concede me a very large part of my argument, were he not somehow convinced that I have established a "deterministic model" which consistency will not allow me to modify. He would even concede me "more American than Latin American Sambos" if the contrast "could be reduced to a matter of degree," though my own model would then "fall." But it was never my intention to establish a deterministic model, and I would be more than happy to settle for "degrees." (For instance, something less than absolute power produces something less than absolute dependency.) I have said as much throughout my book, and I do not think my argument would "fall" if I said so again.[24]

[24] E.g., "The American slave system, compared with that of Latin America, was closed and circumscribed, but, like all social systems, its

I assumed all along that any sustained relationship of power
and dependency in human affairs can have consequences
which are psychologically infantilizing (the degree of the one
depending, as I said, on the degree of the other), and I am
not surprised at the evidence Genovese has produced from
other slave societies that show this. Nor need such evidence be
restricted always to slavery. But it is one thing to cite instances, and quite another to conclude from them that a
cultural tradition as extended and deep-rooted as that of
Sambo in the American South can be postulated for any
society in which slavery existed. *That* case is as yet not
proven, and if it were to be, more flexible techniques would
be needed for doing it than those he has used. A study of the
Negro in Brazilian literature, for example, reveals no such
tradition. There, the slave appears in a variety of types: he is
filthy and bestial; he is a fighting ruffian; he is resourceful,
intelligent, heroic. But there are no lovable, irresponsible
Sambos. The literature of the American plantation, on the
other hand, as I have elsewhere suggested, tells a very different story.[25]

---

arrangements were less perfect in practice than they appeared to be in
theory. It was possible for significant numbers of slaves, in varying degrees,
to escape the full impact of the system and its coercions upon personality"
(137).

[25] Nowhere in antebellum American fiction have I seen the typical
"faithful slave" portrayed, as he is in Brazilian, as one who will *fight* for
his master or mistress and perform heroic acts. The *bad* Brazilian slave,
on the other hand, is a treacherous beast of prey. (The bad female slave is
unfaithful to all her lovers.) See Raymond S. Sayers, *The Negro in Brazilian Literature* (New York, 1956), 81, 148–51, 174–75, and *passim.* "In
Brazilian literature there is no Uncle Remus and there is no tradition of
happy days on the old plantation." *Ibid.,* 224. To the Portuguese, African
Negroes were, to be sure, inferior beings, but not Sambo types. "Deformed,
horrible, cruel, bestial, ferocious, these are the characteristics attributed to
the Negroes by Barros, Castanheda, Góis, and Osório." Jose Honório Rod-
rigues, *Brazil and Africa* (Berkeley, 1965), 6.

I would agree that the day-to-day reality of American slavery contained many more contradictions than my discussion seemed to allow for. But to formalize this idea and to erect "contradiction" itself into a principle of explanation, historical or any other kind, is something (here Genovese is quite right) that I am hardly prepared to accept. The metaphysical side of Marxist theory, unlike many another side, is one I could never take very seriously or regard as very scientific. Genovese takes my argument to task "because it proves too much and encompasses more forms of behavior than can usefully be managed under a single rubric." And yet he does much the same thing, going even further and with theoretical underpinning far more questionable, when he argues that Sambo—having internalized *all* the contradictory elements of the system—could, if "the psychological balance was jarred," rise up and become the negation of himself (Nat Turner), the total dependent becoming the total rebel.

With this, I fear, Genovese has shouldered a very cumbersome dialectical apparatus and at the same time pushed the argument down a road that leads nowhere. Rebellions have never been a major issue in the history of American slavery, and he himself has said as much elsewhere.[26] There were none of any consequence after 1831, and the historical Nat Turner, from all indications, was himself anything but a Sambo. He was psychologically able to do what he did precisely because he was so situated in the system that he could resist the full impact of its Samboizing coercions. Moreover, Turner was an exception. There were few like him, and *this* is the thing

---

[26] "The Nat Turner Case," *New York Review of Books*, XI (Sept. 12, 1968), 34–37. An excellent study of the very special social conditions required to produce a rebel in the American context—in this case, Gabriel Prosser—is Gerald W. Mullin, "Patterns of Slave Behavior in Eighteenth Century Virginia" (Ph.D. diss., Berkeley, Calif., 1968), Ch. 6.

that has to be explained. Genovese has not yet, to my satisfaction, located the true mechanism of rebellion, such as it was, on the North American continent; nor does he seem willing to consider the full extent to which the South was able to organize itself—militarily, psychologically, ideologically—to discourage *all* forms of resistance, well short of open rebellion. There was a strain toward consistency in the South's own self-mobilization here that I, for one, have not been able to perceive to a like degree in any other slave society.

An argument to which I find it somewhat easier to adjust my own thinking is that based on Erving Goffman's theory of "total institutions."[27] George Fredrickson and Christopher Lasch in their essay, and Roy Bryce-Laporte in his, have proposed this theory as a more refined substitute for my concentration camp analogy. They do so on the ground that it allows for a wider range of slave behavior, embracing various forms of independence and non-cooperation with the slave-holding regime. The line of thought they propose is one I find most suggestive.

According to Fredrickson and Lasch, such "total institutions" as asylums and prisons, being more flexible, are for that reason better than the concentration camp for purposes of analogy with the slave plantation. They are especially useful in analyzing resistance to the system. They allow not only for a large measure of psychological coercion and for a scarcity of open revolts, but also for a considerable variety of adjustments short of full internalization of the system's values. Fredrickson and Lasch cite Goffman's four categories of the inmate's adjustment: (1) situational withdrawal (apathy);

27 See Erving Goffman, *Asylums: Essays on the Social Situation of Mental Patients and Other Inmates* (Chicago, 1961).

(2) colonization (a kind of practical adjustment to the world of the total institution); (3) conversion (internalization of the institution's definition of him); and (4) intransigence (a sometimes violent but essentially personal and therefore largely non-political rejection of the institution). The inmate can alternate in these roles, occasionally even playing all of them at once—unlike the case of the concentration camp, where the choice is simply that of situational withdrawal (and death) or of conversion. Such a formulation allows for a wide range in between, as well as for the real problems of discipline—such problems, that is, as a limited sense of obligation to obey, the need for rewards and punishments, and the expediency of various compromises within the system. In such a setting the long-time inmates become the "master opportunists," the "virtuosos of the system" whose personal style is "playing it cool," those who, "neither docile nor rebellious . . . , spend their lives in skillful and somewhat cynical attempts to beat the system at its own game." The point of all this, of course, is that theoretically it should apply to slavery as well.

Bryce-Laporte's work, indeed, is an effort, more detailed and extended than that of Fredrickson and Lasch, to adapt the theory of total institutions to North American slavery. Bryce-Laporte is especially interested in the possibility of some kind of independent subculture in the slave community, and in the conditions under which such a culture might function. Following Goffman, he postulates two major categories of adjustment made by the inmates of a total institution, adjustments which by analogy applied, he believes, to slave society as well. One consists of "primary adjustments," or those which correspond directly to the roles officially demanded by the institution. The other concerns the "secondary adjustments"—the behavior patterns that either deviate from or run counter to the official role-expectations. Bryce-Laporte is particularly concerned with the "secondary adjustments." He further subdivides these into "contained" and "disruptive," the former being adjustments not prescribed by the institution but representing no direct threat to it, and the latter, those either actually or potentially dangerous to the institution. This complex of both "contained" and "disruptive" secondary adjustments that any total institution creates goes to make up its "underlife."

Bryce-Laporte has no extravagant illusions as to the "political" character of this underlife. Such a character would require stable and sustained group loyalties, which would in turn create a strong degree of independent social control. But he does believe that the plantation system permitted, overlooked, or tolerated a series of activities—religious services, spirituals, folk tales, holidays—which allowed the slave a measure of protection for his individual autonomy and which blunted the full impact of the system upon his personality. The slave family, moreover, truncated as it was, represented a truly subversive element, a crucial factor in the underlife of the plantation. All in all, Bryce-Laporte believes, the underlife could sustain the widest and subtlest variety of activity, including the activity of protest: "slowing down work, misuse of implements, resistance to acculturation, apologetic and fantasy folklore, religion and exorcism, malingering, running away, suicide, infanticide, stealing, poisoning, murder, and arson."

Bryce-Laporte's specific criticism of me is similar to that of Fredrickson and Lasch. He denies, as do they, that the psychological impact of the slave system, heavy as it may have been, "reached the dimensions of creating a prevailing and crystallized *personality*." He thinks that if slaves had fully succumbed to the conditions of the system "they would have been all zombiefied or psychologically dead," that the typical adjustment lay somewhere between this and intransigence, and that Sambo was a product of role-playing rather than a true internalization of the master class's picture of him.[28]

The great virtue of this work is that in it the problem of *resistance* is at last fully contained, and contained within a theoretical framework far more subtle and scientific than any previously devised. It makes many useful conceptual distinctions. It does not require "revolutionary" or even "political" activity; nonetheless it leaves room for a wide range of overt, covert, and even unconscious forms of resistance. Nor do I think my own work, generally speaking, need be regarded as incompatible with it. To be sure, there are certain points on which Fredrickson and Lasch and Bryce-Laporte obviously would not agree, and I shall have to comment on those points. Yet I made a number of efforts in the course of my book to provide spaces into which just such a theory might fit, however crudely in comparison to their work I may have roughed them in.[29]

I am particularly intrigued by the conceptual possibilities Bryce-Laporte has outlined—to which should be added the

---

[28] I ought, in passing, to correct at least one misreading of my text. Bryce-Laporte, following Ralph Ellison, believes I extended the Sambo personality to present-day Negro Americans. This is simply not true; indeed, such an extension would have contradicted my entire argument. If one is accounting for dependent personalities in terms of a peculiarly coercive slave system, then it ought to follow that those same personalities would be profoundly affected in the reverse direction by the collapse of that system. The historical evidence, moreover, tends to bear this out; for confirmation one need only examine the experience of emancipation and Reconstruction. I have elaborated this point in Nathan Huggins, Martin Kilson, and Daniel Fox, eds., *Key Issues in the Afro-American Experience* (New York, 1971), vol. I.

[29] *Slavery*, 133–39. Another writer who has experimented with Goffman's theories in connection with slavery is Raymond T. Smith, "Social Stratification, Cultural Pluralism, and Integration in West Indian Societies," S. Lewis and T. G. Mathews, eds., *Caribbean Integration: Papers on Social, Political, and Economic Integration* (Rio Piedras, P.R., 1967), 226–58.

findings of Sterling Stuckey on slave folklore—for an "under-life," a subculture of great richness and variety. The suggestions of Bryce-Laporte and others on music, conjuring, prayer meetings, and escape lore, the descriptions of Negro night life in the cities by Richard Wade, Stuckey's studies of double meanings in work songs, spirituals, and the Brer Rabbit cycle —all these represent a vast treasury of materials, much of it still waiting to be mined.[30] Nor, incidentally, do I see why such a concept as "underlife" cannot itself be extended to comparative examinations—say, with Latin America. The terminology would be particularly congenial to such a setting; Catholic cultures have traditionally taken "underlife" for granted and have in fact encouraged it. Bryce-Laporte argues, for example, that although an underlife does not ordinarily change an institution by revolution, it can, over time, force a series of long-term evolutionary adjustments. We do not as yet know how much of this occurred in America, but it certainly occurred in Brazil. The wild *candomblés*, the cults of black madonnas and black saints, the African folk festivals that could dominate the routine of a Brazilian city for days, the activities of the black brotherhoods—together, all such aspects of slave underlife in time altered not only Brazilian Catholicism but also Brazilian slavery.

But the great problem, returning once more to the main argument, is that of "infantilization" and "internalization." I made many efforts to hedge on these questions and to allow for wide variations. I also tried to allow for the emotionally loaded quality of the semantics, recognizing that the most

[30] Sterling Stuckey, "Through the Prism of Folklore: The Black Ethos in Slavery," *Massachusetts Review*, IX (Summer 1968), 417–37, included in this volume; Wade, *Slavery in the Cities*, 143–79; Harold Courlander, *Negro Folk Music, U.S.A.* (New York, 1963); Arna Bontemps and Langston Hughes, eds., *The Book of Negro Folklore* (New York, 1958); and J. Mason Brewer, *American Negro Folklore* (Chicago, 1968).

technical formulations of all such questions, especially when analogy is being used, must necessarily partake of the metaphorical. Moreover, having convictions of my own as to the nucleus of irreducibility in the human spirit, I recognize that the very nature of the argument is such that it can never be finally settled. Or at least so I hope.

As for "infantilization," Fredrickson and Lasch categorically rule this out, calling such a hypothesis "quite untenable." They do refer—rather vaguely, I think—to "psychic damage," which could imply an alternative model, theoretical or at least descriptive, of psychic events. But they do not seem interested in pursuing this. As a result, they ignore a problem that to me was central. That problem concerned styles of behavior within a structure wherein the lines of authority are vastly more simplified than those which operate in the normal world of adult life. I assumed that these styles themselves fell short of the complexity one normally associates with full adult behavior. (And I am sure one may observe them to great advantage in the world of total institutions.) I should probably point out, resorting again to metaphor, the quite obvious fact that short of adulthood there are still infinite degrees of maturity, and that in such metaphors there are many choices. One need not be stuck with that of "infancy," or even of "childhood." My own experience in the army, for example, convinced me that whereas this particular "total institution" may have "made men of us," in other more pervasive respects it turned us into boys.[31] I venture to guess that prisons and asylums may produce much the same effects, without necessarily "zombiefying" their inmates.

On "internalization," Fredrickson and Lasch see a "curious contradiction between the difficulty of discipline and the

[31] There may be some ritual connection between this and the perennial behavior of aging "boys" at conventions of veterans' organizations.

slaves' professed devotion to their masters." This contradiction, in which "slaves could have accepted the legitimacy of their masters' authority without feeling any sense of obligation to obey it," is resolved in the theory of total institutions. I would quite agree (though I never thought of this as a contradiction), and would add that it might also be resolved in any of several theories of adolescent behavior as well. As for the pervasive effects of slavery upon personality, I note a deep reluctance—in Bryce-Laporte particularly—to face this problem fully, a very American unwillingness to believe that even slavery could really touch the "inner man." I can only suggest that it is still possible to romanticize the spaces in the system. There was a time when Ulrich Phillips was rightly censured for doing something not unlike this, and one might still unwittingly do much the same thing for purposes quite different from Phillips's.[32] It was, after all, a very hard system, and we would do well not to forget it. I would concede that there must have been room in it for the virtuosos, the master opportunists, the ones who "played it cool." But how much room? And how much of the system's infinite variety of coercions could the individual slave absorb without his finally internalizing the very role he was being forced to play? I remain uncertain, and can only repeat my willingness to settle for a "broad belt of indeterminacy between 'mere acting' and the 'true self.' "

Where does the argument go from here? Obviously it could go in any of several directions. I am struck by the possibilities for a new departure that are inherent in certain observations of Bryce-Laporte himself. Bryce-Laporte takes note

[32] This is what Earl Thorpe tends to do in his "Chattel Slavery and Concentration Camps," *Negro History Bulletin*, XXV (May 1962), 171–76 (included in this book).

of Goffman's statement that staffs of total institutions "tend to evolve what may be thought of as a theory of human nature," and to this he adds something very interesting of his own. "Such a theory," Bryce-Laporte says, "really is a composite ideological justification of the various interests and responsibilities of the total institution. . . ." What would we discover about these and analogous institutions by examining the ideological context in which they function? I would guess that a scrutiny of such ideologies on their own terms—their elaborateness, their complexity, the conviction and intensity with which they are held, their pervasiveness not only within the institution in question but in the larger society in which the institution operates—should tell us a very great deal, if done in comparative terms, about how coercive they might be upon *all* the individuals in any way concerned with such a system.

And yet, paradoxically and perhaps perversely, I fear that this would be the very point at which I would find prisons and asylums *least* satisfying as analogies to antebellum slavery. No doubt the employees of such institutions do operate, during their working day, upon something approximating an ideology, one that encompasses most of their relationships with the inmates and which they find generally serviceable for keeping the place running. Yet the degree of explicitness with which such an ideology is articulated and diffused throughout the environing society is another question, and a dubious one, while even the employees' own personal stake in either the ideology or the institution's survival is surely something less than total. It is under those circumstances, as well as all the others we have noted, that room is made for the "corruption of authority," for the seasoned inmate who becomes the master opportunist, "plays it cool," and exploits the system.

But then turn it around and consider the slaveholding ideology of the antebellum South. Consider its infinite permutations, and how thoroughly it dominated the entire political, social, economic, and psychological life of the Southern states. It left no realm of thought or feeling untouched. At its highest political reaches it generated a theory of state sovereignty at the root of which, as William Freehling has shown, lay the South's extravagant need to protect the institution of slavery against any and all federal encroachment, and in the end, with no sense of inconsistency, broke up the national party system with its insistence upon positive protection of slavery in the territories. It developed an elaborate "sociology"—the first Americans to use that term were the proslavery theorists—to expound the beneficent effects of a patriarchally organized society. Its economic rationale was "Cotton Is King," a theory which warned of the ruinous consequences of challenging either King Cotton or his legion of white and black retainers. And most pervasive of all, this ideology contained assumptions about race that governed every action, every attitude, every response, every relationship of white men to black. And the custodians of *this* institution were of all ages and of both sexes, and were located everywhere, all throughout white society and at all levels of it, and were on duty, as it were, at all hours. *Their* commitment was as close to total as anything could be. A full appreciation of this might give us yet another view of the system's resources for discouraging Sambo from becoming a Nat Turner, and of the limits the system placed on even its "master opportunists."

IV

The final section of my book, concerning abolitionism and the intellectual and institutional context in which it functioned, was not as widely noticed as the others. The issues it

raised were in certain ways quite different from those considered in the previous sections, and though it too has come
in for some lively criticism, such criticism has been of rather
a special sort. It has tended to come either from persons not
inclined to challenge positions I have taken elsewhere on personality and on cross-cultural comparison, or else from those
whose primary interests, being more or less exclusively tied
to the American abolitionist movement rather than to slavery
itself, lay outside such realms. Of this criticism the most
prominent representatives are Nathan Glazer and Aileen
Kraditor.[33]

Their basic objection is that I am unfair to the abolitionists
and give them short shrift. I find both the abolitionists and
their procedures distasteful; I blame them, as Glazer puts it,
"for being moralistic, fanatical, uncompromising, vitupera-
tive," and deplore their refusal "to consider practical measures." "Elkins," according to Miss Kraditor, "regrets that
slavery was not ended gradually, by piecemeal adjustments
of the institutional arrangements that supported it." I "obviously" disapprove of "their alleged anti-institutional bias"
(which she claims they did not really have), whereas, as
Glazer insists, "because of the South's monolithic resistance
to any change in the slavery system" the abolitionists in effect
had no choice. It "was necessary for abolitionism to develop
its own absolutism."

It appears that one of the things least controllable in one's

[33] Nathan Glazer, "The Differences among Slaves," *Commentary*, XXIX
(May 1960), 454–58, reprinted as Introduction to 1st paperback ed. of Elkins,
Slavery (New York: Grosset and Dunlap, 1963), ix–xvi; Aileen S. Kraditor,
"A Note on Elkins and the Abolitionists," *Civil War History*, XIII (Dec.
1967), 330–39 (included here), and *Means and Ends in American Abolition-
ism: Garrison and His Critics on Strategy and Tactics, 1834–1850* (New
York, 1969), esp. 11–38. Another work in which similar criticism is made is
Bertram Wyatt-Brown, *Lewis Tappan and the Evangelical War against
Slavery* (Cleveland, 1969), xii, xv, 355.

writings is their overtones, and what they may betray about one's temperamental inclinations at the time they were set down. When I first encountered this line of criticism, I reflected with some irritation that it missed what I was really saying. Since then, the civil rights movement and the intransigence which it encountered have permitted me to empathize somewhat with the abolitionists of a century and more ago, and to experience in a vicarious way what they experienced directly. Consequently going back over what I wrote about them, I note with a certain discomfort a tone that would probably not be there if I were doing it now.

The rest of it, in all likelihood, still would be there. I do not believe the argument I made need depend in this case on the tone in which it was couched, or on whether I believed then, or believe now, that the abolitionists were my kind of people. Those things are essentially not debatable, but they can, I think, be separated from those that are. The two main problems now are the same two that concerned me then. One is that of locating the abolitionists in their culture, and the other is locating them in the general movement that led ultimately to emancipation. As to the latter, I would say now what I did not specifically say then, that the abolitionists and their activities were indispensable to that movement. Exactly how is, of course, another question and a very complex one. As to the former, I find myself quite willing to amplify my position, and less willing to shift ground on it than at any other point in the book.

Miss Kraditor accuses me of wrongly connecting the abolitionists with Transcendentalism in my effort to show the anti-institutional character of their crusade against slavery. I did indeed so connect them, though I think not wrongly. The connection was not intended as a "causal" one; it was intended to exhibit certain cultural attitudes characteristic of the age that were held in common by Transcendentalists, abolitionists, and a host of evangelists and reforming spirits of every sort in the America of the 1830s and '40s. "The perfectionism of Garrison and other reformers," as R. Jackson Wilson has put it, "was, like Transcendentalism, insistently antinomian; both implied a thorough, even ruthless, criticism and repudiation of existing social institutions."[34]

Miss Kraditor is herself ambivalent on the question of institutions, and is quite uncertain as to just where, and with what emphasis, she wishes to place the abolitionists generally in relation to it. On the one hand the Garrisonians, according to her, "insisted they were not anti-institutionalists," and she adds that "most abolitionists" were quite willing to "use institutions to destroy slavery." But on the other hand, "most radicals, including most Garrisonians and many other abolitionists . . . did not share the conservatives' reverence for institutions as such." She is not sure it is proper of me to imply that Garrison and his perfectionist cohorts represented more than a small and idiosyncratic group within the movement as a whole. But then in her own book she repeatedly puts Garrison forward as representative of all that was best and most effective in that movement.

Not that these various positions are necessarily incompatible. I would even, up to a point, support them myself. But I do not think they add up in quite the way she thinks they do. The abolitionists were, to be sure, quite willing to "use" institutions. But they and most other men of that age who were concerned in any sense with moral regeneration viewed institutions, as well as the individuals who "used" them, in a very special way. Their attitudes and assumptions were strik-

---

[34] R. Jackson Wilson, *In Quest of Community: Social Philosophy in the United States, 1860–1920* (New York, 1968), 13.

ingly divergent from those with which men and women in European cultures had traditionally regarded institutions and their own relationships to them. Whether this was a good or a bad thing ought not to concern either of us; the important thing is to recognize that such a distinction existed. Miss Kraditor further pictures the abolitionists as calculating realists, concerned with tactics. As to this I have my reservations. But she also stresses their overriding concern with principle, upon which I am in full accord. Their objective, she says, was above all to combat racism. This, I think, is factually incorrect. The technique of action they put the most store by—whatever the varying degrees of concern for institutions or for racism, and regardless of other dissidences within the movement on doctrine and tactics—was the technique of conversion.

The anti-institutionalism that I and others have found so impressive in the cultural attitudes of this period was in fact perennially inherent in American experience virtually from the first. John Winthrop and those who accompanied him to America in 1630, whatever they might subsequently do, had in their way been challenging institutions in the name of liberty for years before their voyage, which was itself a plenary repudiation of institutional continuities. A dynamic cycle was thus established then and there, one that would repeat itself over and over throughout the ensuing 200 years. It always began with an assertion of freedom, of freedom *from* something—from tyranny, from constriction, from stultification, and from the institutions that supported and perpetuated them. By the 1830s the other side of that coin—a transcendent individualism—was overwhelmingly evident in every mode of thought and feeling, be it economic, theological, political, philosophical, or literary. The "liberation" of the individual from the perennial constraints of institutions was a process—

again using Wilson's words—that "comes as close as anything can to constituting the relative distinctiveness of men's experience in America."[35]

Behind the extraordinary impression made by America on Tocqueville in 1831 and 1832 was something that enabled him to perceive with great clarity any number of distinctive features in American society. This something was a set of gross cultural contrasts between what he was seeing and what he had left behind, involving a series of traditional European assumptions and understandings with regard to institutions. He found it hard at first to believe that America could even exist, much less survive, so little "reverence" did Americans have "for institutions as such." Much of his scheme of organization for *Democracy in America*, indeed, may be read as a systematic search for those social devices and mechanisms that Americans did respect, and for those principles of order that filled the place of institutions as he in his own society had known them. In his experience it was institutions that formed men; in America it was, if anything, the other way around.

In French society institutions provided a frame, a kind of given, within which a man pictured himself and the things he might legitimately do with his life. His family represented to him with some precision who he was, the kind of history he could claim, the connections he was entitled to form, and the responsibilities he would assume. His class position defined both his limits and his opportunities; from it might be projected his education, his career, his values, his very character. His school was not so much an institution where his "natural" potential might be released, as one that prescribed a certain form and order for his mind. Whatever might be the degree

[35] *Ibid.*, 3.

of his preoccupation with religion, the authority of the Church over various aspects of his life was taken for granted. (Nor did one innovate in the field of religion, at least not lightly.) In short, a man viewed himself and his actions and aspirations as moving through a series of institutions, and in the light of this it was far less easy to imagine the mark he might leave on his society than to understand the sort of impress his society would make on him. In America, on the other hand, a major cultural fact was the general inability to see any clear relationship, except perhaps a negative one, between institutions and individual character. The individual was what he was in spite of institutions; they stood in the way of his "real" self; "under all these screens," Emerson would say, "I have difficulty to detect the precise man you are."[36]

Institutions themselves, such as they were, thus assumed a very different character from that in which they had traditionally functioned. They were at best a convenience, something that men might deliberately bring into being and then "use," transform, or abandon as it suited them: the test was not the historic attachments such institutions generated, for they generated few, but rather the extent to which they released the creative energies of individuals for specific and immediate ends. They thereby became something different, almost requiring a different name, and the distinction might be called that between "institutions" and "organizations." Such devices—Tocqueville called them "associations"—were created for a bewildering variety of purposes. "In the United States associations are established to promote the public safety, commerce, industry, morality, and religion. There is no end which the human will despairs of attaining through the com-

[36] "Self-Reliance," in *Emerson's Complete Works* (Boston, 1883-93), II, 55.

bined power of individuals united into a society." In sheer
organizing energy, the Americans exceeded anything he had
previously seen, and we do not need Tocqueville to remind
us that this was the very age in which the promoter came fully
into his own. James Willard Hurst has described the transforming of the entire idea of the "corporation" at this time
from a body clothed in public interest to a device for facilitat-
ing the fullest sweep of individual enterprise. The churches
themselves, as Sidney Mead has shown, owed their vitality
not only to their evangelical zeal but also to their promotional
activities. (The same thing, transposed, could be said of the
new business ventures.) Even the family—judging from
Catherine Beecher's treatise on that subject which went
through innumerable editions—was not really a given, something that one inherited and in which one assumed a place;
it was rather something one created anew with each generation as an act of free choice, and subsequently maintained, as
it were, through force of individual will.[37]

A major corollary of all this was the logic of evangelical-
ism, which suffused and permeated every notable reform
movement in America from the 1830s to the Civil War. To
effect moral transformation, it was necessary not simply to
change institutions, but more fundamentally to change and

---

[37] Alexis de Tocqueville, *Democracy in America*, ed. Phillips Bradley
(New York, 1945), I, 192; James Willard Hurst, *Law and the Conditions of
Freedom in the Nineteenth-Century United States* (Madison, 1956), 15–29;
Sidney E. Mead, *The Lively Experiment: The Shaping of Christianity in
America* (New York, 1963), esp. 102–33; Catherine E. Beecher, *A Treatise
on Domestic Economy, for the Use of Young Ladies at Home and at
School* (Boston, 1841). On the distinction between "institutions" and "or-
ganizations," see Eric L. McKitrick, "Goodbye to All That," *New York
Review of Books*, VI (June 9, 1966), 6–7; on individualism, see John Wil-
liam Ward, "The Ideal of Individualism and the Reality of Organization,"
in *Red, White, and Blue: Men, Books, and Ideas in American Culture* (New
York, 1969), 227–66.

reform individuals. This was done not through institutions, but directly: by liberating men's natural benevolence rather than by strengthening those institutions which might discipline men's natural selfishness. The instrument was conversion. Sin was no longer a matter of original depravity but of willful perversity, and could itself be cast out by an act of will if men could once be convinced, first of their perversity and then of their perfectibility. By manipulating individual guilt, by making the inspiration direct enough and powerful enough, the thing could be done: a man's eyes were opened, his heart was changed, he was converted. And the same logic applied to social evils, which were simply individual sins compounded. The primary object, therefore, was still conversion: to persuade enough people directly enough and powerfully enough, that the evil existed.[38]

Such was the cultural context in which the abolitionist movement developed, and it is within such a context that its many ambiguities are to be understood. Whatever the doctrinal emphasis—immediate or gradual emancipation—and whatever the range of individual types, from the extravagantly abrasive Garrison to the extravagantly self-effacing Weld, the technique of the revival set the tone for the entire movement. Any purely intellectual rationale, any cold calculations on "tactics," were always subordinate to the basic effort to convert. "If your hearts ache and bleed," Weld urged, "we want you, you will help us; but if you merely

[38] On this point see John L. Thomas, "Romantic Reform in America, 1815–1865," *American Quarterly*, XVII (Winter 1965), 656–81, and "Antislavery and Utopia," in Martin Duberman, ed., *The Antislavery Vanguard: New Essays on the Abolitionists* (Princeton, 1965), 240–69. "The criticism and attack on institutions, which we have witnessed," Emerson asserted, "has made one thing plain, that society gains nothing whilst a man, not himself renovated, attempts to renovate things around him. . . ." "New England Reformers," in *Works*, III, 248.

adopt our principles as dry theories, do let us alone: we have millstones enough swinging at our necks already."[39] That the abolitionists effected many conversions is hardly to be denied; this was after all their primary object. But the dynamic of conversion was not the same as the dynamic of institutional change; when that occurred, it occurred in very different ways. Many of them might indeed "work within institutions," and just as readily abandon them. To those institutions that resisted their will, they were ruthless. One does less than justice to Garrison in suggesting that his position in this respect represented merely a "tactic." When Garrison insisted that a "Union with slaveholders" be torn in two, and that a Constitution sanctioning slavery be burned, he was acting on pure principle. True, they formed organizations of their own; those organizations were chronically unstable. The moral tensions *within* the movement, indeed, are as striking as any feature of it, in the light of which the logic of conversion, the manipulation of individual guilt to effect it, the anti-institutionalism, and the insistent primacy of individual will, all seem peculiarly of a piece. When Garrison called the churches "cages of unclean birds" despite the numbers of clergymen being daily converted to abolition, he was acting out the major fragmenting element of the movement. This was an unanticipated consequence, perhaps, but an inevitable one: an intense competition for moral purity among intensely dedicated men.

Only in such a context, moreover, is it possible to understand the bitter quarrel between the Garrisonians and Frederick Douglass. It does not seem fair to accuse Garrison and the other abolitionists of "marked race prejudice," as some

[39] *Emancipator*, July 28, 1836, quoted in Gilbert H. Barnes, *The Antislavery Impulse, 1830–1844* (Washington, 1933), 79.

have done; in this respect they come off better than any other group in a prejudice-ridden society. But neither does it make much sense to represent the eradication of racism as their overriding aim, and here the Peases do have a point: "When immediate emancipation as a plan of abolition was translated to mean only immediate repentance of the sin of slavery," they observe, "the needs of the human beings who were slaves were ignored."[40] In any case, for the Boston group Frederick Douglass represented a major difficulty. Douglass' independence, his decision to speak with his own voice rather than theirs, his repudiation of their extreme anti-institutionalism, his assumption of leadership for Negro aspirations, his efforts to improve the condition of free Negroes in Rochester and elsewhere, all added up to the profoundest challenge, and brought down their full wrath upon him. At the beginning of their association, Douglass' principal value to the Garrisonians was as a symbolic abstraction rather than as a man who might have both group and personal interests of his own to promote. As soon as he showed signs of dissatisfaction with that role, he began getting into trouble. He was told, in effect, that nobody would believe he had ever been a slave unless he behaved and talked more like one when he lectured: "Better have a little of the plantation speech than not; it is not best that you seem too learned." They were piqued by his successes in England. Their displeasure, when he decided to establish his own newspaper which would compete with theirs, was such that they tried to persuade his English benefactors to cut off his support. They were furious when Douglass was "not disposed to denounce as knaves those who believe that voting is a duty," and when in 1851

---

[40] William H. Pease and Jane H. Pease, "Antislavery Ambivalence: Immediatism, Expediency, Race," *American Quarterly*, XVII (Winter 1965), 695.

Douglass announced his opposition to Garrison's stand on the Constitution, Garrison exploded. "There is roguery somewhere," he raged, and moved that Douglass' *North Star* be stricken once and for all from the approved list of abolition newspapers. This the convention of the American Anti-Slavery Society promptly did. Douglass' plans for an industrial college at Rochester, as well as his pleas for its support, were brushed aside by the Bostonians. When he combined his paper with that of the Liberty Party, he was denounced for compromising his principles to gain the financial support of Gerrit Smith, and was ostracized at the Society's 1852 convention for consorting with political antislavery people. Eventually Garrison, after a preface that breathed more sorrow than anger, loosed a sweeping attack on Douglass' integrity, his motives, and his character, and even cast aspersions on the morality of his private life.[41]

One might regard all this as mere personal spite. But that would not be wholly fair either. The entire logic of reform placed enormous burdens on the individual and the individual conscience, and grossly magnified the personal aspect of everything. To be eligible for a meaningful role, a man had to have been converted and purged, which meant that he was convinced of both the enormity and the nature of the evil he was committed to fighting—and to challenge his definition of it was to challenge *him*. This self-righteousness, which in some sense was a necessity for psychological survival in such

---

[41] Accounts of this affair (which is strikingly reminiscent of Harold Cruse's recent complaints in *Crisis of the Negro Intellectual* about white radicals who presume to speak for black radicals without consulting them) are in Benjamin Quarles, "The Breach between Douglass and Garrison," *Journal of Negro History*, XXIII (Apr. 1938), 144–54; William H. Pease and Jane H. Pease, "Boston Garrisonians and the Problem of Frederick Douglass," *Canadian Journal of History*, II (Sept. 1967), 29–48; and Philip S. Foner, *The Life and Writings of Frederick Douglass* (New York, 1950), II, 48–66.

a movement, and this endless competition for individual moral purity were hardly better illustrated than in Garrison's ineffable public admonition to Douglass in the columns of the *Liberator:*

> One thing should always be remembered in regard to the anti-slavery cause. . . . Unswerving fidelity to it, in this country, requires high moral attainments, the crucifixion of all personal considerations, a paramount regard for principle, absolute faith in the right. It does not follow, therefore, that because a man is or has been a slave, or because he is identified with a class meted out and trodden under foot, he will be the truest to the cause of human freedom. Already, that cause, both religiously and politically, has transcended the ability of the sufferers from American slavery and prejudice, as a class, to keep pace with it, or to perceive what are its demands, or to understand the philosophy of its operations.[42]

It is no wonder that Douglass, upon reading this, should have devoted a whole issue of his own paper to pointing out, among other things, that having been a slave did give a man some understanding of the institution of slavery.[43]

To return momentarily to my critics. Miss Kraditor says I "regret" that slavery was not ended gradually by piecemeal adjustments; Glazer believes that I "criticize" the abolitionists for failing to pursue institutional means of undermining the system prior to its eventual elimination. This is a misreading of something I intended neither as a "criticism" nor as an expression of "regret," but as a deliberate counterfactual projection. It was designed to exhibit those very choices which a culture so constituted as this one would *not* allow. As to

[42] *Liberator,* Nov. 18, 1853.
[43] *Frederick Douglass' Paper,* Dec. 9, 1853.

why I should have bothered, there were at least two reasons. I was entitled, I thought, to ask questions about conceivable alternatives to the holocaust that did occur, before concluding —as I have—that such a holocaust was necessary. And with such a model, I hoped, one might be somewhat better sensitized to the limitations as well as the vitality of the abolitionist crusade.

Coming back to the main theme of this essay, I would predict that further progress on this subject, perhaps to a greater extent here than with the other aspects of it I have discussed in the foregoing pages, is most likely to come through studies in ideology. This would both impart a greater precision and supply an ampler framework than most of our work has so far done, and would do much toward releasing us from the closed cycle of debate in which we find ourselves. How did an ideology develop that could prepare the entire North psychologically to take up arms against the slaveholding South, and what exactly was its nature? And what relation did the abolitionist movement itself bear to that development? That there was, indeed, a relation is hardly to be questioned.

But what can and should be questioned is the extent to which the content of this ideology was a calculated logical extension of the abolitionists' work and doctrines. As the extremists of the antislavery movement these men played a vital role. But the very conditions of the culture in which they had to function, and the very dynamic which those conditions imparted to their efforts, made it sociologically impossible that they should ever assume charge of the larger movement that did eventuate in the destruction of slavery, or that they could even contribute, other than indirectly, to the making of its ideology. With their own ranks in chronic fragmentation, institutionally and psychologically, they were in no position to do either.

The role of the extremist nonetheless was vital. It was not a political role he played, or even primarily an intellectual one; it was moral, and one of his functions was to establish the outer moral limits of the antislavery movement. In this he could hardly be "moderate," and his chief weapon, indeed his only weapon, was the manipulation of guilt. To play such a role at optimum did seem to require the insulation of a special kind of personality, and how "likeable" he was may remain an open question. But his other major function—the key one, I think—lay in his willingness to take risks.

The manner in which the abolitionists went forth to confront a hostile society has been set down as something of a "martyr complex." But it is hard not to admire the fortitude with which Weld, Garrison, and a host of others faced both potential and actual violence in locality after locality. Each occasion, considering the only thing they were armed with, was inherently unstable, and for the spectator, the experience on the one hand of coming to scoff and remaining to be converted, or, on the other, of mobbing the speaker, were seldom more than a hair's breadth apart. And with this process, one comes to the true functional link between the abolitionists and the growth of a sectional ideology—or, more accurately, of two sectional ideologies, one for the North and one for the South.

On one level, acts of martyrdom or graded equivalents of martyrdom (the killing of Lovejoy, the manhandling of Garrison, or the wrecking of Birney's press) served to engage a whole series of libertarian values not originally connected with slavery but shared by the entire Northern community. This is a process that has already been well described.[44] On another level, however, the impact of abolitionism on the South and the process of response and counterresponse embracing ever widening clusters of emotional and intellectual commitments: it is this dynamic that must be followed out in all its complexity of detail in order to reconstruct the two massive ideological constellations that confronted one another by 1860.

By the decade of the 1830s, with the initial coming into prominence of abolitionism[45]—to which the South's own response contributed much—the process was fully launched. The South's immediate intransigence—the interference with the mails, the gag on petitions, the violence in Southern communities—was accompanied by a course of complicated political and social theorizing that began inexorably to set the South apart, and to make the South appear more and more in Northern eyes as a deviant and subversive cultural salient within the American Union. With this, the ideological cycle took on a life of its own, almost irrespective of what abolitionists might thereafter say or do. It came to involve everything

[44] By Barnes, *Antislavery Impulse*, and Russell B. Nye, *Fettered Freedom: Civil Liberties and the Slavery Controversy, 1830–1860* (East Lansing, 1948). The terminology I myself used in dealing with this phenomenon was that of the "democratization" of antislavery feeling, in the course of which the movement was broadened and altered through—among other things—the "fellow-traveler" principle. And yet this need not be the only way to describe it. A more sophisticated and more inclusive approach might be in terms of ideology and its growth, a concept which has the advantage of containing its own dynamic.

[45] Though I have not as yet been challenged on this, one point in my book at which I now think I was mistaken was my implication (207) that the proslavery movement did not require the appearance of abolitionism in the 1830s to set it on its way. Narrowly speaking, this may have been correct. But if one takes proslavery in its broadest ideological sense, it is apparent that its full development was in fact greatly stimulated by the sort of threat that abolitionism seemed to represent, and that the growth in scope and complexity of the two sectional ideologies was a product, from the 1830s on, of an oscillating process of challenge and counter-challenge.

from the nature of the Union, the Constitution, the Bible, majority rule, and democracy, to the very meaning of work.[46]

Most pervasively of all, it involved the entire meaning of the future. The previous experience of Americans had given them every reason to think of this in terms of land. "Territory" was above all else a moral metaphor for the future, and territorial expansion meant not simply physical but moral expansion. Thus the new cycle of ideological escalation that was touched off by the Texas question in the mid-1840s reflected a rising competition for nothing less than the country's moral future. Whether slavery should or should not be brought into the territories was more than an economic or even a political question. It was the question of whether those places would be dominated by one total ideological configuration or by the other.

By the middle and late 1850s the other side of the process, the mentality of imagined *conspiracy*, was fully evident. Neither the "Slave Power conspiracy" to fasten slavery on the entire North or the "Black Republican conspiracy" to destroy the South's domestic institutions may have drawn much reality from direct and immediate experience in either section. But with those "conspiracies" as part of an ideological dynamic, as elements of a struggle to control the entire country indirectly by controlling its future character, their power becomes very understandable and real.[47]

---

[46] Two works which contribute greatly to an understanding of this process are Eugene D. Genovese, *The Political Economy of Slavery: Studies in the Economy and Society of the Slave South* (New York, 1965); and William W. Freehling, *Prelude to Civil War: The Nullification Controversy in South Carolina, 1816–1836* (New York, 1966). Eric L. McKitrick, ed., *Slavery Defended: The Views of the Old South* (Englewood Cliffs, 1963), is a convenient compendium.

[47] See, e.g., "The Great Slave Power Conspiracy," Ch. VIII of Nye, *Fettered Freedom;* and Larry Gara, "Slavery and the Slave Power: A Crucial Distinction," *Civil War History,* XV (Mar. 1969), 5–18. Bernard Bailyn

That a New England businessman, a New York lawyer, a Midwestern farmer—whatever their feelings about race—could feel just as threatened by 1860 as any Alabama planter, and that the ideology that sustained them had its own coherence and content, is apparent from a multitude of public and private writings. Such persons felt threatened, as Eric Foner has brilliantly shown, by a power that fostered what they saw as a whole set of deeply un-American values, subversive of majority rule, democracy, Union, and the dignity of free white labor.[48] Such an ideology constituted the fullest preparation for the North's response to the firing on Sumter. It had combined all the North's major convictions, including even its racism, into a party program. It had thus been placed in an institutional framework, the only one the culture really possessed, and fashioned into a powerful instrument for striking down slavery.

---

puts special emphasis on the "conspiracy" component of the Revolutionary ideology in *Ideological Origins of the American Revolution* (Cambridge, 1967), 144–59.

[48] Eric Foner, *Free Soil, Free Labor, Free Men: The Ideology of the Republican Party before the Civil War* (New York, 1970). My reading of this work has been of great assistance in shaping the thoughts of the foregoing paragraphs.